D1381094

SHAPING LONDON

Terry Farrell

SHAPING LONDON

The patterns and forms that make the metropolis

A John Wiley and Sons, Ltd, Publication

Page 1: Somerset House on the Strand (mid 18th century)
On the sweeping bend of the river there have always been formal bank-side palaces, with water gates on one side and road entrances on the other from the great street that runs continuously one block inland.

Previous page: Queen Mary's Garden, Regent's Park, 1986
The royal parks were formed from earlier monarchs' hunting grounds. Uniquely retaining their essential character of 'trapped countryside' within the urban realm. The park was opened to the public in 1838.

Above: Trains at Paddington Station, 1910
Paddington has always been a primary transport hub, where Roman and medieval roads, modern elevated motorways, canal basin, the world's first tube line and London's first bus service all meet.

© 2010 John Wiley & Sons Ltd

Registered office
John Wiley & Sons Ltd, The Atrium, Southern Gate,
Chichester, West Sussex, PO19 8SQ, United Kingdom
For details of our global editorial offices, for customer services and for information about how to apply for permission to reuse the copyright material in this book please see our website at www.wiley.com.
The right of the author to be identified as the author of this work has been asserted in accordance with the Copyright, Designs and Patents Act 1988.

Executive Commissioning Editor: Helen Castle
Project Editor: Miriam Swift
Publishing Assistant: Calver Lezama

ISBN 978-0-470-69996-6

Cover design and book design by Karen Willcox
Cover and book production by Kate Ward

Printed in Italy by Printer Trento

Contents

Acknowledgements

This book is a first for me – in that it is not directly to do with my work and was instigated by someone else and not me! I met Helen Castle as a guest at Charles Jencks' posh lunch at his club, the Athenæum, with Professor George Baird, Robert Maxwell and Professor Colin Fournier. One or two months later Helen rang me and suggested I write about London, and as I got into it I found I really enjoyed it as an unexpected indulgence – a chance to wander, walk and ramble the physical domain yes, but also to follow mental paths of ideas and patterns of thoughts about the place that has been my home for most of my life. For those for whom writing and criticism, the word, sentence and grammar is their expression, I have to emphasise that I am, and always have been mostly a visual person. I do find it easier to draw, talk and explain than to write; and so I have based these chapters on sketches, talks, lectures and dictation. If there is a stream of consciousness and conversational meandering in what appears in print, I do not apologise as it is the only way I do it, and together with the visuals it does, I believe, add up and come together with its own logic and narrative; I hope so.

I am very appreciative of the particular help I have had from Howard Watson, who rescued as much as possible of my grammar and thoughts into some kind of legible word order; to Harvey Van Sickle for helping me with history and facts (as he has done for me for over 25 years!). Helen I have mentioned as setting me on a course, she then later became a very enthusiastic and helpful critic and editor as the book entered its final phases. I have always worked with, off and through others, so many at the office – there is a wide indebtedness to work colleagues, architects, urban planners and indeed the many clients and consultants with whom I have worked on urban planning projects over the years.

This book was the particular mission in the office of the indefatigable Emma Davies who multi-tasked on a heroic scale – words, pictures, meetings, people, I leaned on her and she as ever really delivered for me. Thank you Emma.

The A40 Westway at night
Beneath the elevated Westway, new uses have gradually begun to urbanise the road, connecting up, around and under it.

Introduction

As the writing of this book comes to a close, the surface of my desk is completely covered with piles of books on London – old and new; big and glossy as well as closely typed and modest. The metropolis has been an endless source of fascination for authors and readers across the centuries. Heather Creaton's *Bibliography of Printed Works on London History to 1939* lists over 22,000 separate publications dedicated to the subject and that is only up to the

Second World War. The city has been examined numerous times by historians, biographers, chroniclers and the curious, and now the psycho-geographers: so why the need for yet another book on London? Despite the abundance of literature, there is little that fully captures the messy complexity of the present whole. Accounts of the city and its built fabric tend to either drill down to the frozen past or isolate the same shiny contemporary parts.

**River Thames at dusk with *HMS Belfast*
and Tower Bridge in the background**
This was the former Pool of London,
with Customs House on the left. It was
London's primary dock and harbour right
in the heart of the city. Today it is much
more still and quiet. In the distance is
the Victorian lift bridge which is really the
gateway between the outer docks and
inner London.

Here I have attempted to use my many decades of experience as an urban planner and architect in London, constantly engaging with the form, shape and history of the city, to highlight the many layers that inform it as a place, both natural and man-made; so the Thames and the natural landscape get as much attention as the railway infrastructure, the canals and the roads. The intention is to provide an entirely fresh view, which is interpretative rather than scientific, largely based on my own informed personal observation. It reveals patterns of behaviour, past and present; albeit often hidden under layers of tarmac, traffic lights and roundabouts. The patterns tell us how a city works and how it fails, but they can be both hard to discern and complex, particularly in a metropolis like London that has evolved for almost 2,000 years since its Roman origins. The snatches of accumulated history that are recounted here are often partial, they are not intended to be in any way comprehensive or represent fresh research. They are applied as part of a diagnostic process – part Sherlock Holmes, part Sigmund Freud. Backgrounds and patterns are traced and stitched together in a greater case history of the metropolis, which aims to shed light on why things are as they are and how they have shaped the present, while also stressing the conflicts and continuities between individual places. Like Freud, in order to understand my patient on the couch, I am attempting to piece together a full picture of its ambiguities, contradictions and suppressed aspirations.

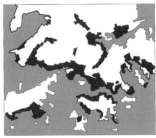
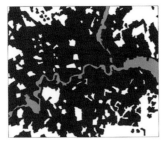

to recognise its prominent position in London's infrastructure as a central spine with all of the city's major railway termini strung along it (see 'Railways' chapter) with Regent's Canal at their rear (see 'Canals' chapter). More than even a great rail and road junction, it may also be regarded as a partition – a social-historical boundary dividing the affluent great estates of 18th-century Marylebone to the south from the 20th-century social housing of Somers Town to the north (see 'Inner Roads' chapter).

The patterns of London's core infrastructure – railways, tubes, roads and canals – provide the framework for much of the book's observation; they are concentrated in the six chapters that form the second and third sections of the book. These linear physical movement lines not only link the places, as destinations and points of departure, but also inform further layers of patterning in terms of walking distances or proximities to each other, or in constellations of similar elements of city form. We might see, for instance, London's original villages interspersed at walking distance from one another, or north London's early 20th-century Metro-land laid out around the Metropolitan Line's tube stops within a 10-minute stroll from housing. Then there are the underlying patterns of the natural terrain, the green infrastructure of hills, the main river and tributaries, and tidal flows. There are patterns of layering, time-based episodes of different building periods, different cultures. These layers are often in wave patterns, sudden bursts or groupings of growth and change. It takes a certain kind of archaeological detective work to peel back the layers of history.

The Thames, which along with its tributaries, is the subject of the first section and five chapters of the book, is a great example of this patterning of layers of urban history, with its width and

If this book is to make a difference, it should do so by providing a better understanding of exactly what kind of metropolis, or urban phenomenon, London is. Rather than describing the city as a static collection of buildings replaced over time, like worn out or discarded clothes, it looks beneath the fabric to the forces that shape the body; driven by often organic or haphazard growth. It should effectively impart the importance of place and the connection between things, creating insights into how specific areas link up and piece together. It is very much my hope that it should prove to be in some degree revelatory, providing readers with new insights and fresh perceptions of what may have become ordinary or banal to them. So that having made the same commute every day to Euston Station, a reader might emerge afresh on the Marylebone-Euston Roads, and see beyond the noise, pollution and congestion of that tarmac stretch to the world's first bypass – the New Road from Paddington to Islington, built in 1756 to re-route livestock from Oxford Street – and go on

Farrell, Patterns of open space (top line) and occupation (bottom line), 1999
These drawings compare London with Hong Kong, all at the same scale.

alignment changing over time, sometimes naturally, sometimes as a result of human intervention, and always when changed altering the course of subsequent human settlement and activity. From glacial times to the Romans and Vikings, to medieval and modern times, each era used and developed and reacted to the river in different ways, and if you look you can see all this; it is all present in today's city form. Like a psychoanalyst, we need to divine the layers so that we can understand the childhood of the city at the same time as we are looking at the grown-up character and personality of the adult. Without an understanding of its unique evolution in each area, from its landscape and parklands, to its transport infrastructure, to its residential growth, we cannot hope to understand what is there now and how to move on, to grow it, change it or improve it.

One overarching pattern is a kind of field patterning, often referred to as 'urban grain': here, the textures of different grains manifest themselves into distinct districts or areas of development, such as the 18th- and 19th-century areas of the West End, Mayfair, Marylebone and Bloomsbury that are gridded with rectilinear streets, or areas of medieval maze-like streets, such as the tight alleyways of the City around Mansion House and the Bank of England. There is also the endless outer expanded suburban field pattern of repeated separated units of semi-detached and detached houses with gardens that is so characteristic of the areas around the North Circular Road – Wembley, Harrow and Pinner – and further out west in the extremities of suburbia in Middlesex and Surrey – Sunbury, Staines, Egham and Englefield Green – where the lazy curved, private car-based geometries that were so pervasive in the 1950s and 1960s can be found. From these patterns – their forms, densities, building materials, street

geometries – whole areas can be classified by looking at aerial photos say, on Google, as belonging to this or that socio-economic grouping, revealing lifestyle characteristics, or whole areas of industry, or office or shopping concentrations. Monoculturalism is part of the patchwork of all city developments, each area with its own character but the whole collaged together in one giant, self-made tapestry or, as is so often the case with London, layered on top of each other where 19th-century roads, for instance, dissect an earlier street pattern of medieval ones. When writing about self-made tapestries in *The Self-Made Tapestry: Pattern Formation in Nature* (2001), the author, Philip Ball, wrote of natural organic patterning:

**A German Heinkels 111 Bomber
over London, 9 July 1940**
This remarkable photograph taken from
an escort plane during a bombing raid of
London reveals the urban grain of the city
dramatically contrasted against the curve
of the Thames.

For all the infinite variety of patterns here, one can pick out a menagerie of characteristic forms that tend to recur again and again – rather like the coherent structures that occasionally arise out of turbulence. These forms seem to have a life of their own – they possess certain properties, and carry out specific roles within the community.

A key to understanding London is to recognise it as a natural city, collectively planned over time, built by many hands working with natural forms, with no grand overarching, superimposed design hand or ordering plans, or geometries. In contrast to a natural, collectively planned city is the designed, the more artificial city, usually laid out so for urgent, often economic or military imperatives – or the city, like Paris or Beijing, that expresses the overriding power of governance of an emperor or dictator. North American city grids are for rapid real-estate disposal, they are surveyors' and land agents' cities; Roman formalism and encirclement of walls and grids are for military expansionism and rule.

In the 20th century there was a worldwide resurgence of the 'designed city' due to historically unequalled economic and population growth. Invariably mistakenly, city planning was seen as needing to be highly orchestrated, designed and artificial – the pervading culture, Modernism, took its inspiration from mass production and its reliance on engineering, on 'design', the man-made, the city as a deliberate predetermined product or artefact. Many of these designed cities had one well-known architect, as epitomised by Le Corbusier at Chandigarh in India and Lúcio Costa with Oscar Niemeyer in Brasilia, Brazil. The UK's poor-imitation postwar New Towns, such as Basildon, Harlow, Crawley and Telford, often failed to provide attractive modern urban centres or even a viable sense of place. London, however, seemingly untouched by these criteria, went on growing and succeeding because it is a natural city and has always been collectively grown. Again, pattern theorists have often recognised the cultural dilemmas of city planning.

It is scarcely surprising that, since the major preoccupation of urban planners is with the design of cities, they have generally attempted to analyse city forms in terms of the effects of their efforts. That is to say, theories of urban planning have tended to focus on cities in whose form the guiding hand of human design is clearly discernable.

The trouble is, hardly any cities are like this. In spite of the efforts of planners to impose a simplistic order, most large cities present an apparently

Farrell, The self-ordering collective of a woodland, 2009
Edge trees grow lopsidedly and mid-woodland trees grow tall reaching for the light, but have spindly lower branches. A rich flora exists below, varying according to the position in the woodland. This is horticulture close to urbiculture.

Farrell, Trees in their isolated state on grassland, 2009
How signature architects and their clients prefer to see their work and the city: stand-alone, but with no connectedness or rich undergrowth. There is a parallel in urban culture; separate grand architectural statements alone do not make for rich urbanism.

disordered, irregular scatter of developed space…
mixed haphazardly. By focusing on regions where
planning has created some regularity…urban theorists
have often ignored the fact that overall, a city grows
organically, not through the dictates of planners.
(Philip Ball, The Self-Made Tapestry, 2001.)

The 'natural' is not, though, necessarily a result of no order. Nature is highly ordered but in an organic, self-organising, evolutionary way. D'Arcy Wentworth Thompson's classic book *On Growth and Form,* first published in 1917, influenced me greatly as a student. As he states, there is order behind the biological forms of flowers, bees' wings, trees, waves and clouds.

The waves of the sea, the little ripples on the shore,
the sweeping curve of the sandy bay between the
headlands, the outline of the hills, the shape of the
clouds, all these have many riddles of form, so many
problems of morphology and all of them the physicist
can more or less read and adequately solve.

Not only is this order highly complex, it is also inherently beautiful. Formally, nature retains a kind of effortless casualness in its complexity rather than the hard rigid rule of simplistic geometry.

The analogy between nature and London as an organic city can be extended beyond D'Arcy Thompson's view of the individual organisms and elements. It is now almost a century since he wrote his book and his ideas about biological forms have been overtaken by the more dynamic collective science of ecology. A city can be better viewed as an assemblage of interactivity, more like a woodland than a tree. It has its own collective ordering like a river valley or a forest, a lakeland or fenland region. Recently in autumn just after the leaves had fallen, I was observing and sketching a small woodland across the walled garden of a Lutyens house in Kent where I spend my weekends. A woodland is made from organic elements each individually following inherent, self-ordering patterns, as recognised by D'Arcy Thompson. But collectively each tree has adjusted its pure designed geometry of individual elements to its position in a higher layered ordering – edge trees grow lopsidedly, sideways; mid-woodland trees have to grow taller to get to the light and have magnificent crowns but spindly under branches in the shadow below. Under the trees live plants and life generally in great variety within the woodland shelter, each different in growth and species according to where naturally yet opportunistically it sat within the larger plan. The whole thing is an entity. A 'woodland' just like any village, town or city is in its own way an interactive, collective element. The relationship between British settlements and nature has not been entirely accidental, a city like London growing out of a group of villages: Mayfair and Chelsea were still ostensibly villages, albeit fashionable ones, until the early 18th century.

The relationship between the natural, or the rural, and London is not, though, just an evolutionary one in which a grouping of agricultural communities were transformed over the centuries into a world metropolis. It is, as discussed in the penultimate chapter of this book, 'Landscapes, Parks and Gardens', a cultural one. And it is reflected in the great traditions of landscape design of Capability Brown and Humphry Repton, which have transferred so readily to city design. This is most apparent in the picturesque handling of the Italianate villas in the Regent's Park

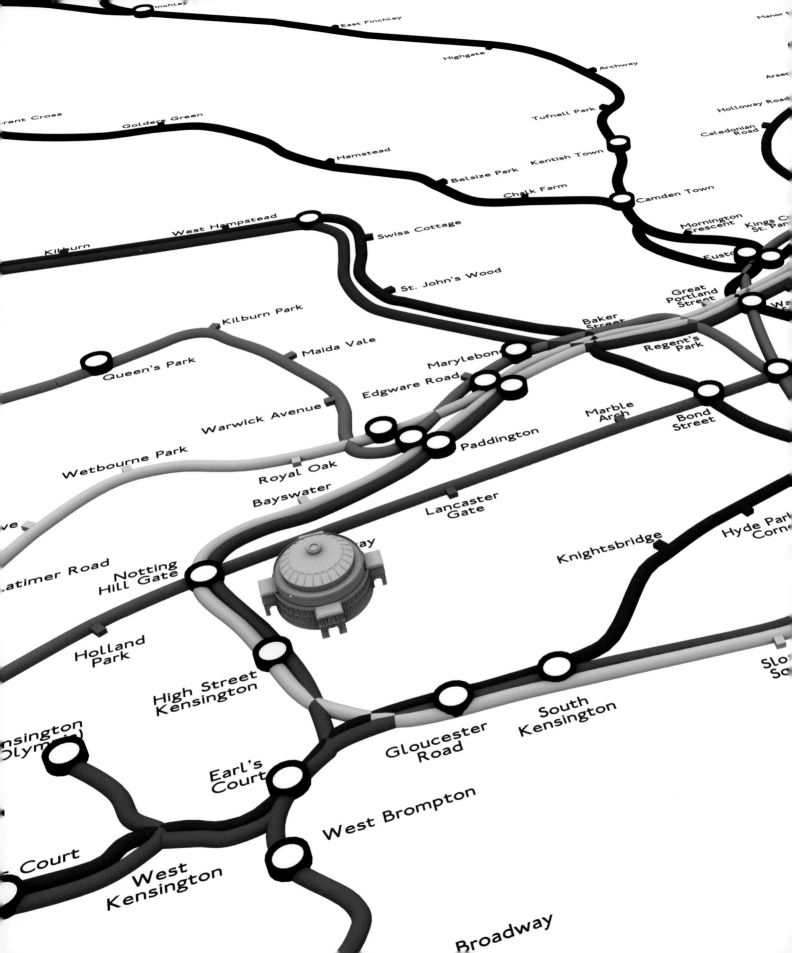

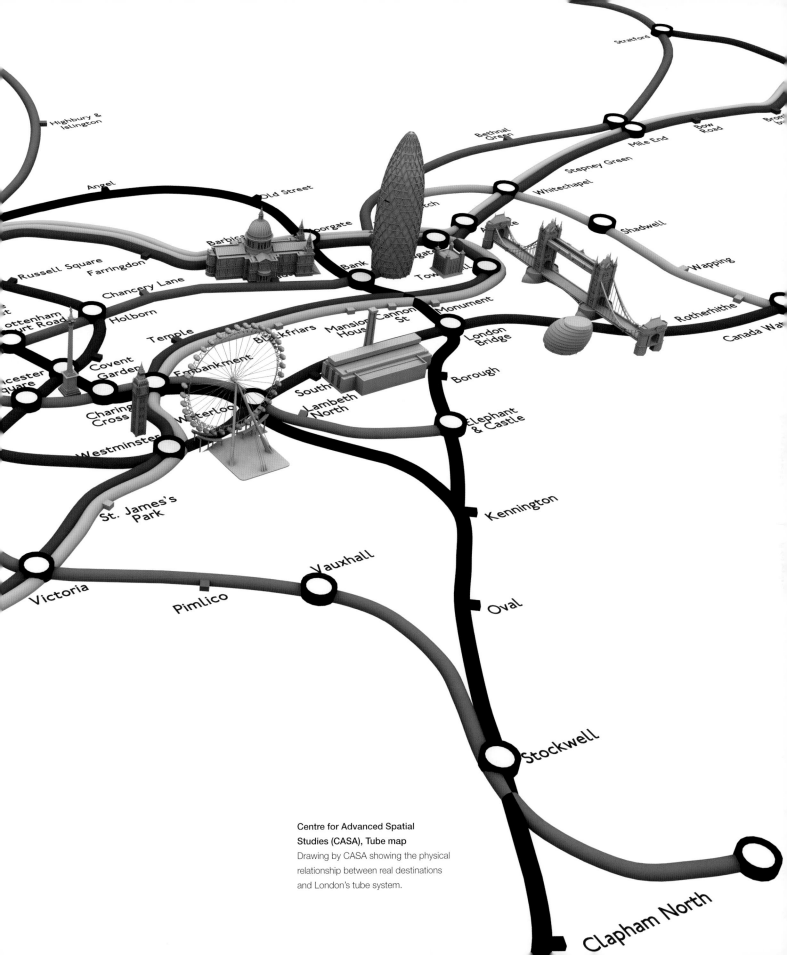

**Centre for Advanced Spatial
Studies (CASA), Tube map**
Drawing by CASA showing the physical
relationship between real destinations
and London's tube system.

villages, developed by Repton's partner John Nash in the 1820s, and the early 20th-century Hampstead Garden Suburb, with its central square designed by Edwin Lutyens. In Colin Rowe and Fred Koetter's 1978 seminal book *Collage City*, Rowe distinguished between the geometric cities of France and Italy, and London, and made the parallel observation of the similar differences in garden and landscape design. Versailles was a precursor and the same family of planning form as Haussmann's Paris and we here, with Nash and Repton, applied British natural evolutionary landscape design to city plan layouts.

The decision in this book to concentrate on the hardware, the infrastructure, the fixed underlying bits of London – both natural and man-made – rather than human occupation, human use and interaction with the fixed elements was entirely intentional. I take my cue here from the great urbanist, Christopher Alexander, who provides a vivid depiction of the difference between the fixed and human in his paper 'A City is Not a Tree', where he writes of a mini-place, a corner of a street, a microcosm of the larger city. On this corner there are traffic lights, a shop, a newsrack. And then upon this physical world the people move, interact with each other

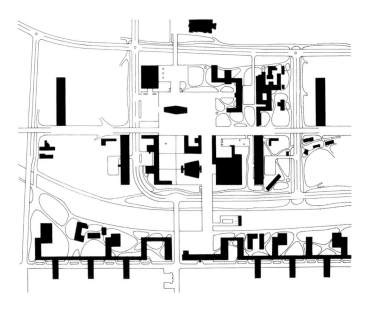

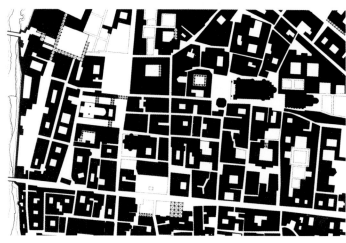

City figure-grounds from *Collage City*
Above: Le Corbusier, project for Saint-Dié, France.
Above right: Parma, Italy.
Colin Rowe and Fred Koetter's book *Collage City* (1978) shows the difference between Le Corbusier's 'designed city' and Parma's 'natural city'. These two excellent examples of their type emphasise the spatial differences. Corbusier emphasises

the object (object fixation in an agoraphobic setting), and the natural city emphasises space (space positive and place-making).

and the physical events, reading or buying newspapers, standing, waiting, silent or talking. It is the infrastructure that provides the key essential framework for human interaction to take place:

> The effect makes the newsrack and the traffic light interactive; the newsrack, the newspapers on it, the money going from people's pockets to the dime slot, the people who stop at the light and read the papers, the electric impulses which make the traffic lights change and the sidewalk which the people stand on, form a system – they all work together ... they form the fixed heart of the system in which the changing parts ... people, newspapers, money and electric impulses, can work together ... all as one system.

The 12 individual chapters of this book that centre around some of the most significant aspects of London's fixed infrastructure are organised under four subheadings; no hierarchy is intended in terms of elements. These sections are 'The River: Liquid History' (the Thames and its tributaries); 'London's Infrastructure: Inventing the Metropolis' (the canals, railways and the tube); 'London's Roads and Pavements: Emerging Conflicts' (inner roads, outer roads, pedestrians, cyclists and buses); and 'Occupying the Land'

(landscapes, parks and gardens). Though separate elements may be emphasised, the way that different aspects 'all work together' and how they came about are also highlighted. The topics of these chapters do not represent a finite set of elements, as there are, of course, far more elements to a city. The book is in no way intended to be an all-inclusive, academically watertight thesis. It is rather demonstration and part exploration. More than anything, it is the result of an enthusiast's observations and thoughts that have arisen while actively engaged in planning and making sense of this fascinating city over a long career.

Survey of air pollution by the Centre for Advanced Spatial Analysis, 2007
New kinds of patterns are made possible through the use of computers. Here are different kinds of patterns from pollution, heat and movement etc.

Redrawn by Farrell, Francesco di Georgio Martini's studies for ideal cities, 2009
Architects and planners invariably fall back on pure geometrics when designing cities afresh.

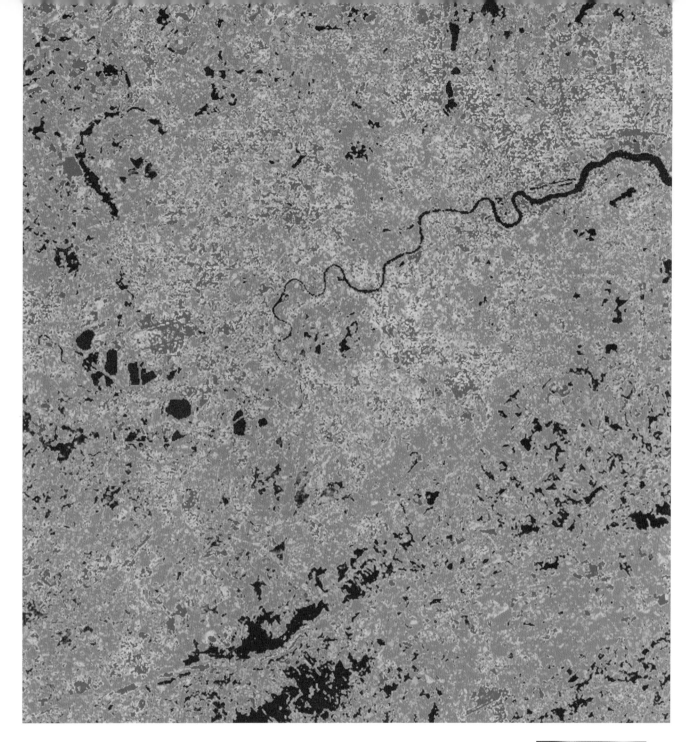

**Land-surface temperature
variations, 9 September 2004**
Computer-generated image showing
data from the ASTER 90-metre spatial
resolution satellite with temperature
variations across London.

50°C  32°C

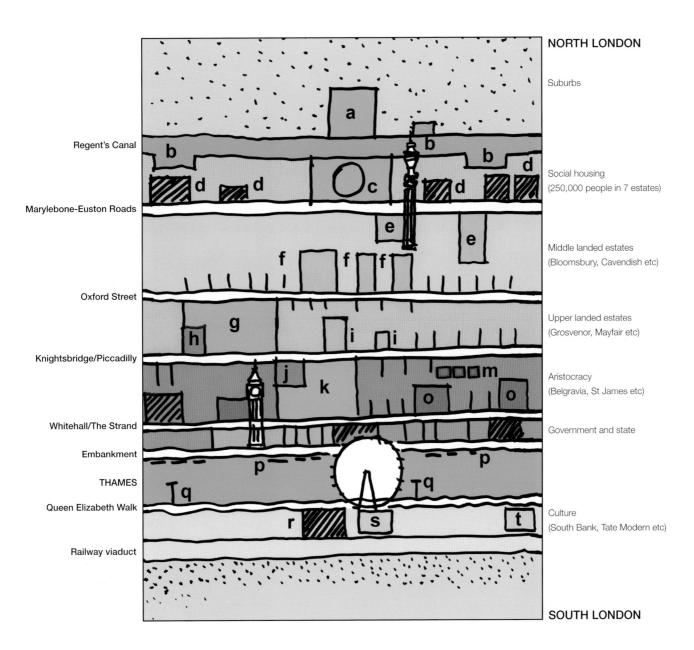

NORTH LONDON

Suburbs

Regent's Canal

Social housing
(250,000 people in 7 estates)

Marylebone-Euston Roads

Middle landed estates
(Bloomsbury, Cavendish etc)

Oxford Street

Upper landed estates
(Grosvenor, Mayfair etc)

Knightsbridge/Piccadilly

Aristocracy
(Belgravia, St James etc)

Whitehall/The Strand

Government and state

Embankment

THAMES

Queen Elizabeth Walk

Culture
(South Bank, Tate Modern etc)

Railway viaduct

SOUTH LONDON

Farrell, London layers, 2009
The layers of occupation of the central
West End follow a clear hierarchy in terms
of power and status, gradating outwards
from the river. Each major street divides
bands of land like social strata.

a Primrose Hill
b Canal and basins
c Regent's Park
d Mainline railway rtations
e University campuses
f Department stores
g Hyde Park/Kensington Gardens
h Kensington Palace
i Great houses
j Buckingham Palace

k Green Park/St James's Park
m Gentlemen's clubs
n Parliament
o Main railway stations
p Near bank moorings
q Piers
r Waterloo Station
s Arts centre
t Tate Modern

The River: 'Liquid History'

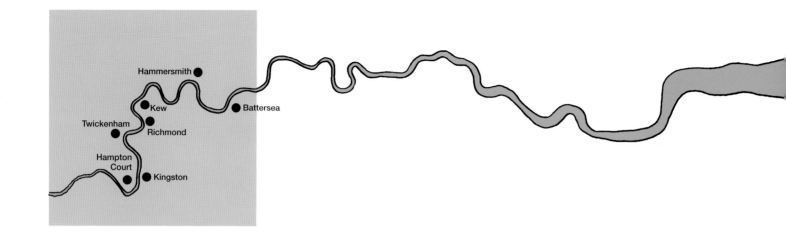

Rural Upper Thames

The Great Metropolitan River

In 1929, in a riposte to an American visitor who referred to the River Thames as 'puny', Battersea MP John Burns aptly coined the phrase 'The Thames is liquid history'. Any study of London, its shape, form and patterns has to start with the fundamental influence of the metropolis' great river. The geological formation of the Thames, which took place millions of years ago and gave the river its characteristic deep curves and squiggle-like line on a map, can still be perceived in today's urban form. The city's original settlements were generally located at fordable points or where the river could be easily crossed by boat or bridge. When the Romans built Londinium in the 1st century AD, on the site of what is now the City of London, they established it at a place where the Thames was narrow enough to build a bridge but deep enough to handle sea-going marine vessels. The modern London Bridge at Southwark remains close to the site of this Roman wooden bridge.

Away from the city, in the upper reaches of the 'rural' westerly Thames, which is the main subject of this chapter, villages and towns also grew up in the countryside around the river's crossing points. This can be seen to this day with Kew and, on its opposite bank, Brentford, Isleworth and Chiswick clustered around Kew Bridge; and Richmond, Petersham, Ham and Twickenham grouped around both sides of Richmond Bridge. Later on in this chapter, it will be shown how this pattern of overgrown villages on this lush stretch of the Thames has been further overlaid by being interspersed with parkland.

London itself is situated within a bowl – the saucer-like form of the London Basin – which is now mainly drained by the River Thames. This indentation is the result of earth movements some 25 million years ago, which formed a downwards sloping fold between the Chiltern Hills to the north and the North Downs to the south. The Thames itself originally flowed further to the north but was blocked by great glaciers during the last great ice age, which diverted the river to its present southerly location.

Previous page: Aerial view of the Thames, 2007
The present state of the Pool of London with very few seafaring ships, but with museum ships such as *HMS Belfast* in the centre. The river beyond goes to Canary Wharf, representing the shift of London's business centre out eastwards and the changing nature of the urban landscape, the river and its territories.

William Westall, *View from Richmond Hill*, **1828**
Famous view from Richmond Hill showing
the landscape, winding river and island
aits (or eyots) – an Arcadian scene.

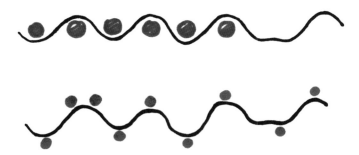

After these original ruptures or disturbances came a succession of cold and warm phases that varied the river levels according to the quantity of ice and ice-melt and the flow of the river. As the Thames grew and shrank over time, a succession of gravel terraces formed where the river's edge reached different stages. The greater the volume of water melting from the ice, the greater the strength of the river itself and the deeper the channel that was cut, and with each deeper channel, the setting would be more firmly laid. However, with each change the floodplain was spread out and left as a layer, a terrace, stepping down towards the river itself. It is this period of evolution that gave the river its winding quality, meandering through the great saucer-like bowl between the chalk uphills to the north and south. It is a legacy that has persisted in the landscape that the Thames sits within today.

It was, though, the great thaw, which came at the end of the glacial periods about 13,000 years ago, which brought about an irrevocable change for Britain and the Thames. As sea levels began to rise, Britain was cut off from the land mass of Europe. Previously a tributary of the Rhine, the Thames now became a great river in its own right, and the main artery of the newly formed island.

This original connection of the Thames to its 'mother' river is a key bit of its history. Despite the geological 'schism', the Thames remained immediately opposite the Rhine on the North Sea. Across from this great highway of Europe, it became the obvious inward route to Britain for European colonisers and traders alike. Waves of immigrants made the crossing from the Continent to the island; you can imagine many of them returning, generations after Britain's separation by the sea to what had once been part of their tribal lands. Julius Caesar described later immigrants as 'Celtic people who came to plunder and stayed to till'. And that seems to have been the immigration pattern right through the ages. It was the Celts who gave the river its original name, *Tamesas,* which is thought to mean 'dark river', after the heavy, muddy sediment carried out to sea. These murky deposits were picked up from the clay beds and swirled about by the considerable tidal shifts racing in and out twice a day.

The river's shape has given many of London's villages and towns their names. The Saxon word '*hamme*', for instance, means 'sheltered place'. Upstream from Kew, the Hams – Ham, Petersham and Twickenham – are located on fertile land where the water meadows flooded. From the vantage point of Richmond Hill, cattle can still be seen grazing on the lush fields of Petersham Meadows adjacent to the Thames; a view that has changed little, in its verdant sweep, since Turner and William Westall painted the Thames at Richmond in the early 1800s. The Thames' broad flood plain, the bowl of the saucer, is always visible from within urban London and from towns and villages up and down its banks, right into the estuary.

The presence of England's rolling countryside in the centre of its capital has been a constant for Londoners through the

Farrell, Places on the rural Thames, 2009
The seven main bends, with open spaces (green dots) on the convex banks: Hurst and Bushy Parks, Hampton Court Park, Ham Lands, Petersham, Richmond Hill Old Deer Park, Syon Park and Kew Gardens. The towns and villages on the outside bends (red dots) are: Hampton, Thames Ditton, Kingston, Teddington, Twickenham, Ham, Richmond, Isleworth and Brentford.

ages. London's pastoral setting is as present in Dickens as the grime and poverty of the city's Victorian streets: with Pip in *Great Expectations* walking out from Jaggers' office in Little Britain in the City to the Pocket family's house on the riverside at Hammersmith; and Arthur Clennam's movements in *Little Dorrit* taking in visits to Amy and her father in the Marshalsea Debtors' Prison, in Southwark, as well as trips to the Meagles family at their cottage between Richmond Bridge and Teddington Lock, where 'within view was the peaceful river, and the ferry boat'. Even today, though the land at the centre of the Thames Valley remains relatively flat, from any tall building or vantage point within London the hills and trees and distant 'rural' villages that edge the bowl are very much apparent: Hampstead, Highgate and Harrow to the north; Crystal Palace and Greenwich to the south; and Richmond and Kingston to the west.

The Thames Defined

For the purposes of this book, the Thames has been grouped into four chapters that highlight the particular character of each stretch of the river. The upstream, or 'Rural Upper Thames', ranges from Hampton Court, where resident royalty had the uppermost formal influence upon the banks, down to Kew, equally rooted in royal estates but now an area of parkland and villages. The royals adopted this part of the Thames as their corridor of connection from Windsor and Hampton Court down towards London. The tidal limit is now the lock at Teddington, a name thought by some to mean 'tides end town', but it predates the first known weir by some centuries and actually refers to the 'tun', or settlement of Tuda's people (the latter comes from a deduced Saxon name

deriving from the three place-name elements in Teddington: 'Tedd', thought to be a derivative of the Saxon name 'Tuda'; 'ing' (ingas), referring to the dependants or relatives of; and 'ton', the Saxon word for a farmstead. So Teddington could be read as 'Tuda's relatives' farmstead'.)

At Kew one enters a set of more closely spaced bridges and a more urban terrain that continues right through the centre of London. I have called this the 'Urban Thames' with the easterly end of this urbanity very much historically based at the Pool of London, where Tower Bridge has provided the lowest urban bridging point since its opening in 1894. Beyond this are the 'Docklands' Thames between the City of London and Woolwich, where extensive docks were built in the 19th century, and the 'Estuary Thames', which is the place of trade, the point of connection to the sea and global exploration; with its power stations, sewerage works, landfills and great industrial complexes, it has an enduring role as the 'engine room' that drives the city.

Kew Palace, 1631
Formerly known as the Dutch House, Kew Palace is the earliest surviving building in Kew Gardens, and was built by Flemish merchant Samuel Fortrey.

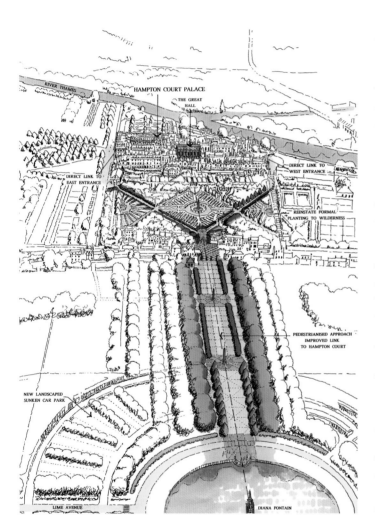

Image labels:
RIVER THAMES
HAMPTON COURT PALACE
THE GREAT HALL
DIRECT LINK TO EAST ENTRANCE
DIRECT LINK TO WEST ENTRANCE
REINSTATE FORMAL PLANTING TO WILDERNESS
PEDESTRIANISED APPROACH IMPROVED LINK TO HAMPTON COURT
NEW LANDSCAPED SUNKEN CAR PARK
LIME AVENUE
DIANA FONTAIN

**Farrell, Proposed view of improved
link with Hampton Court, Royal
Parks study, 1994**
Part of Farrell's Royal Parks study
showing how the Bushy Park and
Hampton Court vistas across the
Thames could be linked together.

The Westerly Rural Thames

By way of contrast to the easterly stretches of the river, the rural
Thames to the far west of the city, from Hampton Court to Kew,
offers unpolluted sunlight, leisure and a healthy quality of life in
an extraordinarily pleasant valley, a kind of Utopia or Arcadia, a
bucolic model for many of the perfect life. It is an idyllic place.
(This is the case to this day with Richmond remaining a highly
desirable residential area with some of the highest property prices
in outer London.) For many centuries this rural valley was a place
of escape from London. There was a royal residence established
at Sheen Palace in medieval times, which became known as
Richmond Palace when it became popular with the Tudors. In
1625, Charles I brought his court to Richmond Palace to escape
the plague. Richmond Palace and Hampton Court were within
easy river transport from the Palace of Westminster but away from
the prevailing wind that blew pollution and smoke downstream
eastwards and out to sea.

In the late 17th century, royalty moved permanently upwind
from Greenwich and the central London palaces. William III and
Mary II, who did not care for Whitehall, commissioned Christopher
Wren in 1689 to rebuild Hampton Court. The Old Deer Park at
Richmond, which had been sold off with Richmond Lodge and
Richmond Palace by Parliament under the Commonwealth, was
also reassembled. This resulted in the nearby hunting grounds
being regenerated as the home of royal and courtly society. The
formal hunting grounds of Richmond Park and Bushy Park were
quite different in character to the urban Royal Parks, which were
rooted in an earlier period of royal 'urban' hunting grounds –
such as Hyde Park, Regent's Park, Green Park and St James's Park.

Aerial view of Hampton Court Palace
Hampton Court was well connected to London by the river. It acted as a royal magnet enticing courtiers and nobility to build their own houses on this westerly rural section of the river.

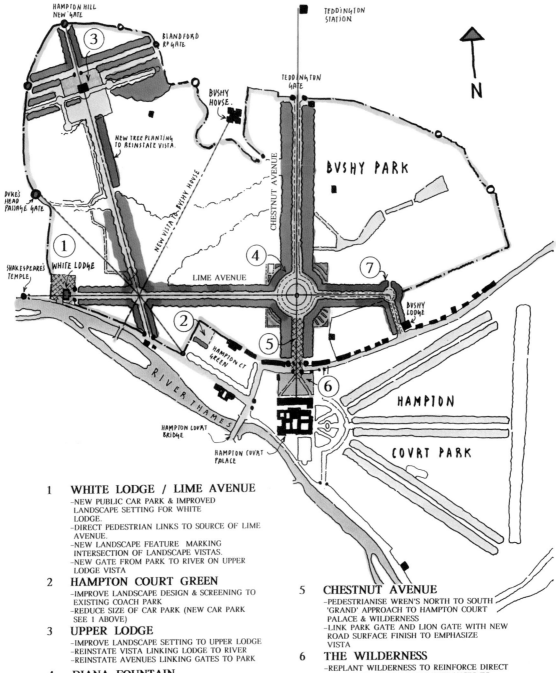

1 WHITE LODGE / LIME AVENUE

-NEW PUBLIC CAR PARK & IMPROVED
LANDSCAPE SETTING FOR WHITE
LODGE.
-DIRECT PEDESTRIAN LINKS TO SOURCE OF LIME
AVENUE.
-NEW LANDSCAPE FEATURE MARKING
INTERSECTION OF LANDSCAPE VISTAS.
-NEW GATE FROM PARK TO RIVER ON UPPER
LODGE VISTA

2 HAMPTON COURT GREEN

-IMPROVE LANDSCAPE DESIGN & SCREENING TO
EXISTING COACH PARK
-REDUCE SIZE OF CAR PARK (NEW CAR PARK
SEE 1 ABOVE)

3 UPPER LODGE

-IMPROVE LANDSCAPE SETTING TO UPPER LODGE
-REINSTATE VISTA LINKING LODGE TO RIVER
-REINSTATE AVENUES LINKING GATES TO PARK

4 DIANA FOUNTAIN

-FORM NEW PLANTED LANDSCAPE SETTING
-FORM NEW VEHICLE ROUTE OUT TO BUSHY
LODGE
-PEDESTRIANISE WREN'S GRAND VISTA TO
HAMPTON COURT
-CLOSE EXISTING & PROVIDE NEW CAR PARKS
DESIGNED INTO NEW LANDSCAPE SETTING
TO DIANA FOUNTAIN
-REINSTATE LANDSCAPE TO LINK TREE PLANTED
AVENUES

5 CHESTNUT AVENUE

-PEDESTRIANISE WREN'S NORTH TO SOUTH
'GRAND' APPROACH TO HAMPTON COURT
PALACE & WILDERNESS
-LINK PARK GATE AND LION GATE WITH NEW
ROAD SURFACE FINISH TO EMPHASIZE
VISTA

6 THE WILDERNESS

-REPLANT WILDERNESS TO REINFORCE DIRECT
ROUTES TO EAST & WEST ENTRANCES TO
HAMPTON COURT PALACE.

7 LIME AVENUE / BUSHY LODGE

-REINSTATE PLANTED VISTA OF WREN'S EAST
TO WEST VISTA
-FORM NEW LANDSCAPE FEATURE AT END OF
VISTA
-FORM NEW LOW KEY VEHICULAR ROUTE OUT
ALONG LINE OF EXISTING LANE ADJACENT
TO BUSHY LODGE

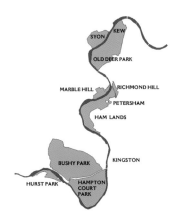

"(The Summit of a far-famed Hill".)

RICHMOND PARK

BY THE

UNDERGROUND

HUMOURS OF LONDON Nº 10

These western parks would never have been considered as part of the city or to be adjoining; they were in the middle of the countryside, in a truly rural setting, rather than trapped pieces of countryside within the town.

The ownership of parkland in this area was not just confined to royalty – many other parks were run by nobles and the church, along with scattered hunting lodges. The Earls of Northumberland, for instance, had their house at Syon since Tudor times, set in extensive parkland which was remodelled in the middle of the 18th century by Capability Brown. York House and its estate in Twickenham was built for Andrew Pitcarne, a courtier of King Charles I, in the 1630s; and Ham House, close to Richmond, was extensively rebuilt after the Restoration in the 1670s by John Maitland, 1st Duke of Lauderdale and Secretary of State for Scotland, in a manner that fully reflected his position as one of the most powerful ministers of Charles II. Hunting took place as a sport and for sustenance on both land and water, as the Thames, as was reported in Tudor times, provided more fish than any other river in Europe. The great parks, such as Richmond, were of considerable size; in 1637 Charles I had established Richmond Park as 1012 hectares (2,500 acres), surrounded by 13 kilometres (8 miles) of brick wall to control poaching and to stop deer escaping. Eventually public gates were made in true people-power style – hard-fought for, and not finally established until John Lewis's famous court victory of 1758 – to enable commoners to exercise their rights and enter the park. This pattern of gradual, evolutionary shift of power expresses itself writ large all over

Opposite: Farrell, Seven-point plan to improve Bushy Park, Royal Parks study 1994
Plans showing how Bushy Park, Hampton Court and vistas across the Thames could be linked together in this Arcadian and sublime landscape.

Above: Tony Sarg, *Richmond Park by the Underground*, poster, 1913
Connected to royalty since the 13th century, Richmond Park now has a long tradition of public access, having been open to 'the common people' since the 18th century. Three times the size of Central Park in New York, Londoners come here from all over the city to walk, cycle, picnic and ride.

Farrell, Position of parks along the Thames, Royal Parks study, 1994
Sitting on the inside bends, the great formal parklands of the River Thames lie in a stretch from Hampton Court to Kew.

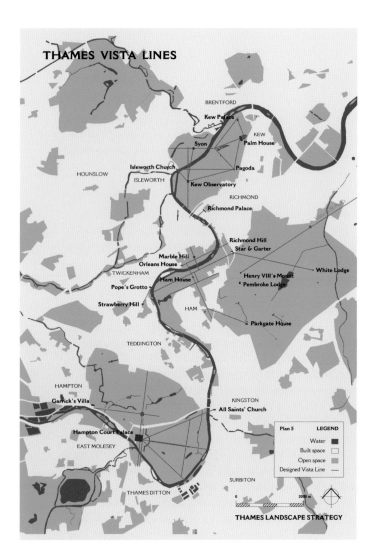

THAMES VISTA LINES

BRENTFORD

Kew Palace

KEW
Syon
Palm House

Isleworth Church
HOUNSLOW
ISLEWORTH
Pagoda

Kew Observatory

RICHMOND

Richmond Palace

Richmond Hill
Star & Garter

Marble Hill
Orleans House
TWICKENHAM   White Lodge
Ham House
Henry VIII's Mount
Pope's Grotto   Pembroke Lodge

Strawberry Hill
HAM

Parkgate House

TEDDINGTON

HAMPTON

Garrick's Villa   KINGSTON
All Saints' Church

Plan 5   LEGEND

Water

Hampton Court Palace
EAST MOLESEY   Built space
Open space
Designed Vista Line

SURBITON
THAMES DITTON
0   2000 m

THAMES LANDSCAPE STRATEGY

Kim Wilkie, Thames vista lines,
Thames Landscape Strategy, 1994
The river is wonderfully varied and the
unique character of the landscape is
defined by a strategy, illustrated here, of
emphasising and reinforcing these vistas
to form a continuously linked landscape.
A brilliant exemplar for how all the Thames
and indeed most of urban London could
be planned.

London; palaces, Royal Parks, great streets are just as layered on the map in present-day London as the terraces and levels of the river and its gravel beds, which are naturally found, and are equally integral to London's urban shape.

Looking at maps and drawings, it is very noticeable how the twisting bends and gentle curves of the river relate to the parks and public landscape. The settlements are on the deeply eroded but stable outer sides of the bends, with Hampton to the north, followed at the next twist of the river by Thames Ditton and Kingston on the other side, then back across to Teddington and Twickenham and back over again to Richmond, across to Isleworth and Brentford and, finally, back over to Kew. As for all London, one is tempted to always call the opposite sides the south and north banks but, as it often confusingly does at other places, the river runs from north to south (as here), and so the banks are to the east and west. Just as the settlements alternate to the outside of the navigable bends, the parks tend to sit opposite them on the low-lying banks on the inside bends, with the gardens at Hampton Court Palace, Ham Common, Richmond and, slightly higher up and further along, Syon Park and Kew all sitting within the sweeping bends of the river.

The Thames Landscape Strategy is one of the few broad-scale studies anywhere in London. Its shape, form and patterns were established as a public project in 1994, and it sets out a 100-year strategy of protection and enhancement for the river and its surroundings from Hampton to Kew. From 2005 this has included the London Arcadia scheme which has restored the view of the Thames from Richmond Hill, linking up the public spaces along the banks, and planting trees, hedgerows and reed beds to recreate a natural but managed environment. The overall Thames

SYON

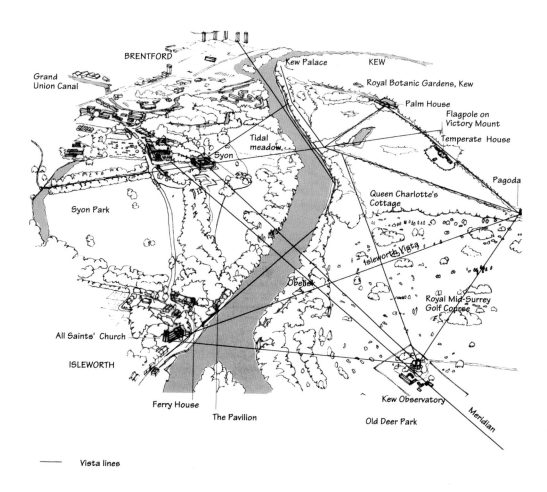

—— Vista lines

Landscape Strategy is led by landscape architect and urban planner Kim Wilkie. This strategy was created originally by a study and exhibition I organised for the Royal Fine Art Commission in 1991–2, the Thames Study, when Kim Wilkie first made public his ideas. This is a format I have pursued continuously, of promoting proactive strategic concepts for planning London's future, all based on the city and its landscape/urban underlying history and character. Wilkie presented proposals for a line of vistas and connecting avenues which were based on the idea that the seemingly natural rural Thames was, indeed, a controlled

Kim Wilkie, Syon, Thames Landscape Strategy, 1994
Vista lines that connect Syon to Kew Observatory, Kew Palace and the Pagoda in Kew Gardens, and All Saints' Church to Kew Observatory and Pagoda, among others.

landscape made for enjoyment and leisure. It was deliberately laid out so that the geometries of vistas were connected to the bends of the river and parklands – very much part of the English landscape tradition, working with not against nature, adjusting and post-rationalising, as it were, the land's innate possibilities.

Of course, it is no accident that this part of the river is more navigable and therefore more accessible along its banks: unlike the urban Thames and tributaries in the central areas, the banks of the upper Thames are natural, while their accessibility is increased because of the limited tidal flow and flooding. Although predictions of both riparian flooding and tidal flooding still remain, the presence of slipways, landing stages, moorings and boat-houses presents a picture of a section of river which, unlike the rest of its subsequent journey down to the estuary and sea, remains fully accessible along almost all of its banks. These elements are also a demonstration of the continuous access to the river from the combination of great Royal Parks and public common lands; it was Queen Victoria who opened Hampton Court and Bushy Park to the public in 1838, and in 1841 opened Kew Gardens as a scientific institution when it became the Royal Botanic Gardens. Marble Hill Park in Twickenham, together with Ham and Richmond, are all extraordinary public landscapes within this section of the river valley.

There are great houses and aristocratic villas within these landscapes and along the banks, which were mostly built during the second decade of the 18th century: Lord Burlington of the Devonshire family designed a neo-Palladian villa for himself at Chiswick (completed 1729); in the same year, Marble Hill House was built for George II's mistress Henrietta Howard, Countess of Suffolk in Twickenham; and the first prime minister's son Horace Walpole built his Gothic Revival 'little castle' at Strawberry Hill (1749–72). Robert Adam redesigned Syon House (1762–9) for the Dukes of Northumberland and a new house at Osterley Park for the Child family, owner of Child's Bank (commencing in 1761). The noble families and the court established their own palaces along the upper Thames for the same reasons that the royal family came here – emulating the sovereign, they could travel up by boat to enjoy the sublime countryside and to escape the pollution of urban London. These houses were very much country retreats rather than true country houses on large-scale agricultural estates. Georgiana, Duchess of Devonshire, describes dividing her time between her London residence at Devonshire House in Piccadilly, the Devonshire estate at Chatsworth in Derbyshire and Chiswick House. The 18th-century aristocracy were itinerant, following the court seasonally to London and their residences to the west of the city, while also maintaining their power bases on their own great estates.

At each bend of the westerly Thames there is a pattern of islands – or more accurately, islets or aits – deposited in the river, splitting the river into channels. As these tree-heavy islands emerge along the winding vistas, they give the Thames a completely different scale, a much narrower intimacy, making the river friendlier for small boats and recreation than the downstream stretches. Spaced at intervals, the islands help to break the main block of the river into separate smaller elements, so there is a linear sequence of villages and small towns each with its own community and identity. It is probably the bulk of Richmond Hill, a large block of slightly higher land, which forces the Thames to run northwards and also to keep bending as it works its way towards the urban city. It is not until it is past this section of higher land,

Marble Hill House, Twickenham, 1724–9
This picture epitomises the great houses on the river's edge. The south front of the house faces the Thames in the foreground. This magnificent Palladian villa was built for the Countess of Suffolk, mistress of George II.

past Kew, that the river returns to a much broader sweep with fewer meandering bends.

Bends in the river, the alternating banks of landscape and urbanisation, the frequency of the islands breaking the stretches of water into reaches of different scales – all of this established a pattern, a rhythm that makes this the glorious section of the metropolitan Thames area. The range of ownership, scale and human occupation give the upper Thames its own enormously varied, rippling, diverse, multi-layered character. The architectural scale ranges from the great palaces to the smaller villas of the nobility, right down to the individual frontages of houses and bungalows. Even on the aits there are little houses with domestic boat-houses, some very small and some converted into villas and bungalows. Moorings and boatyards, and people living in houseboats on quite long sections at Kew, Brentford, Isleworth, St Margarets, Thames Ditton, Hampton and East Molesey, are all part of the riverside scene here, making it unlike any stretch of the urban Thames further east. Along the river there are eight bridges between Hampton Court and Kew, with locks and major utility sites, providing water-handling facilities.

This rural upstream river landscape sets the stage for much that follows in urban London, the docklands and the estuary. London is a city planned organically, upon and close to nature, with the whole metropolis coalescing from a pattern of country villages and towns, with and around the shapes of tributaries, woodlands, Royal Parks and the field patterning of the great landed farming estates (even today it is calculated that there are 500 farms still active in Greater London). London is a natural city, a child of nature much more than a planned urban city. All the way down to the sea the river bends continue to shape settlement patterns just as they have done in the rural Thames, although the scale changes to wider and longer bends. Like here, great parklands are formed on the downstream banks such as Battersea and Greenwich and are formed too around the tributaries such as the central London Royal Parks and Hampstead Heath. There is also a story of continued democratisation of land ownership and accessibility cascading down from Crown to aristocracy to middle classes and commoners, all waves of social change over time evolving and adjusting slowly and peacefully so that the historical layers remain near the surface – the patterns of the past are ever evident.

There are differences that set the rural Thames apart, as lower down there is much less direct access to the water itself, less private ownership of the banks. Further down we find a tougher, harder urban world with a scale change of wider and bigger bends. Prevailing wind blows three days out of five from the west and so smoke and air pollution follows the same direction as the river flows, and with it sewage and city waste. As the density increases eastwards there is a steadily increasing continuum as the people of the city discharge whatever they have used up or do not want, which becomes ever more concentrated on its way down to the sea. In many ways the rural Thames is an ideal or a model for all living in London. One day, with a successful green planning agenda, I would like to think that all the lower reaches could have an air and water quality and access to green space and riverbanks that the residents here enjoy. It is a wonderful idea and exemplar for London generally with the Thames Landscape Strategy galvanising and uniting planners, politicians and the community to work collectively on a place-based focus of common endeavour.

Aerial view of Petersham, 2003
A current aerial view capturing so much of the character of London's rural Thames with parklands and great houses close to the river, small boats in marinas and fine houses built through the centuries. In the centre of this photo are Farrell's three courtyard houses designed in 2003.

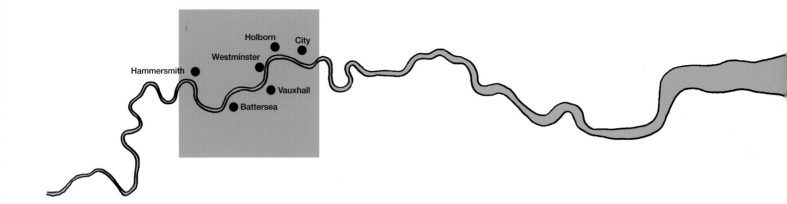

The Urban Thames

The 'Mid-Urban' Thames

The stretch of the Thames between Kew and Vauxhall is neither entirely suburban nor urban, but can be regarded rather as 'mid-urban'. The green wedges of park that characterise the 'rural upper Thames' of the previous chapter, here give way to the residential frontages of Chiswick, Mortlake, Barnes, Hammersmith, Putney, Parsons Green, Chelsea, Battersea and Pimlico. These are affluent areas of west London that are largely made up of pleasant tree-lined streets of Edwardian and Victorian houses, where even the former breweries, dockyards, gasworks and power stations that once lined the banks have been rehabilitated as attractive residential properties. In contrast on the south bank is the monolithic hulk of Battersea Power Station, which seems to elude all redevelopment, and the generous green of Battersea Park. This is counterbalanced on the north bank by the urbane landscaping of the Chelsea Embankment and Christopher Wren's Royal Chelsea Hospital.

On this section of the Thames, the bridges change dramatically. They have a presence, a collective identity that is unique to this part of the river. Hammersmith Bridge, Chelsea Bridge and Albert Bridge are all decorative suspension bridges. It is as though the grand buildings of the central urban Thames need a suppressed expression of bridges, so they are all plain, self-effacing and flat topped. Here, though, where the urban scenery is less conspicuous and often set back from the river edge, it is the bridges themselves that are the divas; there are probably good engineering reasons for all this, but it is the urban theatricality that comes to the fore. Almost wholly residential, this west London stretch of the Thames remains an intermediary to the urban Thames that is the real subject of this chapter.

The Urban Thames Proper

The urban Thames proper can de defined as the section of the river that is 'tourist London' and is associated the world over with the great metropolis. It is the relatively short section from Vauxhall Bridge to Tower Bridge, which is a little more than 4.8 kilometres (3 miles) long. (The mid-urban stretch from Kew to

Henry Pether, *York Water Gate
and the Adelphi from the River
by Moonlight*, 1845–60
Here the water gate that is now
landlocked and located in Embankment
Gardens, is shown in its original waterside
location. It is a marker of how much the
river's banks have been moved inwards.

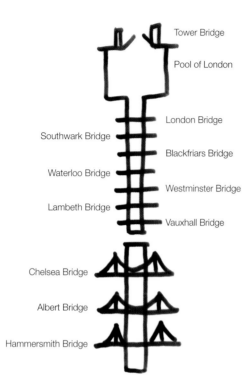

Tower Bridge

Pool of London

London Bridge

Southwark Bridge

Blackfriars Bridge

Waterloo Bridge

Westminster Bridge

Lambeth Bridge

Vauxhall Bridge

Chelsea Bridge

Albert Bridge

Hammersmith Bridge

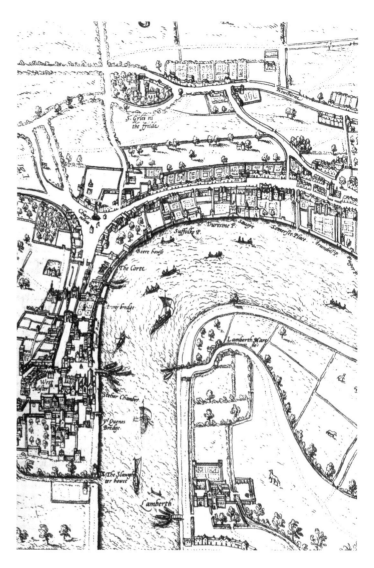

Vauxhall is more like 16 kilometres (10 miles) along the river's edge.) With its landmark buildings, it is these banks that are visually the most potent and pervasive. Having been reproduced for several centuries in paintings and for tourist souvenirs, it is here that the Thames becomes an integral part of the view and integral to London's identity. Edged by Westminster at its westerly end and the City at its easterly end, the Thames is lined by Big Ben, Parliament and Westminster Abbey, as well as newer tourist destinations such as the London Eye and Tate Modern on the South Bank, and iconic buildings such as St Paul's, the Tower of London and Tower Bridge itself. Here, the Thames has a much more elementary pattern compared with the river upstream and downstream. It has a single unifying, underlying geometry. It is a great curved bend; a bow-shaped arc that begins upstream of the Houses of Parliament near Vauxhall Bridge and ends after Tower

Bridge. It is this looping shape that continues to cause visitors quite a lot of confusion in terms of orientation between the two banks. It has, though, significantly given rise to the north and south banks having quite different characters for many centuries, with London proper existing almost exclusively only on the north side.

Farrell, Pattern of the Thames' urban bridges, 2009
In the central area the bridges are flat topped and simple. In the less dense area upstream, the skyline view is dominated not by grand palaces and other great buildings, but by the three decorative suspension bridges, creating a distinctly different visual experience from one part of the river to the next.

Georg Braun and Franz Hogenburg,
Londinium Feracissimi Angliae Regni Metropolis (Map of London), **1572**
The drawing shows the bend of the Thames at Westminster. The south bank was still substantially rural and Westminster itself connected through gates up Whitehall to Charing Cross. Various quays and water gates are clearly shown along the river's edge.

The character of the north bank was born out of its natural features that gave it an advantage in three important respects: the land to the north is slightly higher and the river cuts into it so there is a naturally formed south-facing slope on the north side that enables it to benefit from sunlight and warmth; there is also a deep channel up against the bend as the faster water on the outside of the river catches the bend and scours out the bed so that boats can travel closer to the outside bend, closer to the land; at the close of the bend, near today's London Bridge, the river was fordable, which gave the Romans and their successors the ideal

William Daniell, *The Tower of London*, 1804
Busy trade activity on the River Thames. The Tower of London can be seen on the right of the picture, the Pool of London before the first bridging point.

place to make the first crossing of the Thames inland from the sea. It is the combination of these aspects – such simple matters of natural terrain and geography, and the effect of the forces of nature working together – that meant London was founded here, just where it is. These are all essential characteristics of London's location that we tend to overlook now that our homes are centrally heated, that we do not rely on the river for transport and communication and that there is a proliferation of bridges.

In due course, London was to grow between two points on this bend, where two cities were built: Westminster, upstream towards the beginning of the bend where a pre-Roman ford crossed the Thames at Lambeth, and the City of London itself, towards the end of the bend at the Pool of London. For a millennium or more, London existed at just one end, the City end. Elsewhere along the Thames, the twisting and turning of the river dictated which sides were inhabited and which sides were empty. On the south side, flowing alongside the flatter land, was slow water which deposited mud and material on the inside bend, so the banks were as shallow and muddy as the great Lambeth Marsh further inland. With the tide ebbing and flowing, this meant that access to any possible landing points was much more difficult and could only be made by planks and jetties at high tide – so landing was messy, difficult and only possible for a limited period of time. And so it was that the inside bends of the Thames were less habitable and therefore of less value. Here, at the centre of the great arc, the whole city was lopsided – it grew on one bank only. The north bank was also favoured for its defensive position; it was the best place for invaders to try to conquer from and retreat to – the bulk of the land of England being north of this point, of course.

The Tidal Thames

The tidal presence had an enormous effect on the shape and character of the developing city. Initially, before human occupation, the very width of the Thames was extraordinarily different to what we see today; on the north bank, excavations have uncovered Roman quays some 100 metres (328 feet) beyond the modern riverbank. Over the years, the Thames' natural width was adjusted, adapted and moved ever inwards in order to narrow the river and to control the banks and their access, especially on the north side. Now, as archaeologists excavate continuously, particularly among the foundations of the north bank, they have put together different stages of development, with Roman, Viking, medieval and Victorian lines all moving the bank inexorably further south, further into the Thames. Gradually, the south bank has also encroached, with the result that the river is now a greatly narrowed man-made channel which has created an 'artificial' tidal range of up to 7 metres (23 feet) and is totally unlike its original, natural form.

One particular example of this transition is The Strand, which takes its name from the Old English word for beach or shore. In medieval times, The Strand was the main street running alongside the river between the City of London and the Palace of Westminster. This made it a popular location for residences of nobility and bishops seeking influence at court. In the 18th century, much of the former foreshore was covered by rubble from the demolished Tudor palace, Denmark House, in order to create a large platform for the building of the new Somerset House.

The Strand is today located well inland some several blocks from the present river's edge, having been pushed further back still by the construction of the Victoria Embankment between

Tower Bridge on the River Thames, early 20th century

A similar view to William Daniell's view of the Thames, looking in the opposite direction, this aerial photo was taken a hundred years later. It was the arrival of the lifting Tower Bridge that enabled sailing boats to enter the Pool of London.

1864 and 1870. Midway between The Strand and the river, though, is an intermediary riverbank stage, now marked by a 'folly' in Embankment Gardens. This is the York Water Gate (c 1625), the ornate gateway to York House, which was owned by James I's favourite, George Villiers, the Duke of Buckingham. Boldly rusticated in an Italianate style, it was reputedly designed by Inigo Jones and executed by Nicholas Stone. So much attention was lavished by Buckingham on this riverside entrance for his mansion because it provided the main access from the garden

front side of York House to the Thames at a time when the boat remained the most viable means of getting around the city. After the Restoration, York House was sold on to a property developer who demolished it and redeveloped the entire area, leaving only the water gate behind. Then, when the Embankment was opened in 1870, the water gate ended up truly landlocked some 137 metres (450 feet) from the water's edge.

The narrowing of London's river has had the effect of intensifying the speed of its flow and has altered the range of

Aerial view of London, 2005

This clearly shows the difference between the territories trapped between the raised railway viaducts going into Waterloo and other stations and how the south bank has been heavily industrialised and built up with offices. South of the viaducts, however, are residential areas with green spaces.

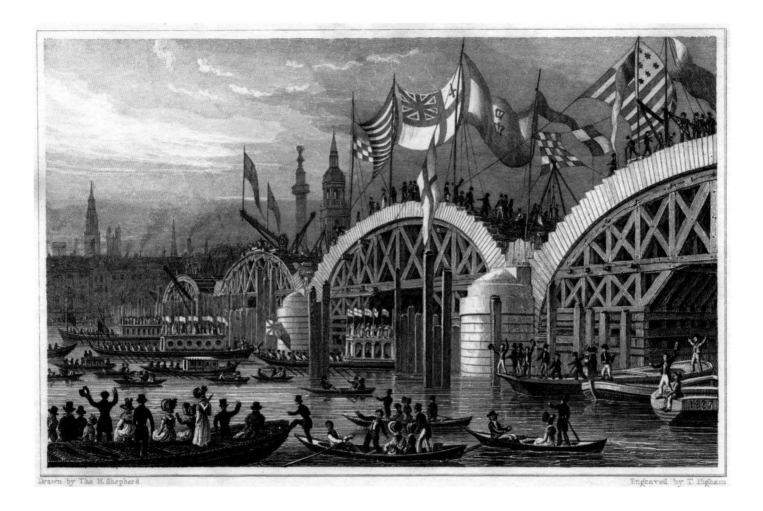

Drawn by Tho. H. Shepherd   Engraved by T. Higham

heights between low and high tide, which all combine to make the Thames increasingly difficult to navigate. One only has to sit by the Seine in Paris, London's nearest comparable capital, placed well inland from tidal influences, to see the effect this has upon a city. In Paris, the river sits in a composed way, flowing leisurely, relatively unvarying in its relationships to the levels of its banks. In contrast, the Thames is wide and quite fearsome: twice a day vast volumes of water race inland and back again in great, unnatural, surging sweeps. The Thames is swirling, speeding and muddy with silt suspended in the water like a continuously emptying dirty bath that refills just as quickly, covering and recovering tidemarks and refuse-filled mud banks; at high tide it can, alarmingly rapidly, fill right up to the brim of the flood walls.

Recently, much has been made of reinstating London's urban public water transport, but the difficulties of the tidal range and the speed of the river have made the use of the Thames very difficult, though not impossible. Before the demise of a scheme at Battersea Power Station, a comprehensive plan was drawn up by the

Boats passing under
London Bridge, 1827
New London Bridge, with the Lord
Mayor's procession passing under the
unfinished arches on 9 November 1827.

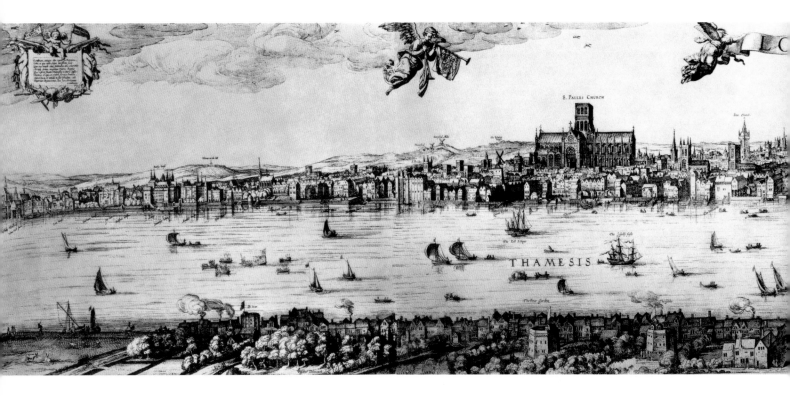

developers for a water service which for the first time would work officially in conjunction with London Transport and be featured on the transport maps of the city. It is still perceived as something of a novel idea for Londoners to have a water transport service, yet in Hong Kong, Sydney Harbour and San Francisco, where other great waters meet the sea, the water forms a major part of the public transport system with hundreds of thousands sailing back and forth on boats every day. Clearly, London would greatly benefit from this direct, quick access, recreating the river once again, as it used to be, as a major public transport route. However, any ideas along these lines have met with considerable difficulties, mostly because of the effects of the tidal rush and its range.

There was a time when the effects of this tidal phenomenon were almost eliminated and the river in central London became a completely different place. This was the later medieval era when the old London Bridge, with its massive close-spaced supports – 19 stone arches of varying width – reduced the tidal flow so much that there could be ice fairs in winter upon the static waters upstream of the bridge. This all came to an end when the 622-year-old structure was demolished in 1832, but the old saying 'London Bridge is falling down' actually comes from the effect of the weirs cascading through the bridge, the price that had to be paid for holding back the static waters of low tide above the bridge. The weirs would have continuously undermined the bridge, which acted like a dam. With the technologies available then, the wooden pile supports would have been endlessly eroding as time passed.

Partly inspired by the idealised pictures of Canaletto's non-tidal river and its flotillas of small boats, and partly motivated by a need to radically address the predicted rise of the river's water

Nicholas Jansz Visscher,
Panorama of London, 1616
Visscher drew the south bank in the early 17th century when the theatres and bear pits were being closed down and the city skyline was still dominated by old St Paul's.

levels due to climate change and global warming, there are ever-present enthusiasts for making the Thames truly non-tidal by creating a tidal barrier further downstream. In 1944, JHO Bunge even wrote a full book on the subject, *Tideless Thames in Future London*, arguing for its feasibility and benefits, but these ideas are always countered by those who enjoy the romantic connection of river and sea, the presence of the wilderness and the great force of nature's powers which Londoners witness as a spectacle twice a day. There are few, if any, major world cities where this scale of tidal range is seen right in a city's heart – it is a very special and unique part of London's identity. But the river level will rise permanently and the streets and underground tube system will be threatened – most probably during the 21st century – so that artificial control and management of some kind will be needed and its form and effect thought through and planned.

The Embankment

A city inevitably grows outwards, like the annular rings in a tree. The further back into the centre, the older the rings. However, because the banks of the urban Thames are man-made, London, at its very heart, does the reverse. As London has changed along its banks over the past centuries, in the very centre the actual edges of the river are newer than the area behind it. As has been suggested in relation to The Strand, the north bank was transformed by the creation of the Embankment at the end of the 19th century. This was substantially the result of a singular Victorian enterprise by Joseph Bazalgette (1819–91), who as Chief Engineer to London's Metropolitan Board of Works was responsible for the implementation of London's sewerage system and street improvements after the cholera epidemics of the

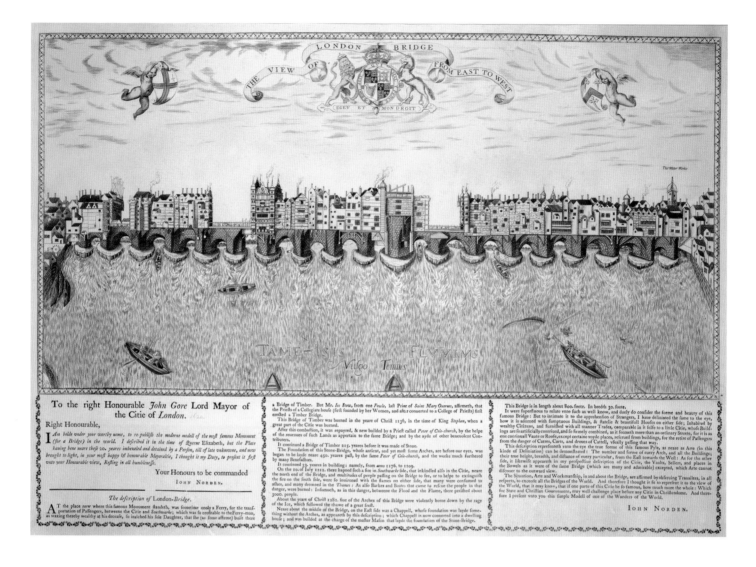

mid 1850s and 'the Great Stink' of 1858. (The Great Stink was the result of an unusually hot summer when the Thames and many of its urban tributaries literally overflowed with sewage, which encouraged bacteria to thrive. The resulting smell was so overwhelming that it affected the work of the House of Commons and the law courts, to the point that plans were put in place to

relocate Parliament to Hampton Court and the law courts to Oxford and St Albans before the weather broke.)

Bazalgette narrowed the river by building a phenomenal structure into the water to define its current edge. He merged a series of major infrastructural improvements as one continuous, spectacular linear project. The most obvious presence of this is

Old London Bridge
Multiple piers slowed down the flow of the water and created a weir that continuously undermined the bridge and created behind it a reduction in the tidal range levels.

the road itself, which sits on top of the structure for most of its length, and runs almost continuously along the riverside, taking in Cheyne Walk, Chelsea Embankment, Millbank and Victoria Embankment, until it is pushed back one block at Blackfriars Bridge and turns into Upper and Lower Thames Street in the City of London itself. Consequently, in central London there is, as

in Paris and much of Manhattan, a major road sitting between the city and the river, but this is no ordinary road. It is a complex structure, a linear 3D building providing several very major metropolitan functions: road, sewerage, mains water supply and underground railway. The first function is the road which is also part of a retaining embankment wall that holds back the tidal

Giovanni Canaletto, *The Thames at Westminster and Whitehall from The Terrace of Somerset House, c 1750–1*
Unlike today, London's river here appears flat and calm like the inland lagoons of Venice.

range. With global warming the water is rising ever higher and would continue to do so dangerously if not for the Thames Barrier down at Woolwich. It is still alarming to see how close to the top of the wall the water comes at very high tides – particularly in the Charing Cross and Waterloo Bridge area. Bazalgette's project provides one of the great significant differences between the north and south banks: the south bank remained in private ownership for a very long time, until halfway through the 20th century, with industrial wharfs and warehouses running along much of its length, while the north bank has been a publicly accessible thoroughfare for over 150 years.

Below the road and behind the embankment wall are the most extraordinary elements of Bazalgette's design and the real innovations for London. In the middle of the 19th century, the

Thames Embankment, 1867
Bazalgette's astonishing Victorian achievement of the new Embankment that moved the retaining wall further into the River Thames to allow for sewerage, water supplies and the arrival of the underground steam-driven rail systems of the District and Circle lines, and above it the construction of the new road system of Embankment Road.

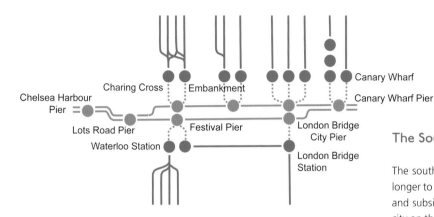

sewers and the rivers containing a great part of the metropolis's waste were intercepted in one great underground main sewer, which sent the waste downstream to the great outfall sewers at Beckton and Crossness. Water mains also run below the road in this linear edifice. Bazalgette's project enabled the extension too, in one inner circular loop, of the world's first completed underground railway system – the Circle Line. This part of the underground railway sits on top of the old river bed with the wall, sewers and road built around it in one singular edifice.

There have been some ridiculous proposals to eliminate the north bank, demolishing all that Bazalgette designed and built by sinking the road beneath the waters. This would be an extraordinary engineering extravagance when all that is needed is the extension of the system of traffic management on London Marathon days to more days of the year. The Bazalgette road surface could be reopened for pedestrians by closing or part-closing it to traffic at weekends. The adjacent Embankment Gardens, built as part of the Bazalgette plan, the surface of the road and the great walled river edge could together become a more regular public space – which would be a very formal, large-scale civic parade, a contrasting but complementary linear expression to the ad hoc, picturesque, piecemeal walkway that is now permanently on the south bank.

Farrell, Riverbus connections, 2009
Proposed riverbus connections as part of the redevelopment proposals for Battersea Power Station showing the integrated connections between the river and other major transport systems.

The South Bank

The south bank was of a much lower elevation and took much longer to develop than the north bank. It tended to have a service and subsidiary role, supplying what was needed to the growing city on the north bank. The Roman walled city on the north bank was safe for centuries even after the Romans left, particularly at night after curfew, which encouraged later invaders such as the Vikings to make their camps on the south bank. This set a

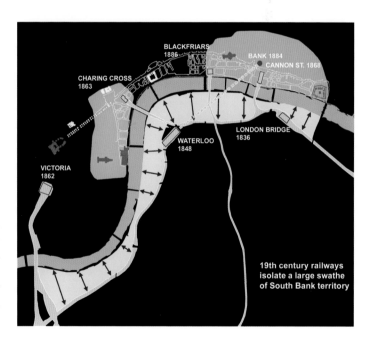

Farrell, 19th-century railways, 2007
The effect of the arrival of the railways from the south of London on elevated viaducts that isolated territory up against the riverbank.

As the north bank enlarged and became more densely populated, the south bank in the 18th century became a place of pleasure gardens easily accessible by private boat or by the many wherries, which with their notorious water men were as ubiquitous to London as the present-day black cab. The short-lived Belvedere Gardens – opened in 1781, as an inn with 'pleasant gardens and variety of fish-ponds', and closed by 1785 – were where the present Belvedere Road is now, running behind the Southbank Centre; by far the largest cultural complex in Europe, the Festival Hall and National Theatre continue the theatre and performance traditions that date back to Shakespeare's time on the south bank. South of the river were also the Cherry Gardens at Bermondsey, where Samuel Pepys visited the 'Jamaica House'

pattern and, during the late Middle Ages, it was the place for entertainment outside the curfewed and controlled city limits. It was Shakespeare's world, the alternative to the highly regulated urban life of the City, a kind of early 'Left Bank' or Soho or Greenwich Village; a world of creativity, invention and culture. The Globe and Rose theatres were here, as were bear- and bull-baiting spectacles. It also contained the lawless, the underworld of prostitution, drinking and gambling with all the dysfunctional and disruptive aspects which are the alternative life of all cities.

Thomas Rowlandson,
Vauxhall Gardens, 1808
Opened in 1661 and also known as
Spring Gardens, Vauxhall Gardens
reached the height of their popularity in
the early 1800s. They were the inspiration
for the Tivoli Gardens in Copenhagen as
well as other European pleasure gardens.

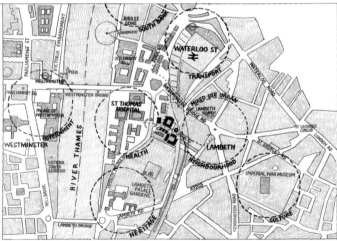

Farrell, South bank regeneration, 2001
Regeneration of the south bank with ideas
for Waterloo and areas around St Thomas'
Hospital all relating to Waterloo Station.

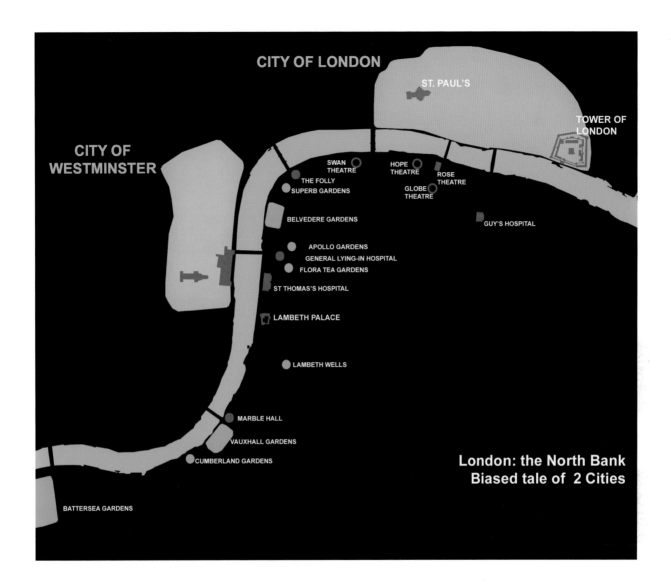

CITY OF LONDON

ST. PAUL'S

TOWER OF LONDON

CITY OF WESTMINSTER

SWAN THEATRE

HOPE THEATRE

ROSE THEATRE

THE FOLLY
SUPERB GARDENS

GLOBE THEATRE

BELVEDERE GARDENS

GUY'S HOSPITAL

APOLLO GARDENS
GENERAL LYING-IN HOSPITAL
FLORA TEA GARDENS

ST THOMAS'S HOSPITAL

LAMBETH PALACE

LAMBETH WELLS

MARBLE HALL

VAUXHALL GARDENS

CUMBERLAND GARDENS

**London: the North Bank
Biased tale of 2 Cities**

BATTERSEA GARDENS

and recorded in his diary that he had left it 'singing finely'; as was the Cuper's Garden, also known as Cupid's Garden, which was opposite Somerset House and once famous for its fireworks. It was named after the original proprietor, Abraham Boydell Cuper, who set up the gardens in the 1680s. Formerly the gardener

of the Earl of Arundel, Cuper procured a collection of antique marbles from his former employer with which he decorated the gardens. A long landing stage in the river known as Cuper's Bridge acted as a popular entrance. The garden, however, gained a notorious reputation and was suppressed in 1753.

Farrell, The north bank
of the Thames, 2007
The primary buildings of the two cities
of the north bank. Along the south bank
stretch various gardens and theatres.

The long-lived Vauxhall Gardens, however, which opened in 1661 and closed in 1859, survived in various forms for almost two centuries; and at their height were the very epitome of leisure gardens. With music from concert orchestras, sideshows, masquerades and lights on brackets, sconces and chandeliers, Vauxhall Gardens inspired the Tivoli in Copenhagen, which today perhaps gives some idea of what the Thameside gardens were like. On the north bank, on the site of what are now the grounds of the Royal Chelsea Hospital and the annual Chelsea Flower Show, were the more fashionable Ranelagh Gardens. Opened in 1742, they were more fashionable than Vauxhall Gardens (the entrance fee was two shillings and sixpence, rather than a shilling at Vauxhall) and were also accessible from the river by people wearing rich silks, embroidered coats, wigs and powder.

Today the south bank has steadily gained momentum again after over a century of an industrial period of wharfs and warehouses. This stretch of the Thames is now a parade of attractions from the Design Museum, just south of Tower Bridge, to the new vast Tate Modern inside Giles Gilbert Scott's Bankside Power Station, the Southbank Centre, Jubilee Gardens and the huge wheel (London Eye) and along to Battersea Gardens with its arts fair and long inner frontage of lawns and trees. Prior to this, though, in the 19th century, this whole zone of land on the south bank was cut off from the villages and towns to the south of London by elevated railway lines. This trapped the south bank, making its primary connections northwards. If one looks at the maps at the end on the 19th and first half of the 20th centuries, it is striking how the whole of the south bank was for a period totally industrialised with, at one side, privately owned warehouses and wharfs creating linear forms at the water's edge and, at the other, southern side, service road access. This industrial landscape, with many chimneys, breweries, brickworks, etc, was arranged so that

The Isle of London
Fanciful ideas, such as Nicholas Hare's, for islands in the Thames have continued through the years.

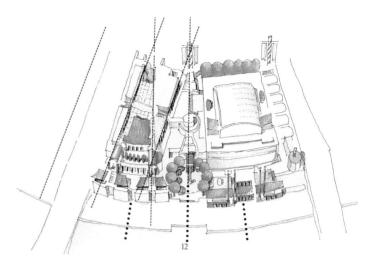

12

the bank was split into a thousand ownerships on this great bend, all adding to the pollution and industry of London.

The first real change began in 1917–22 with the very deliberate gesture of building County Hall, the new HQ of the government of the metropolis, proudly on the south bank – a visual challenge to the national government in the Houses of Parliament on the opposing bank and establishing its own clear, separate identity. It was built by the architect Ralph Knott as a result of a competition which many entered, including Edwin Lutyens. Its grand form still dominates the south bank and established, in front of it, the first piece of civic walkway and embankment that matched that on the north side. This development was embryonic to an extended pattern of public frontages and river walkways running from St Thomas's Hospital to the west and, to the east, in a very emphatic and public gesture in 1951, it connected County Hall to the Festival of Britain and its Festival Hall.

I clearly remember all the 1951 Festival of Britain's temporary cities laid out at Crystal Palace, and on the south bank around the Festival Hall and in Battersea Park, where there was a tree walk and the Guinness clock. As a child visiting from Newcastle, I had no mental map of London – it seemed to be a huge collection of different places – but the festival was a world created for a moment in time. With the Skylon and Dome of Discovery on the south bank, it helped me to see the force of design and introduced me to Joseph Paxton's original Crystal Palace, a surviving remnant of which had been erected on the south bank (its third home). The Festival came towards the end of Clement Attlee's Labour government, probably the most radical government of the 20th century, when the returning war heroes built a brave new world under socialist rule. The gesture of the Festival of Britain was part of this new spirit and the succeeding Conservative government wanted to remove all evidence of it, but they could not be seen to demolish two bits of lasting legacy (it would have been a step too far!): the Festival Hall, which became the core of the much loved recolonising of the south bank for the arts and entertainment, and, probably even more important for London's infrastructure, though less recognised, the new Embankment Walk with its dolphin lamps, its stone walls, its broad and generous walkway, and its tree planting.

The river and its banks are now recognised once again as the *genius loci*, the heart of London. The celebration of the millennium in 2000 took place as a royal barge paraded downstream and past Greenwich, in a scene that Elizabeth I would have recognised, with the monarch sailing under the bridges to the Millennium Dome before the public crowds. Substantial numbers of Londoners still gather to celebrate and watch the fireworks here on New Year's Eve and at major events on the bridges and embankments. The south bank walkway now has its own event, the Mayor's Thames Festival in September, the biggest public festival in London, that draws on the largest gathering/public realm space. To add to this the north bank is intermittently closed for public events, including the London Marathon and occasional parades.

Farrell, The Southbank Centre, 1984
The ongoing redevelopment of the Southbank cultural centre and the new editions during the late 20th and early 21st centuries.

The south bank today has moved from being a world of introverted, inaccessible private utility to its opposite, to a world of public recreation with access for all. This pattern is being repeated along embankments on either side of the Thames downstream and in many of the other dockside gentrifications around Britain. It has been a radical town-planning shift – the transfer from the exclusively private to the unambiguously public. Naturally, the pattern of private ownership and its very patchwork nature resulted in the south bank's reclamation being agonisingly slow and piecemeal. Parts of it, particularly the most ancient bits around Southwark Cathedral, have still not yet succeeded in full riverside access but the walk continues past Tower Bridge to a fine piece of new walkway and gradually comes to a halt at Butler's Wharf, just past the Design Museum, where the pattern of the 19th century still remains.

Travelling west, the walkway does not come to an end until a group of exceptionally ordinary office buildings on land owned by the Prince of Wales's Duchy of Cornwall Estate, but it

Lambeth waterfront from Lambeth Bridge, 1860
This is the riverbank on which now sits MI6. This scene of waterside small-scale industry would have been replicated along most of the south bank from Battersea to the sea.

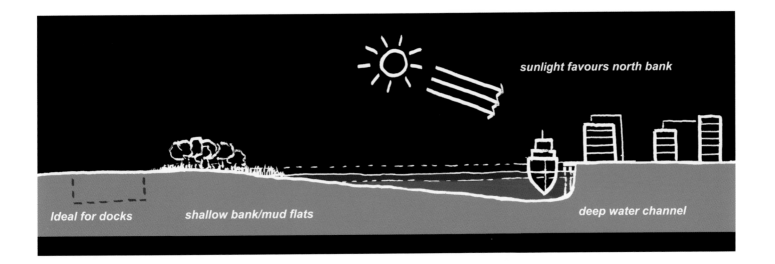

sunlight favours north bank

Ideal for docks   shallow bank/mud flats   deep water channel

returns again with a new walk in front of the MI6 building and from thereon the bank is being connected up and continuing its piecemeal accretive progress.

The Thames as the Shaping Force

It is interesting to think of the phenomenon of the central River Thames in terms of its effect upon the patterns and shapes of the urban territory. It is an enormous shaping force upon the activities, the energies, that pass from it and through to the banks; it is at once in itself a large force, almost a field force, like something of heat or magnetism. In a way, the water is a surface force or pattern, but it has changed radically. Pre-urbanisation, it was a surface of variable width and depth, taking the effects of the tides on to its banks, expanding and contracting, with its edges being entirely at the whim of the gravitational effects and the height of the water as it spreads over the banks. Then, as it was gradually channelled, the river was given fixed edges, but its surface, albeit narrowing step by step over time, was for many centuries of its urban life a thing of utility. In fact, it was very much an attractor – it was the highway for sewage, boats, cargo and movement. Everything happened on the river and, accordingly, its banks were intense interactors with its surface. One only has to look at the Canaletto paintings and other drawings of the Thames, right up to the Pool of London, to see that the whole trade of the metropolis and Britain's empire was happening upon this very surface. The Bank of England's boardroom still has a wind vane attached to a dial on one of its walls, a remnant of the time when the bank's directors needed to know which way the wind was blowing; if it was blowing inwards on an inward tide then the board members knew that ships that had been waiting at sea would now be arriving and there would be heavy business and heavy demand for money.

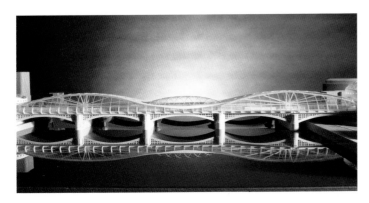

Top: Farrell, Deep water channel drawing, 2007
The deep channel, the built embankment and the shallow riverbank opposite. This is the fundamental reason why London is built as it is, primarily on the north bank facing the south and the sunshine. The shallow mud bank on the opposite side is ideal for industry and docks.

Farrell, Blackfriars Bridge proposal, 1993
One of many proposals for rethinking Blackfriars Bridge to straddle the railway with the building of the new Thameslink line.

However, the attractor era finished when, in the 20th century, shipping as an economic life force in London ended and the river ceased to be the primary utility surface for trade transport. Bankside buildings along either side were once characterised by their proximity and interaction with the water's edge. Times have changed from when the interaction with the water was to get as many ships as possible to each and every building in a competition for connection, to a point where today virtually no building in the centre directly interacts with the water's edge. The surface of the water is now a parkland; it is a 'scene', a vista to be enjoyed and looked at as it is a novelty and a contrasting feature to urban life – a thing of the wilderness. In the world of modern life, with its inevitable artificiality detached from nature, here we have 'Exhibit A' of nature's wilderness right in the heart of our urban lives, and the linearity of its edges has an increased intensity adjacent to this energy field.

One remaining interaction that does exist is the floating museum-park, mostly along the north deep-water bank between Westminster Bridge and Tower Bridge, where historic boats are permanently moored. Their primary function is as corporate party boats but one dramatic exception is the *HMS Belfast*, a Second World War battleship moored on the south bank within the original Port of London. The other boats that still connect to the banks, but in a more active way, are the ferry boats with their stops and landing stations. They naturally moor differently on each bank; on the north bank, they are close to the wall, in the deep water and accessible by short jetties, but on the south bank they can only be reached by long projecting piers, reaching beyond the mud banks and out into the water so that they can work at low as well as high tide.

The Bridges

The river is now, as it were, a divider rather than an attractor because it separates two banks and disconnects one side from the other, which thereby, in a new land-based urban realm, intensifies the importance of the crossing points, the bridges. They have become the key elements, increasing from the original, Tower Bridge, and then Westminster Bridge, to about 25 bridges between Tower Bridge and Kew Bridge. The roads, the banks, the connecting bridges and the linear developments to either side have become the primary attractors.

In grouping and patterns, the bridges have a collective character, too. Tower Bridge, completed in 1894, is itself a solo act – the gatekeeper – and immediately became the most recognisable symbol for London; an extraordinary concoction of Englishness and of Victorian quirky historicism, it was created by the engineer John Wolfe-Barry, with the City Architect Horace Jones providing the ornamentation. Designed in the spirit of its outer historical clothing, it is a work of brilliant engineering innovation. The rest of the urban bridges can be placed in groups. The least interesting are the railway bridges, all eight of them from Kew to Cannon Street, clunking, hefty things for which no civic pride or finesse was thought to be needed – hence *Punch*'s depiction of Hungerford Bridge (built in 1864 as a replacement for Isambard Kingdom Brunel's elegant pedestrian suspension bridge) as a sea monster. Grouped in the central urban sweep between Tower and Vauxhall Bridges is a series of flat-topped bridges in a pattern all following a collective idea that the clear open view over them is their vital significant feature. Each is designed in a different era, with Waterloo Bridge, completed in 1945, probably the most recent and one of the finest.

Upstream, the next grouping is the suspension bridges which begin in Chelsea, where views over the water become less important as they are in residential areas, the great parade of palaces and close proximity of buildings to the river having ended. The suspension bridges themselves have become central to the landscape character – ones such as Albert and Hammersmith (both particularly at night when lit up) are large urban statements that are like sculptural objects, becoming dramatic urban focus points.

Back in the central urban area, the most recent innovation in bridges has been the building of two pedestrian bridges, with the Millennium or so-called 'wobbly' bridge linking the steps at

Foster + Partners and Arup,
Millennium Bridge, 2000
Pedestrians crossing the 'wobbly' footbridge that links the south bank with the City.

St Paul's Cathedral to Tate Modern (or at least sort of, as the front door of the latter has been placed perversely around the corner). And then there are the walkways either side of the re-fashioned Hungerford Bridge – a third reincarnation, completed in 2002, of a dedicated pedestrian bridge at this point. The first was a brilliant pedestrian-only suspension bridge by Brunel that brought south Londoners directly into Hungerford market, which had been built in the vain hope that it could rival Covent Garden. Brunel's bridge was cannibalised by the railway company that brought trains into the new Charing Cross station on the site of the failing market. The suspension chains went to provide the supporting harness for the Clifton Suspension Bridge (it is bizarre to contemplate when looking at them in Bristol that they began life on the Thames

rather than the Avon), while the two massive bridge pillars were integrated into supports for the new (ugly) railway bridge. The second and intermediary pedestrian bridge was then provided in 1951 for the Festival of Britain when Hungerford Bridge was double-sided by temporary Baileys (floating bridges) – a clever re-utilisation of a wartime ad hoc invention.

In this chapter, the differences between the north and south banks of London have been highlighted as most clearly observed today in the linearity of access along the river banks: the route on the north bank is a road – Bazalgette's extraordinary engineering cocktail of linear elements for water, sewerage, tube, etc – while on the south side the route is a pedestrian walkway done in a rather incremental and irregular way. The linearity of buildings, though, has some similarity north and south. On both banks there is a parade of grand palazzi, of grand statements of a scale that befits the long vision lines. Public government buildings such as the Houses of Parliament and Scotland Yard all parade along the north bank, alongside grand buildings such as the Savoy, Hungerford House and Somerset House, which, like their clerical and aristocratic predecessors, have front doors to The Strand and river access to the rear.

County Hall, the GLA Building, the headquarters of Shell and other offices parade along the other side, as do the series of previously mentioned warehouses that had a continuing presence on the south bank during the 19th century and much

Farrell, Hungerford Bridge proposal, 1993
A later Farrell scheme for Hungerford Bridge to transform it into a transport hub with small rail links and new pedestrian connections.

Farrell, Hungerford Bridge proposal, 1985
Bridging the river in modern times has developed ideas for pedestrian-only links such as this one by Farrell.

of the 20th century. On the north side, the parades of great lines emanate as roads out from the river's edge until eventually they get lost in the urban terrain. By contrast, on the south bank the steep bend of the river has the opposite effect, creating a radiating road pattern from Elephant & Castle, around which the bend spins. All of these fascinating patterns, partly geometric, partly natural, which are rooted in the geographical features and similarities and dissimilarities of the Thames' two banks, have had a formative and enduring effect upon the shaping of present-day central London.

Lifschutz Davidson Sandilands, Hungerford Bridges, 2002
Eventually two pedestrian bridges were built either side of the railway bridge across the Thames by Lifschutz Davidson Sandilands.

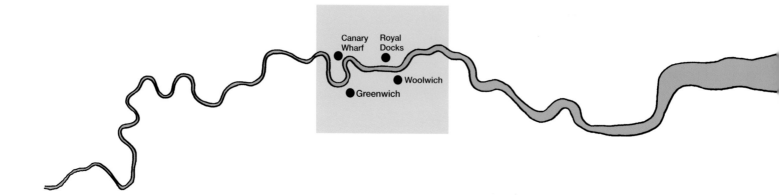

The Docklands

Transforming the Pool of London

Downstream of Tower Bridge, east of the City of London, is the metropolitan sub-region that has become known as the Docklands. In the 19th century, the landscape here experienced an even more radical and blanketed process of industrial transformation than the railways brought to central London (see 'Railways' chapter, p 132). The escalation of trade that was brought about by Britain's world dominance and ever expanding empire in the late 18th century had an immediate impact on the short stretch of river between London Bridge and Rotherhithe, known as the Pool of London; the furthest navigable point that could be reached by tall-masted vessels, the Pool with its small quays had been the centre of London's port since Roman and medieval times. By the early 19th century, it was so congested that it was said that it was possible to step across the river from ship to ship. The Pool was also so rife with pilfering that by 1800 an estimated 11,000 people made a dishonest living on the river.

New warehousing, offloading and docking facilities were required to handle the increase in traded goods that came from all over the world to the ever-growing capital. As with the railways, this was inevitably done on an ad hoc and incremental basis. Unlike Second Empire Paris, there was no Baron Haussmann in London. There was no autocratic ruler or governing body with a grand, centralised plan. London was transformed in discrete parts through small and medium-scale local plans, all of which may have been operationally sound within themselves, cleverly thought through, invariably pioneering, inventive and revolutionary. There was never much thought about how one part related to the other or what might be the next phase. Each entrepreneurial endeavour stood alone as a self-contained enterprise.

Embracing the Sweeping Thames

One of the most singular characteristics of the docks is that they utilised the patterns of bends in the river. It was outlined in the previous chapter, in relation to the north bank of the central

Sailing ship in London Docks, 1880–90
An early photo of a sailing ship in a London dock, showing the immediate adjacency of large ships, dock workers and the river's edge.

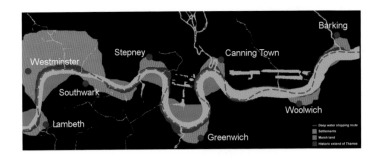

London Thames, just how the river's current scoured out a deep water channel on the outer curve of bends, leading to settlement and communities on those outer curves, where boats could dock and water passage was possible, whatever the tidal level. Concomitant with this pattern is that on the opposite bank – the inward bank where water moves more slowly, sediment settles and mudbanks grow – which was becoming a place of lower value and so of less immediate usefulness. With the pressure of development, this under-utilised land was eventually absorbed by the city. This pattern, though, intensifies here in the Docklands where the river has more bends and the difference in bank utility becomes more imbalanced. From Tower Bridge to Woolwich, the river sweeps in bends that are more acute than in the urban upstream section or, in fact, immediately downstream in the estuary. There is a steep trio of bends from the Pool of London through to Woolwich itself: these commence with the hump of Rotherhithe and are at their most accentuated in the great historic curve around the Isle of Dogs that is reflected in the counter arc around the Greenwich Peninsula.

The construction of the 19th-century docks used the natural swerving shape of the Thames, cutting across the bends to create channels or wet docks – what amounts to artificial bits of river – in order to bring waterways to the places where existing communities lay. At its extreme manifestation, this concept led to the suggestion by W Reveley in 1796 to straighten the entire Thames and make the original Thames the docks (a similar scheme was carried out on a smaller scale at Bristol), but this required a grand plan, a more French or North American approach. This being Britain, a whole sequence of docks was built instead, incrementally and piecemeal, with each one learning from its predecessor but of added scale and size.

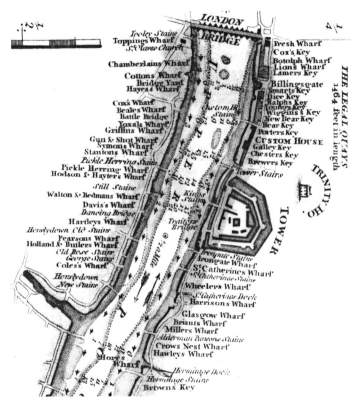

The overall aggregated pattern – an extraordinarily straightforward idea, once grasped – was to straighten the Thames by a series of set-piece docks between the bends, with an inlet and an outlet upstream and downstream, taking advantage of the tide,

**Wine and spirits stored
at London Docks, 1946**
Thousands of barrels of wines and spirits from Europe were offloaded and stored at London Docks in the run up to Christmas. The whole of the Docklands was divided into secure zones behind high walls creating inward islands broken by the big new water spaces, custom compounds and security barriers.

Top: Farrell, Historic settlements along the Thames: their relationship to the shipping channel and the narrowing of the river, 2007
The docks were built on the less used and more redundant inside bends away from the human settlements of the towns along the river.

The richness of London's riverside activity
Before the main docks were under way it was the river's edge that provided the wharfs, particularly around the Tower of London in the old Pool of London. This illustration shows the intensity of these wharfs which in time continued right downstream into the centre of the Docklands themselves.

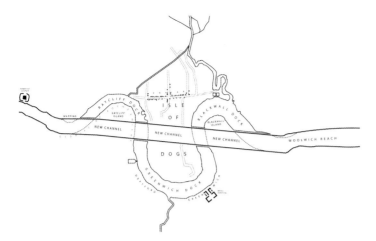

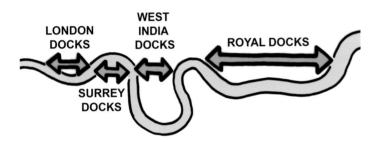

The excavation of docks also further pronounced the physical isolation of the river's peninsulas. The construction of the West India Docks and the City Canal, for instance, made the Isle of Dogs a true island, cutting it off from the mainland. To add to this discontinuity, the only river crossing points in Victorian and early 20th-century times downriver of Tower Bridge – itself dating to the 1890s – were the Blackwall and Rotherhithe tunnels of 1897 and 1908 and the pedestrian tunnels at Greenwich (1902) and Woolwich (1912). It was not until the building in 1967 of the second Blackwall Tunnel (which I was involved in as my first ever architectural project) that cross-river road traffic gained any kind of density at all. Otherwise, virtually all crossings of the river happened upriver in the middle, urban section of the Thames.

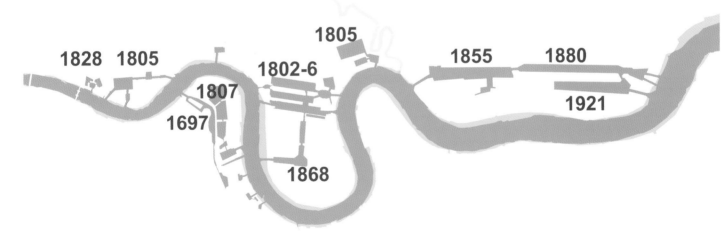

Top: Redrawn by Farrell, Straightening the Thames, 2009
Drawing based on a historic vision by W Reveley in 1796 of the new straight River Thames with the cut-off bends used as docks.

Centre: Farrell, Docks sketch, 2007
The original vision was inverted and the docks were constructed between the bends of the river.

Above: Farrell, The straightening of the Thames over time, 2007
Between the 18th and 20th centuries, the realisation of the docklands epitomised the age of Imperial trade.

Dockland Redevelopment

The docks' demise happened very quickly from the late 1960s to the early 1980s. This was brought about by technological changes and new cargo-handling methods, including the invention of the cargo container and a whole new system of ship design with special cranes for loading, which relied on the advent of larger lorries travelling on the new motorway road networks. The Docklands docks had been purpose-built for now outdated

cargo-handling methods, while particularly inflexible union practices meant that they could not enforce the radical changes needed to face the comprehensive new system. The unions proved non-negotiable, so to avoid conflict new cargo terminals were built far away in Felixstowe, Hull and Southampton. The distance was irrelevant, as the new terminals could use lorries on the motorways to deliver speedily to anywhere, including London, with less conflict and much more efficiency and cost effectiveness.

The docks began to lie idle from 1967–8 with the closure of the East India, St Katharine and Surrey Docks, and soon became the focus of new ambitions – partly to grow London and partly to regenerate the land and, of course, to provide jobs for those people whose livelihood had vanished. As the pollution levels of London also declined, there was the potential to develop the Docklands as new places for living and working, and white-collar and middle-class residential areas began to emerge. London Docklands Development Corporation (LDDC) was established in 1981 as one of the Thatcher government's regeneration initiatives, with the explicit intent of removing regeneration from the realm of local authority politics. The results were very mixed and there sits, particularly in the Isle of Dogs, an extraordinary juxtaposition of the way some of the world sees urban development and the way the British do, in that there is a piece of what to the British mind is an over-planned, over-regulated territory called Canary Wharf.

Canary Wharf is a slice of Manhattan: its planning is traceable back to the French architecture and planning culture of the 19th century which was established by the Beaux Arts academic system and was then adopted in the late 19th and early 20th century in the US, particularly in Chicago and New York through the work of planners such as Daniel Burnham.

Aerial view of the King
George V Dock, 1954
The Royal Albert Dock (background) and the King George V Dock (foreground) with ships and cranes idle as a result of the London dockers' strike. 16,000 men and an additional 8,000 ship repair workers downed tools due to a breach of a long-standing agreement that the last to be employed should be the first to be laid off.

View of Greenwich and the Canary Wharf Tower, 1985–1995

With the arrival of Canary Wharf a new juxtaposition of scales becomes apparent with the beginnings of tall buildings. This is 1985, when controversy surrounded the erection of the tallest building in Europe in view of the World Heritage Site at Greenwich.

Opposite: Looking east over London's Docklands
Above: Looking west over London's Docklands

The formal layout and organisation of Canary Wharf looking east and west is in complete contrast to the disorder and chaos around it. It represents two extremes – American formalist Beaux Arts planning as opposed to British laissez-faire and significant disorder. The docks themselves are barely visible, being partly filled in to get the new layer constructed. In the distance is the Millennium Dome – the focus of the 2000 millennium celebrations – and the Thames Barrier and Royal Docks: a complete change in the landscape of east London.

Skidmore, Owings & Merrill (SOM), the masterplanners of Canary Wharf, indeed originated from Chicago and now have major offices in New York, London and all over the world. With SOM at the helm, this cultural and planning tradition recrossed the Atlantic and settled upon the West India Docks. Aided by cheap land opportunities and generous UK tax breaks, the American developers created a new, highly planned mini-city which sits in an area where everything else was laid out randomly in the most haphazard and casual 20th-century British 'non-plan' way. Much of the rest of the Docklands – from the Isle of Dogs, Poplar and

Docklands Light Railway (DLR), 1993
The first new transport infrastructure into the Docklands, the DLR opened in 1987, followed in 1999 by the Jubilee Line. The newest addition to the Channel Tunnel rail route stops at Stratford and Ebbsfleet, and there are plans for the Crossrail route, which will further improve the Docklands connectivity (2017).

Wapping right through to Canning Town and the Royal Docks – was scattered with patterns of development where the only unifying characteristic was that if a developer could be enticed to settle there when they saw an opportunity, then they were allowed to do virtually as they wished and make the best of it.

This has now led, in typical London style, to a further rethink later on. The oncoming 2012 Olympics being planned for the Lea Valley and the tremendous commercial success of Canary Wharf, with its virtual completion at the end of the 20th century, has made everyone ask whether this all adds up to anything more than casual chaos. Unlike many Victorian developments or elsewhere in the world, like the Far East, all the transport systems, including the Jubilee Line, Crossrail and Docklands Light Railway (DLR), were brought in after the development: there was little early coordination of public transport investment and land development. But now there is a more settled and determined approach. The Olympics in 2012, the establishing of a new London government and city mayor from 2000 and the designation of all the estuary as one regeneration area are all gradually helping to form a collective way among local boroughs, agencies and developers. Furthermore, the fast Channel Tunnel Rail Link now stops at Stratford, giving a huge connectivity boost to the Lea Valley, Canning Town and Bromley-by-Bow.

Several new hopeful lines of change of urban planning speculation are emerging. One is that the reversal of the use of waterways from private utility to public amenity needs to be accelerated as the introverted private docks are now part of the public landscape. The idea of using the surface of the still waters of the big docks in a way that is different from the River Thames, with its sweeping, dangerous currents and its tidal range, is one

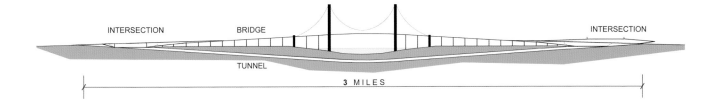

INTERSECTION   BRIDGE   INTERSECTION

TUNNEL

3 MILES

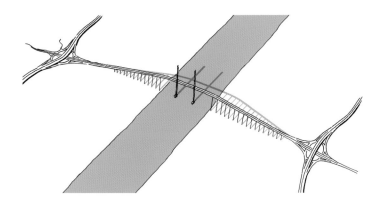

by communities connecting from one side of the river to the other. Historically, this has applied to all great cities and has been an essential dynamic of central London upstream of Tower Bridge and the Pool of London. The logical conclusion of this bank-to-bank connectivity has not been implemented because the lingering authorities that run the trading aspect of the river still dictate its usage. However, by connecting the banks with a new generation of lifting bridges, the new urban order would be completed. Finally, the Docklands could join all of London

that British Waterways is now studying. These vast areas of water could be regarded as parklands, surfaces for leisure, fish farming, floating gardens, islands for restaurants or housing. These docks are so enormous that collectively they form areas bigger than most urban parks.

The second idea is from an observation that the urbanisation of this area following the end of dock activity can never really be seen to be completed until the issue of the bridges is addressed. Urbanisation of these Dockland areas has not been taken to its logical conclusion, which is that urbanity is most deeply enriched

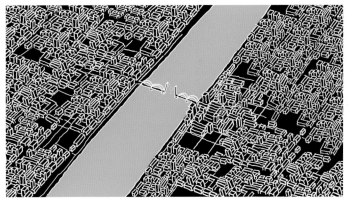

LOCAL COMMUNITY   LOCAL COMMUNITY

Top and top left: Farrell,
High-level river crossings, 2007
High-level river crossings connect motorways either side and create uninhabitable conditions within wide strips of land. This is the kind of bridge that is at Dartford, and has been proposed by engineers and others as the bridge format to be brought further into London.

Above right and above: Farrell,
Low-level river crossings, 2007
Low-level bridge connecting communities either side of the river. Farrell's proposal for community bridges allows for development right up to the riverbank and for people to cross to neighbourhoods either side, just as they do in urban areas of London.

and enable the centre of the metropolis to expand eastwards at least as far as the site of the Thames Barrier at Woolwich. These bridges would be humanly scaled, local community-based links, as opposed to regional transport infrastructure such as tunnels or high, inaccessible bridges. They would make it possible for people to walk or cycle from one side to the other or to take short public transport bus connections from bank to bank, rather than from inland motorway to inland motorway.

With bridge links and the development of a landscape strategy that fits within the ambitions for the Thames Gateway Parklands (a vision implemented over time by a variety of organis-ations, providing an overall framework for regenerating and developing both urban and rural open spaces), the whole potential of this area to build upon the existing communities, to make this a settled part of urban London with quality and livability, can then be realised. As things stand it is an ill-adjusted patchwork of high points and extreme low points, and of opportunities not recognised at all. Within the area are some pieces of historic development that are of world-class importance. Greenwich, which has been designated a UNESCO World Heritage Site since 1997, has a rich royal and maritime history with an almost unsurpassed architectural heritage, which includes Inigo Jones's Queen's House (1614–17), Christopher Wren's Old Royal Naval College (1696–1712) and Wren and Robert Hooke's Royal Observatory (1675); Woolwich, conveniently close to the royal palace at Greenwich, became home to the Royal Naval Dockyard (founded by Henry VIII in 1512), the Royal Arsenal (dating back to 1671), the Royal Military Academy (1741) and the Royal Horse Artillery (1793).

The scale of the Docklands area is one that is not often grasped. It is a very large piece of territory which is, by and large, underpopulated. A lot of densification is possible, particularly towards the eastern end within the boroughs of Greenwich and Newham. It will probably take some 40 to 60 years before this is all fully realised. Its biggest impediment is its lack of connectivity across the Thames and the limitations of the communities being broken up not only by this, but also by some ill-advised arterial roads and, of course, the docks themselves. It is a section of the Thames that is now truly artificial, not in the sense of the middle Thames section, with its artificially narrowed channel and urbanised banks, but rather in the sense of a different kind of urbanisation, a different pattern altogether.

The potential of the Docklands remains unrecognised nationally. Any success has come as a bit of a surprise. Canary Wharf's North American developers in the 1980s and 1990s proceeded with an optimism and an urban planning commitment that no British local or national government has brought to the regeneration of these areas. London has fallen a long way short of taking charge of its destiny here, particularly compared with our Victorian predecessors and the North American, reverse-colonialist, entrepreneurial developers. But, new voices and thoughts are emerging from the Stratford and Olympic initiatives. It has inspired those communities and people around it, and possibly the national government, to see that the Olympics could provide a stimulus and a legacy. When one sails up the Lea river and sees the post-industrial, degenerated landscape with miles of emptiness, one can look across to Canary Wharf and realise that all around and in vast areas of east London there is something of a blank canvas. It is a place where we have not really properly woken up to the sheer scale of the possibilities, as well as the obstacles.

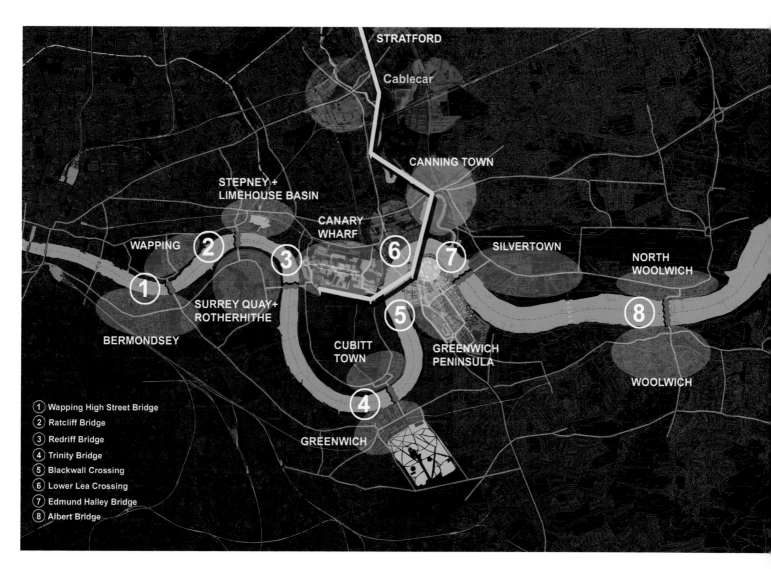

STRATFORD

Cablecar

CANNING TOWN

STEPNEY +
LIMEHOUSE BASIN

CANARY
WHARF

WAPPING ②

③

⑥ ⑦

SILVERTOWN

NORTH
WOOLWICH

①

SURREY QUAY+
ROTHERHITHE

⑤

⑧

BERMONDSEY

CUBITT
TOWN

GREENWICH
PENINSULA

WOOLWICH

④

GREENWICH

① Wapping High Street Bridge
② Ratcliff Bridge
③ Redriff Bridge
④ Trinity Bridge
⑤ Blackwall Crossing
⑥ Lower Lea Crossing
⑦ Edmund Halley Bridge
⑧ Albert Bridge

Farrell, Eight new proposed local bridge connections in the Docklands, 2007
How communities either side of the river can be brought together to realise the true urbanisation of the area. None of this would necessarily restrict the use of river transport. The balance would be more equal between new uses, new communities and the growing population either side of the river and the river traffic.

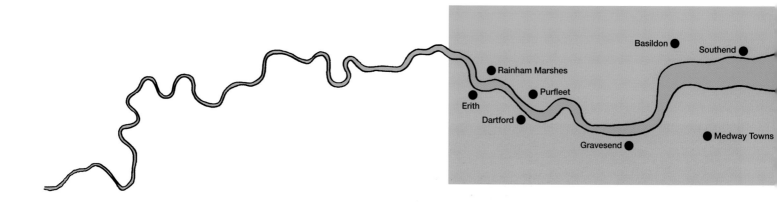

Basildon ●
Southend ●
● Rainham Marshes
Purfleet ●
Erith ●
Dartford ●
● Medway Towns
Gravesend ●

Estuary Thames: London's Engine Room

A View from the Top

The best view I have had of the Thames Estuary and its landscape was from a unique, spectacular vantage point on the roof of a 12-storey tower block in the north Kent town of Gravesend, opposite Tilbury. From here it was possible to look out east from London towards the sea and what seemed to be the entire Thames Estuary. My guides were leading local people, including the leader of Gravesham Council, and various people involved in the area's regeneration, broad landscape and public-realm improvements. And so we all surveyed the riverside town and its hinterland of Gravesham – named after the original title of the ruler, the *greve* – including the landscape inland to the River Fleet's origins at Southfleet, through to Ebbsfleet and then to Thameside and Northfleet itself, which sits facing across the river to Tilbury. We were in the middle of an unprepossessing housing estate and, although in height terms the tower block was rather modest by most standards, it was by far the most accessible tall rooftop as far as the eye could see.

Upstream, sitting on the horizon to the west, were the Manhattan-like tower clusters of Canary Wharf and to the extreme east, to my right, I could see the bright sky merging with the glinting light of the North Sea, with large ships clearly visible on their way in and out of the estuary. The singular impression one has is that this is a landscape of great vastness – a kind of heroic emptiness. There is also, contradictorily, a kind of compression or condensed perspective one gets with any flat landscape similar to that of the Netherlands or the Fens, where one can so readily see a very great distance across the flat landscape. There is a kind of foreshortening that happens – an impression that everything is being looked at through a telephoto lens and that objects standing in the landscape can be placed one against

Tilbury Power Station, 1995
Built in the 1960s, Tilbury is a coal-fired power station located on the north bank of the Thames.

Sunrise on the Thames Estuary

A beautiful aerial view towards the
seaward end of the estuary, approximately
from the line of the Dartford Bridge
outwards. In the foreground is Tilbury
and in the far distance is the North Sea.

The River: 'Liquid History'

the other as the only occasional incidents in an otherwise two-dimensional map-like terrain. Providing one knows how to read these compressed features, the view can be read like a vast map with places' identities as specific, solo incidents, almost in bas-relief. But unlike the Netherlands and the Fens, where windmills, farmhouses and trees make up the identifying features, here there is a 'super enlargement' – a kind of giant scale; as the expansive terrain takes in Europe's largest tower blocks seemingly docked at Canary Wharf and the giant oil tankers and container ships slowly progressing in the North Sea.

The most distinctive building elements are the power stations at the Isle of Grain, Tilbury, Dartford, Kingsnorth, Barking, Erith and Littlebrook. They are like enormous utilitarian industrial cathedrals with their giant smoking chimneys. The effect is quite different from upstream in central and west London, where the large power stations at Lots Road, Battersea and Bankside sit within an urban terrain of large riverside buildings. The estuary stations seem to be of a larger size because of their very isolation from anything of competing scale. All the estuary power stations sit on the Thames riverbank close to where ships bring oil, coal and gas to the river; port and power stations are locked together and distributed along its edges.

Ten per cent of the UK's energy is generated here, on this section of the river. This becomes pretty self-evident when one scans the landscape of pylons and power lines that criss-cross the land to take the power to where the people are, snaking their way inevitably back into London. There are two spectacularly large pylons at the Swanscombe Peninsula which carry the cables in one giant step across the Thames itself, standing head and shoulders above anything around, suspending their great lines in one enormous parabolic loop. I have been told, but have no evidence, that most of the power which is delivered from the south to the north bank is French nuclear power on its way to London; such is the great networked grid of open-market electricity supply; even those who vow to oppose nuclear power could unknowingly be boiling their kettle from such a power source.

Directly across the river from Gravesend is Tilbury, London's main docks and, with over 50 million tonnes of cargo, Britain's second-largest port, downstream of which one can see the regular movement of the Thames' biggest ships – quite a contrast to what happens from this point upstream. There are many other giant chimneys rising from other industrial complexes, but a lot of these are defunct and threatened with demolition, such as the ones associated with the cement works at Northfleet. Local opinion is divided: these buildings are historic grand achievements, built with the labour and the skill of engineers, contractors and their workers; they are one way of giving heroic distinction, identity and generational continuity to the whole region. But they are also still seen as negative reminders of an earlier, grittier industrial age and have an association, for some, with the exploitation, waste, smoke and pollution that caused the decline of this once attractive landscape from its underlying, natural, pre-industrial condition.

The ridge of chalk on the Kent bank, south of the river, has been quarried for its stone since the time of the Romans, and here there are long ridges where scars of the cement industry form huge interruptions in the very gently undulating landscape. These are being filled in with large buildings, invariably of the kind of scale and size that matches this expansive landscape. A particular example here is Bluewater at Greenhithe in Kent. One of Britain's largest shopping centres, it is an extraordinary

motorway-connected and generated alien body, like a landed spaceship – a singular monocultural phenomenon.

Since Tudor times, the estuary river has also been a landscape of forts and defensive lines protecting London, the capital, from invasion. All ages have imprinted their defensive lines across the Thames, and the banks of the river still display fortifications from the 14th to the 20th centuries. Henry VIII's fort of 1539 at Tilbury sat across the river from Gravesend, allowing crossfiring and a defensive boom of boats to repel the Armada in 1588. The ten forts of the Thames and the Medway later defended London from the Dutch and Napoleon, and in 1942 were joined by the Maunsell Army and Naval Sea Forts – groups of concrete long-legged towers housing anti-aircraft batteries. All of these

set-piece war- and peace-time objects are set within a landscape that seems all the more misty because of the contrast between land and water, the very shininess and reflectivity of the latter making land and buildings rather flat and singular in shape, giving a kind of indefinite silhouette-like character to the form of land and buildings.

The estuary has always been London's connection to the bigger world and also where the very business of the metropolitan engine room was positioned downstream, and downwind; goods come in and go out, and not just tradable, desirable goods and products – this is also where the metropolitan waste sewage and polluted water ends up. Barges once carried manure (when London was a horse-powered metropolis) downstream to be

Farrell, Thames Gateway Parklands, natural landscape, 2008
The first step in the study was to establish the area's own identity based on its geography and landscape; it is one place, it is an estuary – it coheres. It is a natural, living landscape, with over 40 marshes, 10 tributaries, creeks, ditches, woodlands, agricultural land and parks.

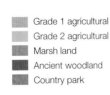

Grade 1 agricultural
Grade 2 agricultural
Marsh land
Ancient woodland
Country park

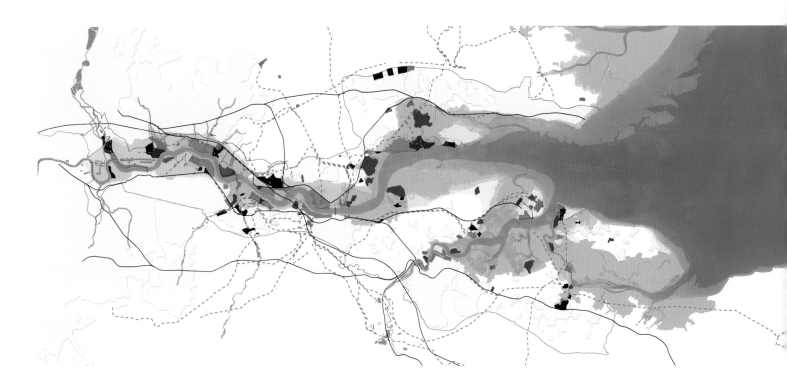

made into fertiliser and today still carry London's waste in giant heaps collected from every household's and office's dustbins and skips before being sent on its way to be processed and returned, or to landfill sites on the estuary banks. It has always been and always will be where the very stuff of London flows in and out, like the tide itself.

The Thames Gateway

There are many who have been sceptical of the government's aim to regenerate this estuary area, under the single project name of Thames Gateway. The massive regeneration project, which is tied into the 2012 Olympics, covers a 64-kilometre (40-mile) stretch from the Lower Lea Valley in the Docklands to Southend in Essex and Sheerness in Kent. One of the most repeated criticisms has been along the lines of 'How can all this large area be seen as one project? – What has the Isle of Dogs got to do with Southend?'

Standing looking at the view from the tower block in Gravesend, it is really clear that the Thames Estuary is indeed one place – first, because of its underlying consistent landscape, and then because of the unifying way that man has occupied and used it and settled in it. Stepney Marsh on the Isle of Dogs was drained and settled in the 13th century, and a revealing map of 1805 shows the marshlands stretching from there to the sea along banks on which Dutch drainage schemes were already well

Farrell, Thames Gateway Parklands, industrial areas, 2008

Parklands is one coherent place: a made landscape. Marshes and swamps have been transformed for over 2,000 years to become a human landscape containing half a million homes, 11 major port clusters, freight yards, power stations and large industrial complexes.

— Rail
– – Major power lines
■ Oil and gas works
■ Industrial land
■ Power station
■ Sewage works
■ Docks
■ Landfill sites

Land Reclamation Pre-1610
Land Reclamation 1794
Land Reclamation 1805
Land Reclamation 1900–2008

under way. Along the edges, unlike the areas above the Thames Barrier where there are unnatural man-made muddy flats, the tide races in and out, and beyond the flats are large areas of flat land, constrained only now and then by raised dykes which are themselves designed to integrate with pieces of naturally raised terrain. Here the Thames is a straightish estuary river and is wide too; it has not been fashioned, hemmed in and manipulated by man. The considerable tidal range – up to 7 metres (23 feet), and taking two to four hours longer to flow out than to flow in – is naturally expressed on its flat banks and into its saltwater marshlands, and it probably still has elements that would be familiar to the Romans. Unlike the urban areas upstream, it is only in the estuary itself that the more natural edges of the river predominate. Consequently, it is, of course, the area where flooding, sea surges and storms take their greatest toll, such as in 1953 when Canvey Island, a reclaimed island on the estuary in Essex, was submerged. It is a pattern that is exercising the Environment Agency engineers and, indeed, the Treasury with the oncoming effects of global warming and rising sea levels. This is the global-warming frontline; this is the defence zone where the long-term future of London will probably be decided.

Further back from the edges the rising land to the north in Essex could hardly be called hilly, but there is a geological ledge which is repeated on the slightly higher land to the south in Kent; the flatness between these ledges defines the estuary, and makes the idea of this being one place and therefore one mega-regeneration project all the more convincing and believable.

Farrell, Panoramic view of Gravesend and Gravesham, 2008
View of the Thames Estuary taken from the roof of the tower block in Gravesend.

The Burgeoning Estuary

The Thames has varied its line along these flat edges ever since its mouth moved (during the last ice age) from near Ipswich to the existing estuary. The 400,000-year-old Swanscombe Man, for example – found in 1935–6 at Barnfield Pit and now identified as a woman – is thought to have lived and died on the north

Bluewater shopping centre, Kent
This great modern 'palazzo' – a shrine to shopping – attracts around 27 million visitors a year. The average shopper walks an impressive 3.6 kilometres (2.25 miles) per visit.

bank before the changing course of the meandering river placed her remains on the south bank. In terms of the way nature has occupied this flat landscape, it is one of the largest wetlands in Britain. Indeed, if all the current projects of restoration work by the Royal Society for the Protection of Birds (RSPB) and others continue, it will be well on its way to becoming the largest collection of wetlands in Europe. It is a place of great natural intensity – bird migrations, fish breeding and the millions of invertebrates that live here create great excitement to those who know about these subjects, and as such their protectors, I have found, have a very wide view of the global interconnectedness of the air and water from this place. It is an area that can truly be called a wilderness, and yet it is right on the doorstep of London and indeed part of London, as the metropolis has come to use, exploit and then depend upon this land.

The history of occupation goes back tens – indeed, even hundreds – of thousands of years but the occupation that affects us most is probably that of the Romans, whose first main battle at Rochester in AD 43 marked the start of 400 years of settled development. For the next millennium, its man-made occupation remained fairly small scale. However, this changed in the 1500s when interest began to grow in the exploration of lands westwards across the Atlantic, southwards to Africa and eastwards to India. From the 16th to the 19th centuries, the estuary area became a kind of Cape Canaveral of the world, with the reused royal palace at Greenwich, and its naval college and observatory that trained officers and logged their observations to catalogue and map the

world, and also the dockyards of Woolwich and Chatham, from where the navy moved its base for journeys to newly explored and discovered lands. All this made the estuary lands London-dependent territories but also, as seen earlier, London-defensive territories. The successes of exploration and the navy led to a radical change in the role of the estuary and its relationship with London, which was becoming the capital city of a large global

Maunsell artillery towers, Thames Estuary
The Thames has always been a first line of defence for London, and here is the early 20th-century version of the ancient port at Tilbury.

empire based on trade. Trade brought in goods and people that required ports and docks on a scale never hitherto built.

Before the age of rail and motorised road transport, the rival ports needed to be right in or near London's docks, on the river above where the Thames Barrier now sits. As a result, the outer estuary remained pleasant, providing a place of escape from London and acting much as a pleasure ground and leisure area for working Londoners from the East End. It was their Lake District or Peak District. Just as those in Manchester, Newcastle and Liverpool could walk, hike and bike, so did the working people of London

Aerial view above Southend Pier
The nature of the estuary, looking across towards north Kent with Canvey Island on the right and London in the distance.

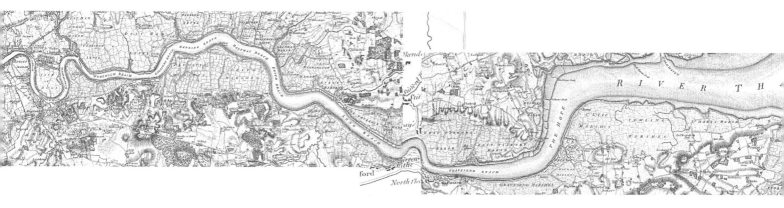

have access to the countryside, until the pollution overwhelmed the area in the 20th century. Working Londoners came out here to hop-pick in Kent and strawberry-pick in Essex. From the first steamer service from Greenwich in 1815 – and especially after paddle steamers arrived in the 1830s – they also came to play. Just as the working people from the Lancashire towns holidayed in Blackpool, so Londoners travelled along the Thames to piers and promenades along the riverbanks.

These raised riverside structures were necessary because of the flat, extended muddy banks and great tidal range. The steel and cast-iron constructions were the means of getting to the banks, and walking above the tidal flats became in itself part of the attraction. Southend Pier – which in 1929 became the longest pleasure pier in the world – travels a whole mile before it gets to the permanently deep water and became a promenade in its own right, albeit out to sea at right-angles to the land. At Erith, Rosherville and Gravesend, the early Victorians built pleasure gardens with zoos, arboretums and other parkland features where ladies in crinolines and gentlemen in Sunday suits promenaded on days out from London.

Of course, London's success began to alter the fortunes of the estuary. On 17 April 1886 the cargo steamer *Glenfruin* was the first vessel to enter the Tilbury Deep Water Dock, heralding

the moving out of the industrial infrastructure beyond the old docks. Power stations were built during the age of electricity and the change in scale that the 20th century brought with London's growing population all gradually doomed large parts of the territory and over-industrialised the landscape. As people began to travel further for their holidays at home and abroad, it lost its appeal as a leisure destination and the estuary became subsumed by its subservient role as engine room to the capital. This truly was

Thames Estuary marshes, 1805

One of the most revealing maps showing the true origins and character of the man-made land that we now call the Thames Gateway. It illustrates the Dutch drainage field pattern; the Dutch did much of this work to bring their livestock, particularly sheep, in from the Continent to sell to the London market.

Canvey Marshes, south Essex

Over the last 25 years up to 40 per cent of the Essex salt marshes has been lost. A coastal realignment project at Abbotts Hall Farm is helping to allow the regeneration of the salt marshes of the Essex coast, along with reconstruction of the sea wall.

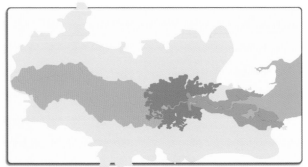

a working landscape that kept London going – fuelled London – for 50 to 100 years. Up until the middle of the 1950s and 1960s, it increasingly became the land of smog, smoke, air and water pollution – it became a land where the inhabitants gave up their notion of the attractive landscape and original beauty that Charles Dickens described, JMW Turner painted and Gerard Manley Hopkins wrote poems about.

Aerial view of the River Thames and Greenwich buildings

The scale of these buildings, the UK's equivalent of Versailles, with the Royal Park beyond and the Thames, personifies the whole approach of the Parklands landscape – part urban, part rural and part river. The pier is in the foreground with the component parts built by the great British architects: Wren, Vanbrugh, Inigo Jones and Hawksmoor. In the distance, on the hill, is the Observatory, the conquest of space where the legacy of Newton and the global explorers established understanding and the Empire.

Farrell, Thames Gateway Parklands Vision, 2008

The great metropolis is further from access to any great areas of wilderness than any other British city. I grew up in Manchester and Newcastle where there are wonderful national parks, but London is a long way from this kind of publicly owned and accessible wilderness. The concept of the Gateway is to make its first infrastructure a landscape one, with the aim that it will have a restored character that will make the Thames Estuary as recognisable in quality and interest as the Thames Valley, with all the implied economic and quality-of-life benefits.

Southend Pier, 1890s

In the 1850s the London, Tilbury and
Southend railway had reached Southend,
bringing with it a huge increase in visitors
from east London. In 1877, the old
wooden pier was replaced with a
new iron one.

Regeneration

In the second half of the 20th century, the docks and smaller ports on the estuary began to disappear with the growing dominance of shipping containers. The larger cargo ships required for containers needed to be docked in coastal deep-water ports, such as Felixstowe and Southampton. It was a situation that was unacceptable to workers' unions and communities who depended for their livelihoods on the docks. As a consequence, the Thames Estuary became one of the few areas of the southeast

Joseph Mallord William Turner,
The Confluence of the Thames and the Medway, c 1808
The Thames was a theme that ran throughout Turner's work. The river has been a continuous inspiration for so many artists, poets and writers.

The River Medway looking towards the Thames
The Medway and the navy garrison towns: a group of five towns arranged around the Thames' largest tributary with the inevitable power station, Kingsnorth, in the distance.

Birmingham was grappling with its horrific ring road, rejuvenating the character of its old canal systems and celebrating the great achievements of the Victorian industrial landscape.

The so-called Thames Gateway project has been slow to get going, and yet it is here that the future of London – and therefore a critical component of the UK economy – has to be addressed: the very sustainability of the metropolis still substantially depends upon this area. The kind of industries that have recently settled on the place are those that are now seen as the green industries, the critical industries of the 21st century that will get us out of the mess that industrialisation has created. A key element of this is dealing with the rising sea levels, protecting the urban territories and the economies that depend upon low-lying ports, dockside housing and office developments, not to mention underground tube systems and electrical installations all lying at levels that, if rising sea levels continue as some predict, will be threatened, thereby placing the capital city in jeopardy. Energy creation and management for the great metropolis lie here within the gateway, with its power stations and its potential for new generations of power creation, through tidal power, through clean energy production, through bio-fuels and perhaps, some say, through nuclear power situated out on islands, away from human habitation. Waste handling and recycling seem a self-evident part of the green industries, as do processes that deal with liquid waste, how to recycle and reharness water that will be in short supply and, of course, how to eliminate pollution from water and land to reduce the effects upon the atmosphere.

If anything, the concept of the estuary as London's gateway has been intensified. This is where the first land-based link to Europe, the Channel Tunnel Rail Link, comes through, stopping on

of England that suffered the same post-industrial problems of the great cities to the north: Newcastle, Manchester, Liverpool and Birmingham. Because it is in the southeast, among the ever-burgeoning economies of the financial centre and virtual world trade that London came to depend upon, the estuary's problems have not been addressed with great commitment. It is where the poorest, most socially deprived people of the southeast live and where the most post-industrial pollution and neglect lie. However, it was not until very recently indeed that the problems began to be recognised – at a time when Newcastle Quayside was already being transformed, Manchester was reinventing itself and

Farrell, Greenwich
masterplan model, 2003
The definition of the Thames Gateway project is that it begins at Greenwich. This model of the Greenwich Peninsula masterplan includes the urbanisation of land around the Millennium Dome. In the background are the Isle of Dogs and Canary Wharf.

**Farrell, Lower Lea
Valley proposal, 2003**
Proposal for the Lea Valley showing
the legacy of new development and
parks after the 2012 Olympics.

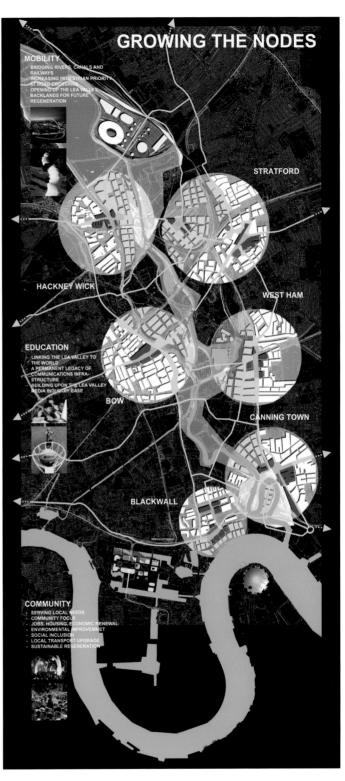

GROWING THE NODES

MOBILITY
- BRIDGING RIVERS, CANALS AND
  RAILWAYS
- INCREASING PEDESTRIAN PRIORITY
  AT ROAD CROSSINGS
- OPENING UP THE LEA VALLEY
  BACKLANDS FOR FUTURE
  REGENERATION

STRATFORD

HACKNEY WICK

WEST HAM

EDUCATION
- LINKING THE LEA VALLEY TO
  THE WORLD
- A PERMANENT LEGACY OF
  COMMUNICATIONS INFRA-
  STRUCTURE
- BUILDING UPON THE LEA VALLEY
  MEDIA INDUSTRY BASE

BOW

CANNING TOWN

BLACKWALL

COMMUNITY
- SERVING LOCAL NEEDS
- COMMUNITY FOCUS
- JOBS, HOUSING, ECONOMIC RENEWAL
- ENVIRONMENTAL IMPROVEMNET
- SOCIAL INCLUSION
- LOCAL TRANSPORT UPGRADE
- SUSTAINABLE REGENERATION

the south bank at Ebbsfleet and the north bank at Stratford and the River Lea area. This is where the major roads express themselves with the M25 rising over the river and the Dartford Bridge, while under it lies the Dartford Tunnel. This is where London's newest airports at Stansted and London City have been built and where Mayor Boris Johnson is campaigning for a new 'Heathrow' in the estuary itself, while Kent is promoting an alternative airport at Manston. There has been a long tradition of the promotion of the estuary as the possible location of London's largest airport and I am sure that the debate will continue.

Mention should be made of the tributaries and the inland water areas of the estuary, as the Thames and its tributaries – 17 in the tidal river, and almost another 40 beyond Teddington – together drain 12,934 square kilometres (4,994 square miles), or about 10 per cent, of the land area of England. (The catchment area rises to 15,343 square kilometres (5,924 square miles) if the Medway, with its dockyards, large power stations and forts, is included.) As has briefly been mentioned before, further upstream is where London's docks meet London's estuary and this is now where the tide of urbanity pushing outwards is at its most intense, with the establishment of the new Olympic City for 2012.

The government has made a commitment to regenerating the whole of the Thames Estuary from its post-industrial state under the project title of the Thames Gateway and is very proud of saying it is the largest regeneration project in Europe. A particular aspect of the project, which will enable London to make better use of these territories, has been to base the regeneration upon landscape and environment. The project's area can be identified as being almost contained within the three major river valleys: the Lea, the Fleet and the Medway.

The most current activity is in the Lea Valley because it is a run-down area contiguous with Canary Wharf and the regenerated areas of London Docklands. It is also the location of the new fast rail line which goes both to the Fleet at Ebbsfleet, providing a convenient station there, and to the Medway which it will feed with commuter fast trains from 2009. In the Lea Valley itself there is not only a new city under way around the station at Stratford; the area will also be the home of the Olympics in 2012. The Olympics, the Olympic Park and everything that goes with the great event will no doubt be the centre of much attention. It will not, I suspect, be the same kind of event as Beijing 2008: it will have its own character and will be a rather British, possibly underplayed event.

For me, the most important thing about the Olympics will be its legacy, its potential to regenerate the area, just like the Millennium Dome did at Greenwich Peninsula. The Dome, much castigated at the time, has actually had a huge regeneration effect just south of the river and, it is claimed, is now the most successful entertainment venue in the world. Hopefully, post-Olympics, the Lea Valley will experience some of this regeneration effect. It is an area that has substantial underlying character because of the network of water courses. The river follows several different lines, having been partly man-made and partly canalised, and there are also proper canals that run adjacent, so there is a criss-crossing network of waterways that leads up to Hackney Marshes and beyond. The idea of making all this a big park, perhaps even a Royal Park, has been mooted, but the proposal that I think holds most credibility is one where the rivers and the water courses will form the feature of a new urban area that will have some parks but also housing, new industry and workplaces, as well as all the other

Farrell, The Hoo Peninsular Vision, A
strategic framework for the regeneration
of the Hoo Peninsular, 2008
The proposal for the Medway and its
adjoining towns shows how the principle
of the Thames Gateway Parklands
strategy can be applied to and regenerate
urban areas.

mixed-use activities that go with the regeneration of Bromley-by-Bow, Canning Town, Stratford and other centres in the area. This was very much part of Farrell's proposal, put forward in 2003, for the Olympic masterplan.

Further downstream, the Fleet river runs through the aptly named Northfleet, Ebbsfleet (I assume the name comes from its place at the former edge of the tidal range) and Southfleet. There has been another concentration of Thames Gateway-style regeneration in this area, which has included the aforementioned shopping centre at Bluewater and the old Blue Circle quarries being filled with housing and, primarily, a new railway station at Ebbsfleet, with a town being developed around it. Gravesend and its borough of Gravesham have had their own active regeneration; the high street, restored pier and country parks have formed quite a cluster with the other new developments to make this, as it were, a regeneration hotspot.

Even further downstream is the Medway. Here, I have been working as design champion for a new 'unitary authority' to reinforce the concept that the five established towns of Strood, Rochester, Chatham, Gillingham and Rainham – which together have a population approximate to Newcastle upon Tyne – should be reclassified as a city. There is an extraordinary physical phenomenon in this area in that the great naval base moved away from here in the recent past, leaving behind it what I have called 'the empty stage': all the riverbanks, the prime centrepiece of this urban conglomeration of five towns, have been abandoned and left empty. The towns, which had substantial supporting roles to the navy, provide much evidence of the fact that they were dependent satellites upon a core which has gone and they now find themselves in a disconnected hinterland. Following the navy's

abandonment, the river, its banks and edges have presented a great opportunity to bring together and regenerate the whole area. Under the title Medway Renaissance, there has been a very active programme of new housing, museums and the restoration of extraordinary dockyard buildings that pioneered all kinds of naval and boat construction.

The Medway and, indeed, the coastline along Kent to Margate and Ramsgate will also benefit from the fast train line to Ebbsfleet and the new Channel rail line to St Pancras via Stratford. These new communication lines are probably among

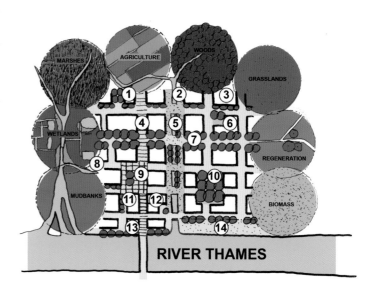

Farrell, Urban Parklands Model – greening the urban landscape and improving access for existing and new communities to significant landscapes, 2008

The urban landscape is made up of all the component parts that go towards seeing our places of urban settlement and human habitation as landscape itself.

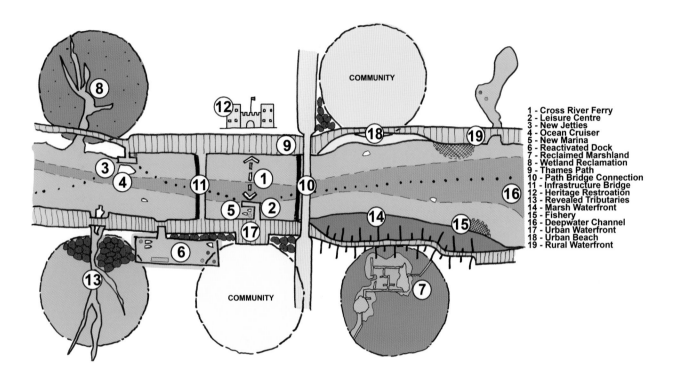

1 - Cross River Ferry
2 - Leisure Centre
3 - New Jetties
4 - Ocean Cruiser
5 - New Marina
6 - Reactivated Dock
7 - Reclaimed Marshland
8 - Wetland Reclamation
9 - Thames Path
10 - Path Bridge Connection
11 - Infrastructure Bridge
12 - Heritage Restroation
13 - Revealed Tributaries
14 - Marsh Waterfront
15 - Fishery
16 - Deepwater Channel
17 - Urban Waterfront
18 - Urban Beach
19 - Rural Waterfront

the most important new energies regenerating the Thames Gateway project. On the north bank, so far the biggest new investment is the rethinking of the container ports at Shell Haven, one of the great ports on the Thames, where DP World is building a dock capable of taking the world's largest container ships and a logistics campus that will change the way in which goods are distributed in the southeast and the rest of the UK.

I sat back and looked at the whole of the estuary when questioning the government's definition of the Thames Gateway project some five years ago. It seemed to me that until recently there was a habit of using economic targets as a substitute for vision and planning – to my mind, targets such as the number of houses built (200,000 being the ultimate target), the reduction in unemployment, the creation of new jobs, and the amount of inward investment being attracted did not add up to the same thing as a vision and a plan. So, after much self-questioning and thought on the subject I offered the idea that the core concept should indeed be that of environmental and landscape regeneration as the first infrastructure. This idea grew from the fact that the estuary region is inherently one of landscape character: what unites it is the estuary valley, the tidal flats and marshes and the human activities that go with this kind of terrain. Eventually, I was appointed by the government to develop the idea of landscape regeneration under the title The Parklands. We drew up a plan where we categorised all the terrain as either the 'blue landscape', which is as it suggests is all the water, water edges and tributaries;

Farrell, Concept sketch of Water Parklands activities on and adjacent to the water and the relation to the surrounding communities and landscapes, 2008

The water landscape, the 'blue landscape', shows how all the river and tributary edges can have their appeal as accessible public landscape restored.

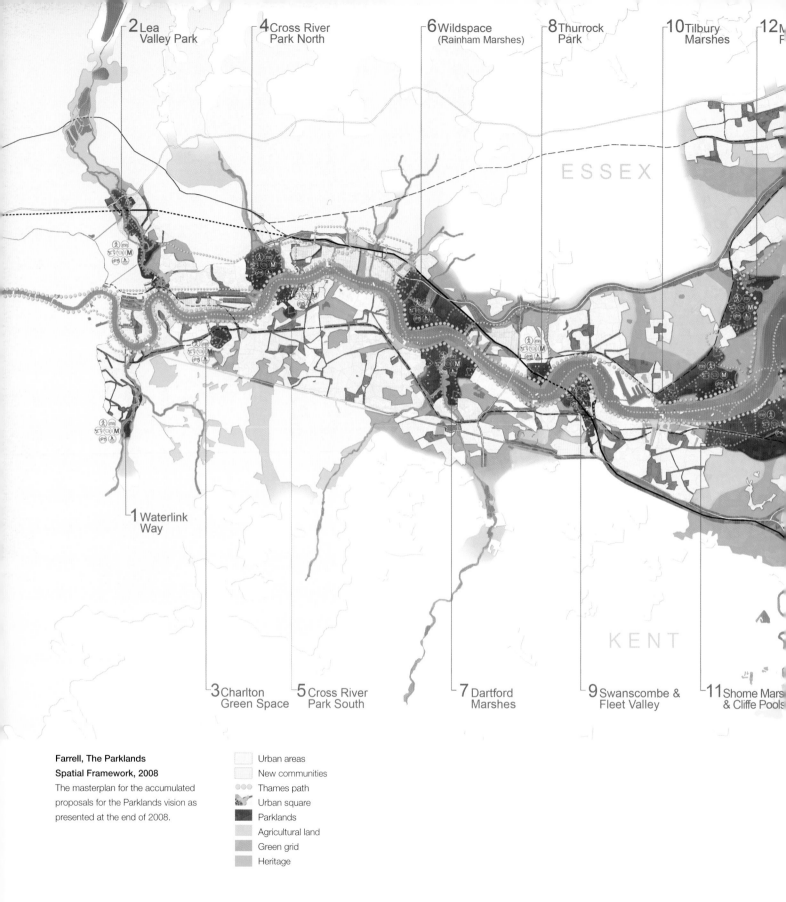

2 Lea
Valley Park

4 Cross River
Park North

6 Wildspace
(Rainham Marshes)

8 Thurrock
Park

10 Tilbury
Marshes

12 M

ESSEX

KENT

1 Waterlink
Way

3 Charlton
Green Space

5 Cross River
Park South

7 Dartford
Marshes

9 Swanscombe &
Fleet Valley

11 Shorne Mars
& Cliffe Pools

Farrell, The Parklands
Spatial Framework, 2008

The masterplan for the accumulated
proposals for the Parklands vision as
presented at the end of 2008.

Urban areas
New communities
Thames path
Urban square
Parklands
Agricultural land
Green grid
Heritage

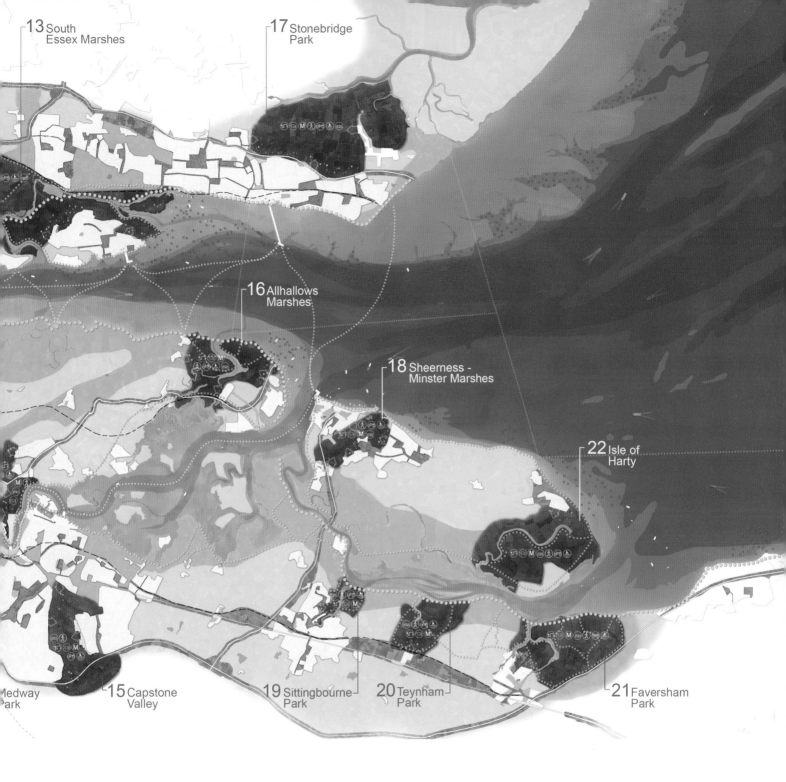

13 South Essex Marshes

17 Stonebridge Park

16 Allhallows Marshes

18 Sheerness - Minster Marshes

22 Isle of Harty

Medway Park

15 Capstone Valley

19 Sittingbourne Park

20 Teynham Park

21 Faversham Park

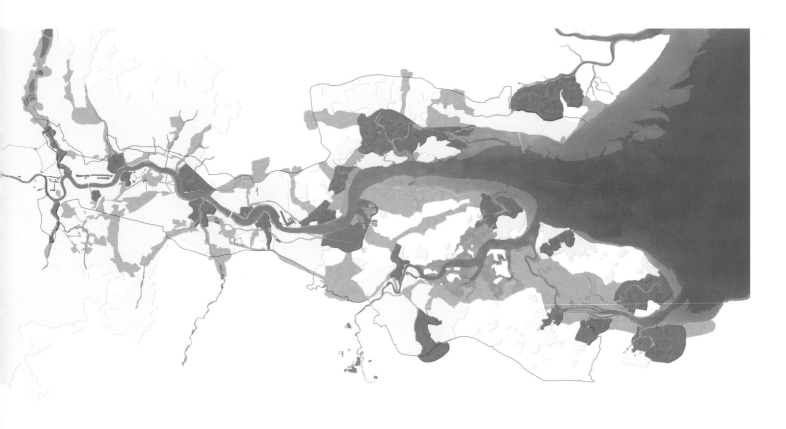

the 'green landscape', which, also self-evidently, is the areas of parks, woodlands and agricultural land; or the 'brown landscape', which represented the towns themselves, in that they could be rethought in terms of their municipal parks, streets, squares, play areas and even household gardens. This led to a plan being published at the end of 2008, which was generally accepted and supported. It now seems that under the title 'Eco-region', a new vision is emerging which to my mind is much more satisfactorily attuned to the issues of this century.

One of the methodologies that we adopted was to talk to as many parties as possible through workshops, and we held one

in each of the categories of blue, green and brown. This provided a very telling insight into all the different voluntary bodies, government agencies and local authorities that are doing such good work in the area – the activities of groups such as the RSPB, Natural England, the National Trust and Sustrans reveal that deep down the English have developed a strong affection for land and landscape. Consequently, many of the pieces of the jigsaw were already there so we felt as though our task was trying to find the picture on the front of the box. We eventually subtitled the project 'One Vision – A Thousand Projects' on the basis that it was a question of giving an overall face, an identity, that could

Farrell, Community Parklands, 2008
Improved access for existing and new communities to significant landscapes.

☐ Communities
▨ Green grid
■ Community parkland

bring together under one flag all the river walks, canal restoration, new piers, country parks, wildlife reserves and wetlands which are already being undertaken by passionate voluntary supporters. This approach was summed up by a diagram we drew that identifies the estuary as a landscape that could share the same qualities and give the same impression as the Thames Valley, which is renowned for its environment and the quality of life of those who live there. So the ambition under the new concept of the Gateway is to make the estuary a really fine place to live again with nature, landscape and the ecological qualities leading the regeneration project.

Pipers' visualisation, Parklands: One Vision – A Thousand Projects, 2008
Visualisation of the model at Thames Gateway Forum, 2008.

Farrell, Parklands: One Vision – A Thousand Projects, 2008
Bottom-up regeneration but with a picture on the box.

The Tributaries

The Hidden Influence

The 55 or so tributaries or secondary streams and water courses that drain into the Thames have been of enormous significance to London, affecting the shapes and patterns of the evolving metropolis, particularly through their draining of the 12,950-square-kilometre (5,000-square-mile) catchment area from the hills to the north and the south. Their existence, especially in the central areas, is now hidden as they have been turned into underground culverts, but their presence is still there in the layout of streets and the undulations of the landscape where long, albeit rather shallow valleys topographically show the original lines of the natural landscape. When looking at the patterns and forms of the tributaries, as with so much of the rest of London, it is fairly straightforward to divide them into two main categories: those that flow from north to south and those that flow south to north to meet the Thames, as they have different characters and different histories in urban planning. The tributaries all begin their gravitational journey from the hills. The hills are relatively small features on the edge of the great London bowl, but within the main part of central London they are recognisable on the skyline at Harrow, Hampstead and Highgate to the north and at Sydenham Hill, where Crystal Palace was re-erected, and Norwood to the south.

On their journey down to the Thames, the tributaries originally did much to sustain local communities. It is no surprise to find that the line of a river or a stream is also the line of settlements – providing them with water supply, sewage disposal and also, depending on the location, the water power for mills and so on. For example, on the maps of Kent are shown the rivers Cray and Darent with a series of mills providing for a variety of different enterprises; water power was developed, as elsewhere in Europe, as a primary power source for several centuries, and in London it was the tributaries that were of the right size to be harnessed and used. There is a natural conflict between mills/mill ponds and water navigation. As the tidal Thames increases water levels far up into the larger streams, navigation was possible right up the Fleet to Camden Town, up streams like Counter's Creek that were

Flock of sheep on Piccadilly, 1930s
This photo shows the dip where the River Tyburn once crossed Piccadilly going into Hyde Park and then St James's Park, and the natural contours lying beneath the surface of London. A charming picture of the days when 600 sheep grazed in Hyde Park and were then driven down Piccadilly to further pasture at Green Park.

partly canalised, and along the two main central rivers, the 32-kilometre (20-mile) long Brent to the west and the 72-kilometre (45-mile) long Lea to the east. Throughout history, from Roman times through to the Viking era and onwards, these two major tributaries were always important navigational channels and continue to be so today. Over the ages their navigational function was enhanced continuously, including through canalisation and links to new canal systems.

The distance between rivers suited land drainage and created a natural pattern, as did their routes towards the mother river. Invariably, the tributaries' point of connection to the Thames would

be at the nearest place on its outer bend, which made the bend the most suitable area for habitation and therefore established an urban geometry. This can be seen at Brentford, where the Brent meets the Thames. It was one of the first settlement areas in London, preceding even the Roman occupation of Britain. Several Celtic artefacts have been found in the area, such as the Brentford Chariot-Horn Cap (100 BC–AD 50) now in the Museum of London. To this day the north bank of the Thames around Brentford remains far more built up than the south bank, which is given over to green space, preserved by the Royal Botanic Gardens at Kew. That there is a natural pattern to all these things is no surprise; it underlies all the systems of habitation and the street patterns emanating from settlements. It is hard to overestimate how much these tributary rivers have contributed to the eventual detailed scale urbanisation of the metropolis, creating a systems pattern that is fundamental to understanding the city.

Parks and the Great Estates

The tributaries have always been associated with historic forests and meadows that eventually became public spaces. This is particularly noticeable in the most well-known Royal Parks in the centre of London, with the Westbourne being a major feature of Hyde Park and the Tyburn similarly forming the primary features of the water and parkland at both Regent's Park and further down at Green Park and St James's Park. Further out, Counter's Creek travels from Harrow through the landscape of Wormwood Scrubs, while the Fleet supplies the parklands of Hampstead Heath and Highgate Woods with their ponds. The Lea runs from the Holloway side of Finsbury Park down through

Redrawn by Farrell, Map showing the main tributaries to the urban Thames and landscape spaces, 2009
Although mainly hidden, the tributaries are of fundamental importance, giving foundation to London's urban geometry.

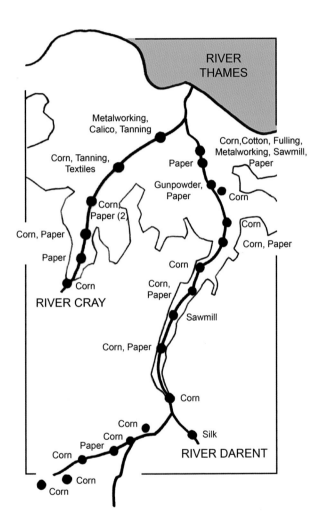

**Farrell, Mills on the Darent
and Cray (1700–1900), 2009**

Water was a main source of power
for industry until the 19th century.
Kent's rivers and streams were dammed,
diverted to turn water wheels that drove
machinery. Later on, steam engines were
also used to power water mills. Note
the diversity of industries along these
modest-sized rivers.

Hackney Brook to Victoria Park, and in a more direct line north it goes over Hackney Marshes and the large open spaces that form the recreation grounds there. To the south of the river, the Ravensbourne travels through Blackheath and its parklands and down into Greenwich, with its Royal Park. Crystal Palace is the source of the Effra, and Richmond Park and Wimbledon give rise to Beverley Brook, which travels down to the Thames at Barnes.

So parkland and evidence of landscape persist wherever the rivers flow, but equally there is a series of urbanisations where settlements have grown along these small rivers. Nowhere is this more evident than in Colin Rowe and Fred Koetter's book, *Collage City* (1978), which includes a plan showing the aristocratic estates and their relationship to development and land ownership in the centre of London. The central rivers run through St James's, Hyde and Regent's parks, which inevitably began as royal domains and hunting grounds, but in the areas where there are no Crown lands, the rivers run through a set of villages. For instance, we can follow the course of the Tyburn as it leaves Regent's Park and travels down through the villages of Marylebone and Mayfair to Green Park and St James's Park along the front of Buckingham Palace, and onwards to Westminster Abbey. Rowe and Koetter's remarkable plan shows that the village centres, originally rural hamlets, are located, as they would still be today in the countryside, along the banks of the tributary. The Tyburn is now underground, but its path can be seen by the informal medieval street pattern that sits above the river, so that Marylebone High Street leads into Marylebone Lane and down St Christopher's Place, across Oxford Street and along the side streets of Mayfair, winding its way through urban terrain until it reaches Green Park and then the Thames. The routes of the Westbourne, the Fleet and the

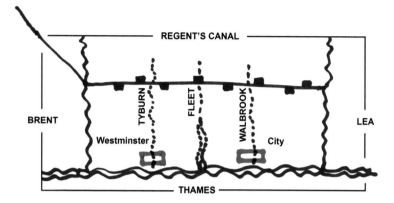

Walbrook have each affected the street pattern in the same manner as the Tyburn: these four key rivers form both the parklands and the detailed urban layout of central London.

Between the four rivers, on the land once owned by the aristocratic estates, there are the grid layouts of each of the estates, remarkably still intact, which together form a patchwork of grids, each slightly differently aligned. This is a most vivid example of the development patterning of streets deliberately laid out by the aristocratic owners after the land changed from agricultural use in the 18th and early 19th centuries. The estates, which still today remain the major backbone of central London's residential areas, were laid out and carefully controlled under long leases by speculative builders to attract the middle classes towards a potentially genteel lifestyle. Consequently, the broad avenues and regular layouts of the streets and squares, the estates of Harley, Cavendish, Grosvenor, Portman and Bloomsbury and the areas of Brunswick and Bayswater right down to Pimlico, sit like pieces of carpet or tapestry arranged by an underlying more geometrical logic between the slightly more irregular flow lines of the streams and the high streets attached to them.

On Professor Shane's map (see opposite) one can see the true genius of London and its layout. It is not a self-imposed overview laid out for princes and dictators like Haussmann's Paris or, indeed, like most Continental cities such as Barcelona, Madrid and Berlin. It is not built upon totally made-up land so that it can be made into invented geometries like Amsterdam, nor upon the real-estate grids, ready for land disposal, of the great American cities of New York, Philadelphia or San Francisco. The layout of London is based upon a much broader and more democratic land ownership (albeit by the upper tiers of society, but nevertheless spread diversely among them), and also upon the gentle undulations of land form and the natural irregular meanderings of tributaries as they run towards the Thames. This patterning is the absolute centre, the *genius loci*, of so much of central London – the stream beds are the first layer and the fields in-between are the second, which were laid out as residential estates and the

Farrell, Pattern of tributaries, canals and major places in London, 2009
Two still accessible external tributaries bookend these underground tributaries; the wider River Fleet divides Westminster and the City.

Drawing showing the source of the River Fleet at Highgate Ponds in Kenwood
The rivers rose from the high points around London and to this day many are retained as major parks and recreation lands.

have been substantially canalised and, while adapted through the ages, left open and navigable and then linked across the top by the Regent's Canal to form a loop with the Thames to the south. In between, the smaller urban rivers are 'lost' because urbanisation has been so intense that the need for land, together with the added problem of waste pollution, caused the rivers to be taken through large sewers underground.

The primary rivers in this central section include the Westbourne which flows from Hampstead through Hyde Park into Sloane Square and on to the Thames, with Chelsea Hospital and its grounds slightly to the west. At different times and places it has been known by various names, all deriving from the river and often giving names to places en route – Kilburn, Bayswater, Serpentine, Westburn Brook and Ranelagh, while Knightsbridge is named after a bridge over this river.

Crown lands of the Royal Parks – St James's Park, Green Park, Hyde Park/Kensington Gardens and Regent's Park further to the north. This makes up the essence, the geometry of what we know of the core, the heart of London.

The 'Lost' Rivers

The tributaries also play their part in the patterning beyond this core. Further to the west, east and eventually to the north is a navigable water ring. This has emerged because, as mentioned earlier, London has two major tributary rivers that are bigger than the others – the Brent to the west and the Lea to the east. They

Professor David Grahame Shane,
Field analysis of central London, 1971
Much of the planning of the great parks and their pedestrian links is a pattern of the river beds. But the river beds also form the high streets of many of London's villages and the fields between them became the great estates of the landed aristocracy in the 18th and 19th centuries.

Drawing of Rosamund's Pond
Rosamund's Pond in St James's Park is an artificial stretch of water fed by the River Tyburn, like the Serpentine in Hyde Park fed by the River Westbourne and the lake in Regent's Park fed by the upstream River Tyburn.

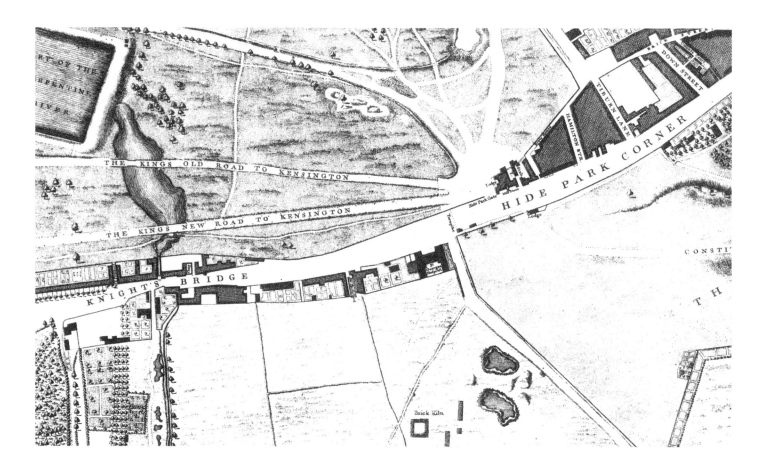

The Tyburn flows through Regent's Park and St James's Park. At the point that it arrives at the Thames, it used to divide into a muddy area that was filled at high tide and created islands, one of which was Thorney Island – the defensive monastic site of Westminster Abbey.

The Fleet rises in two springs on Hampstead Heath and was directed into two reservoirs – Highgate and Hampstead Ponds – in the 18th century. It is now London's largest underground river. At one stage the upper reaches were known as the Holborne, with the lower level known as the Fleet, which is derived from an Anglo-Saxon word for estuary or 'a place where vessels float'. The river goes under King's Cross, which was originally known as Battle Bridge, and ends up at the Thames under Blackfriars Bridge. One of the most important aspects of the Fleet was that its size was an impediment to land traffic. It needed to be forded and was difficult to cross at high tide – hence the separation between the City of Westminster and the City of London. The Fleet and the steep valley of the Holborn area alongside it truly were the line of division between the cities, which did not become seamlessly one place until the building of the Holborn Viaduct in 1863–9.

The Walbrook, the small river in the City, provided water to the historic Roman settlement and was the original off-Thames harbour. It starts in Finsbury and enters the Thames at Cannon

Plan of London
Hyde Park Corner and Knightsbridge with
the River Westbourne crossing over the
bridge at Knightsbridge from the lake in
the middle of Hyde Park.

Street railway bridge, probably getting its name from traversing the ancient wall of the Roman settlement.

London's Bookends – the Brent and the Lea

The Brent and the Lea bookended London in such a way that they became the water-based conduits both inside and around London. They were left open to extend navigability and eventually gave rise to London's industrial areas. Both these rivers and their man-made adaptations form networks of waterways, which will be discussed further in the next chapter on canals. To the east, Regent's Canal terminates at Limehouse Basin. In order to connect the canal to the Lea, without going along the section of the Thames that loops around the Isle of Dogs, various channels like the Limehouse Cut were created. With the Thames Gateway development plan, the river has once again become the centre of attention, after a period of considerable industrial development in the 19th and early 20th centuries. It was a major centre of industrial innovation during the 19th century as well as of immigration. Industrial towns and hamlets, such as Rotherhithe, Poplar, Deptford, Charlton, Canning Town, Plumstead, Dagenham, Greenhithe, Gravesend and Tilbury arose here to house a working population – not dissimilar to those that developed along the riverbanks of the mill towns in Lancashire. The area continues to supply immigrant labour to the city from the East End.

The current excitement around this piece of London's geography is that the Thames Gateway has made it the very centre of the biggest urban regeneration activity in the British Isles. This regeneration focuses not just on the docks to the south and the new railway station at Stratford, where the Channel Tunnel Rail Link arrives before finally going on to London, but also on the Olympics which will be held here in 2012. The navigation systems are being rethought by British Waterways with a new lock at Three Mills Island (Prescott Lock, not named after the previous Deputy Prime Minister!) to hold back the waters at low tide so that they are navigable right up to and beyond the Olympic site. Prescott Lock will restore the navigability of the Bow Back Rivers, a system of waterways which has been largely derelict since the Second World War, but which will now be incorporated into the Olympic Park. Water transport will be restored to the area,

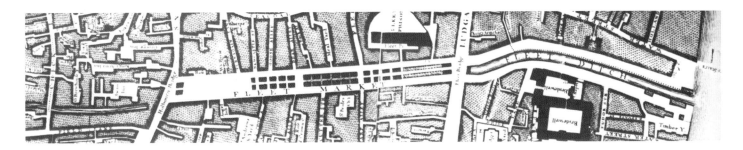

The Fleet before it reached the Thames
Although in the 1730s the Fleet Ditch was covered over north of Ludgate – the Fleet market opened in 1737 – the southern end remained an open sewer until the construction of Blackfriars Bridge in the 1760s.

including both leisure-boat and industrial activity, with barges being used for the removal of waste and recycling from the new residential developments.

Further north, in Hackney, the Lea's network of channels, locks, enhanced natural waterways, man-made canals and established lakes and ponds were all connected to various industries. This makes the whole Lea Valley a water-based landscape and the hoped-for new city which will emerge here one day has already been given the popular name Water City. To the west, the description could just as easily be given to Brentford, with its network of riverways, man-made docks and canal system. The first canal link to London was here, with the Grand Union (the first stretch of which was opened in 1794) running down to the Brent, connecting it to Birmingham and the north and providing the site for a range of industries related to the Great West Road, the route out westwards to Reading, Bristol and Wales.

A Watery Future

It is possible to think of central London as having been created by a simplified pattern of rivers and tributaries. As described, the city is essentially framed by two open, navigable and quite industrialised major tributaries, the Brent on the west and the Lea on the east. Within this frame there are three important rivers, the central one being the formerly navigable and tidal Fleet, which divides the two old cities of Westminster and the City of London. To the west, the Tyburn flows through the great estates down to the historic core of Westminster with the Abbey and Parliament. To the east the Walbrook, small as it is, was very significant in its water supply to the City of London. All of these tributaries link to the Thames to provide a comprehensible pattern, but all this water is managed by different authorities. The Port of London Authority and the Environment Agency both play major roles in the management of the Thames, while the navigational side of the smaller rivers and canal systems is run by British Waterways. Then there is, of course, the sewerage and the water supply side, largely governed by Thames Water, although there are three other companies with regional London interests. Furthermore, the Greater London Authority is also involved in various water management policies. Of course, with global warming there is going to be a considerable change to the way water is viewed across the globe, and nowhere more so than in London. Inevitably, over time there will be a great deal of the wrong kind of water – sewage and waste water – as the population continues to grow and exceeds the Victorian infrastructure, while there will be more flooding due to increased rainfall as well as rising sea levels of salt water. All these will have an effect upon how London plans itself in the future.

It was not until the early part of the 19th century that the problem of sewage, water treatment and the supply of clean water became of such importance to Londoners. This was not just due to population growth; it was also caused by technology, with the invention of the water closet itself increasing the flow and the pollution levels while, during the Industrial Revolution, the number of factories, slaughterhouses and tanneries along the banks of the tributaries and the Thames grew exponentially. These factors led to the cholera and typhoid epidemics of 1853–4 and the Great Stink, as it was called, during the hot summer of 1858 when the rivers overflowed with sewage. Consequently, huge interceptory sewerage networks were laid out by Joseph Bazalgette, Chief

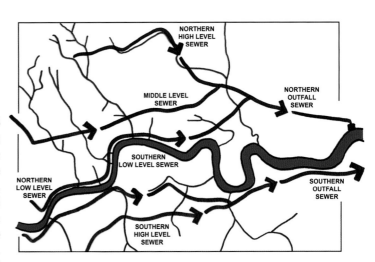

Engineer of London's Metropolitan Board of Works, between 1856 and 1866. These affected central London's tributaries by running across the directions of the streams and literally intercepting them to redirect the sewage to run parallel with the Thames along three main routes on the north bank and two on the south. Eventually, the sewers combined to become the northern outfall sewer and the southern outfall sewer, with the former going to Beckton Works and the latter to Crossness Works. This made the whole of the water system for central London completely artificial. Consequently, there is a substantial reduction in flow down the old tributaries so that small streams like Counter's Creek now have a virtually non-existent flow of water.

The era of pollution and the heavy rainfall run-off into the sewers continues, giving rise to proposals of a fairly dramatic nature to completely revolutionise sewerage management with brand new systems. One such is the Thames Tideway which will be a wide storage and transfer tunnel with an internal diameter of between 7.2 and 9 metres (24 and 29 feet). It will run for 35 kilometres (22 miles) underneath the river bed of the Thames between Hammersmith and Beckton/Crossness. This scheme has been estimated as costing £1.7 billion. It has not yet been started, but with the increased environmental problems and population growth it is anticipated that this huge project will be carried out within the next 20 years.

One of the most surprising developments in recent times has been the rather romantic one of opening up some of the lost rivers to recreate the presence of the tributaries within the central area. As Peter Bishop, Director of Design for London, said in June 2008 at a presentation to the Mayor of London, Boris Johnson: 'When these rivers are opened up I think Londoners will

be absolutely surprised that they [the rivers] have been there all the time, but you never see them'.

Tributaries are already re-emerging as once-again beneficial natural landscapes within our metropolitan urban areas. A section of the River Quaggy has been brought out of its culvert and opened up in Sutcliffe Park, southeast London, while a stretch of the Ravensbourne within Lewisham is also being revived. The new London River Action Plan, supported by the Greater London Authority and the Environment Agency, aims to restore a further 15 kilometres (9.3 miles) of concrete-channelled tributaries to their natural state by 2015, including parts of the Wandle, Roding, Colne and Brent. The major central rivers, including the Fleet, are impossible to revive, although it has been suggested that ornamental stretches could be created along them. However romantic these ideas are, though, they do touch a nerve – they reveal the fundamental importance and attraction of these hidden lost pieces of the natural terrain that underlie London and give foundation to its urban geometry – it is like discovering a hidden part of oneself, one's own identity.

Redrawn by Farrell, Joseph Bazalgette's plan for intercepting sewers, 2009
The great 19th-century sewerage system intercepting London's tributary rivers and diverting them downstream to treatment works along the estuary.

London's Infrastructure: Inventing the Metropolis

Canals

A Built-In Resource

The UK's 18th-century canal network is an outstanding valuable resource. This is not just because of its original industrial purpose and sheer length of over 3219 kilometres (2,000 miles) but because, as I wrote over 30 years ago, in the May 1976 edition of the *RIBA Journal*, the great beauty of this historical achievement is that the network provides so much that can add to today's life. It was at that time, in the 1970s, that schemes for vast, extremely expensive leisure centres were being erected and I was struck by how sizable the leisure resources are in Britain, which we already have built in, just waiting to be better used. The canal system, for example, is a network of precious leisure routes that could be opened up more widely than at present, combining countryside, industrial archaeology, a bit of travel and some physical exercise at the locks. The system provides a linked-up, connected set of threads over so much of the rural and urban landscape that translates into an uninterrupted network of gently graded foot and cycle paths for people. It makes a

continuous ecological pathway for wildlife, both on land and on water, and surprisingly is one of the most penetrating accessible pathways for modern utilities such as telecommunications, gas and water supply.

The canal network carries water everywhere; water is so basic, so much a container of natural wilderness, that it is a highly accessible release from urbanity and modern life. The canal is a man-made, eminently user-friendly waterway: it is shallow, with contained footpathed edges and a consistent and extraordinarily small human scale of bridges and towpath layout and design. It is made 'to fit', like a made-to-measure suit for the human figure. It is not a thing of nature, like a river that responds to the wild, where all that is natural, the varying scales of nature, all evolved independently of man. Instead, the whole thing is an artefact; a product which was as ergonomically designed for human-scale activity and use as today's buses, cars and houses. One feels and senses this from the geometrics, which are based on human and horse movement; the steps, the gradients and the granite edges all respond to the very specific, nationally adopted

Previous page: Alastair Lansley for Union Railways, St Pancras International, London, 2007

The masterful extension and renovation of William Barlow's 1868 train shed, undertaken for the new Eurostar terminal. London built the first railway stations but they can still be added to in a magnificent way, in the tradition of continuous evolution.

Narrowboat cruise on the Grand Union Canal, 1959

An excursion boat passes along a tree-lined stretch of the Grand Union Canal, en route from Little Venice to Camden.

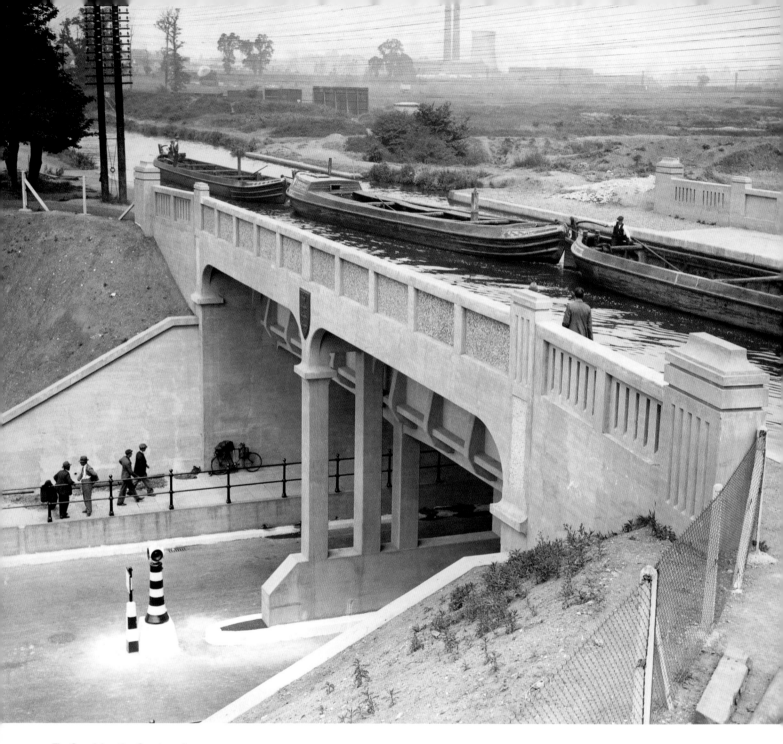

**The Grand Junction Canal passing
over the new North Circular Road, 1939**
The building of new roads in the early
20th century retained the canals, which
then sailed in aqueducts over the new
suburban roadway system.

Barges on the Grand Union Canal, 1931
The Grand Union Canal at Kensal Green
Gas Works, showing the relationship
between the canals and the industrial
backland areas. Note the pollution from
coal-powered boats.

human-use module of the width, length and draught of the canal narrow boat, which itself is a tight-fit universal unit. And finally, the canal network has artificially made docks, ports and harbours continuously along its length, enabling it to 'place make' readily along its urban networks, such as at London's Little Venice, Camden Lock, and the basins at Paddington, City Road and Limehouse, which are man-made water harbours replicated all over the cities, towns and villages of Britain.

The intimacy of scale and air of silence along a canal cannot be found on the other modern throughways of road and rail. The animal world of fish, birds, water voles, rabbits and foxes has fully adapted to this man-made work, as canals are often less polluted than rivers and provide a continuous network in which they can gather, breed and coexist in safety and seclusion. At a smaller scale, the plant and invertebrate world, with its more limited mobility, particularly benefits from these extensive ecological corridors.

Farrell, The major rivers of Britain (1750), 2009
Until 1750 the rivers of Britain (with some man-made extensions) were the only navigable inland waterway system.

Farrell, Connecting rivers with canals (1810), 2009
By 1810 the rivers had all been linked by canals – travelling over central high hills, connecting all of Britain in one inland waterway system.

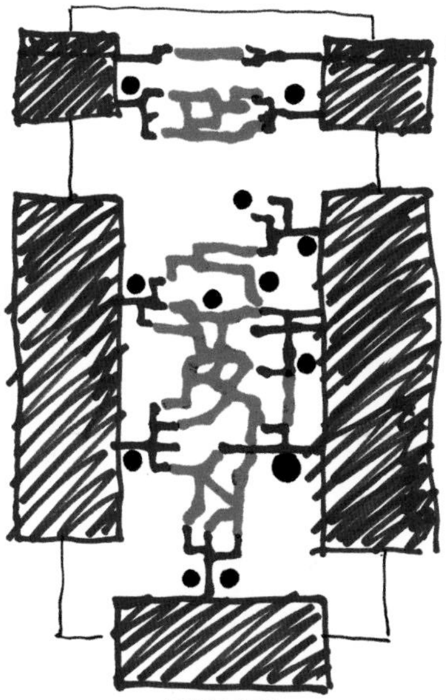

The creation of this magical and romantic natural environment was, of course, very far from the intentions of the speculators and industrialists, whose sole purpose was utility and profit through industry. Nevertheless, over 200 years since it was built, the canal network now provides new benefits more valuable and certainly more long-lasting than the original purpose.

'Canal Mania'

How did this national phenomenon come about and how did it affect London? Until their invention, the first highways were across seas and via land and rivers, followed by the crude but dangerous and difficult road systems of Roman and Saxon times. The natural network for navigation was the river system, but with the growth of trade and the need to deliver new, heavy and bulky goods such as coal, building materials and agricultural produce to growing towns and cities, the rivers gradually filled to capacity. Also, the rivers were increasingly being used, and interrupted in their flow, to power mills and to carry polluted waste. All of this made navigation even more difficult. At the time, nowhere

Farrell, Diagram of UK seas and canal links, 2009
The canals (in red) linked the rivers so the seas and oceans were in turn linked making a totally connected boat travelling 'waterworld' reaching all the land and cities (black dots).

in the world was there more demand for access of goods than in London, which grew from a population of about 200,000 in 1600 to nearly one million in 1801.

There is probably no aspect of planning that shows better what a wonderful thing patterns are in mapping than the general evolution of the combined river and canal systems. They have an added interrelationship with coastal boundaries and Britain's hill ranges from the Pennines down to the Chilterns. The reaction and interaction of these – the natural and the man-made – make the basis of the patterning, a result of a combination of natural water run-off, down contour lines to the sea, and man-made, engineered interceptions to aid and extend by artificial means the routes taken by the natural waterways and to add to their limited navigational benefits.

It is worth looking at a map of around 1750 and comparing it with one of 1810 to see the astonishing and spectacular quantity of work that was undertaken during the short period between these dates – the era of 'canal mania', which peaked in 1793. (In my family, the Farrells came to Britain from Ireland during the 19th-century famines and provided men for a massive workforce of navvies or 'excavators' – the name given to the men who dug the canals and railways.) The main canal age ran from the Bridgewater Canal of 1759–65 to the Birmingham & Liverpool Junction Canal of 1835. Canal mania tailed off very quickly from the 1830s, however, as the railways appeared in the 19th century with their even greater ability to transport larger and larger goods and, of course, at much greater speeds. Some canals, such as the

Industrial estate in north London, 1993
The Grand Union Canal in north London, showing the industrial areas that occur along the canal banks.

Horse pulling a barge on a London canal, 1954
As late as 1954 working boats were still winding their way up and down the canals, shown here at a lock in central London.

Grosvenor Canal and Basin in Pimlico and the canal in southeast London that linked Gravesend to the Medway, were literally taken over by the railways when their gently graded courses and tunnels were sold to rail companies. Indeed, many attempts were made to sell even more lines to the railways, as they provided ready-made land acquisition corridors, but often without success.

A Connected Water Network

Historically, the major rivers varied in importance but all were navigable by sea vessels a considerable way upstream – even Leeds, far inland, was navigable from the sea. London's River Lea, for example, was an important navigation river going back even as far as the Vikings who, in the 10th century, sailed up the Lea all the way to Hertford and ransacked the town. To some extent river navigation had already begun to decline by the start of the

Farrell, JF Pownall's unbuilt Grand Contour Canal (1942), 2009
Travelling at a continuous level of 95 metres (310 feet) above ground, and 30.8 metres (100 feet) wide, the Grand Contour Canal was to link all canals, rivers and UK cities.

canal era in 1750, but it is quite clear from the map that the river system still dominated, especially along Britain's five major estuary rivers – the Humber, the Wash, the Mersey, the Severn and the Thames – and their tributaries. (There are also some important subsidiary ones around the Norfolk Broads, the River Test coming up from Southampton and the Medway in Kent.)

Within only 50 years this had all been radically transformed. The first step in the canal era was to improve and extend the river system. The Fens became the place of most activity because the rivers and the drainage went hand in hand – indeed, some canals here go back to the Romans who had several canal systems in Britain. The big change came with the development and wider application of the long-established navigation (or 'pound') lock – a kind of water staircase that turned the gravitational limitations of water, and therefore its transport methods, on its head. Now, against all logic, if water could not go uphill, then at least boats could.

A whole set of canals were built over and across the long mountain spine of England, with boats now travelling up and down the hills. This made the Pennines and the Chilterns surmountable, so the five great estuaries could be connected: the Mersey was linked to the Humber and the Severn across to the Wash, while London and the Thames was connected to all the major estuary rivers and their industrial and agricultural goods. The whole lot were connected up as effectively as an electrical wiring circuit that literally empowered all the disparate water parts of England. The emphasis on canal systems was emphatically to the north and Midlands, as these were the main production areas. The whole urban scene of some cities such as Birmingham and Manchester became riddled with canal systems, so much so that it was once

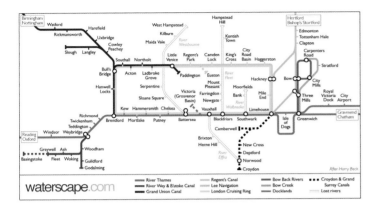

said that Birmingham – very much the central hub of the system – had as many canals as Venice! The new canal system connected the distant production system of these cities to London, without going out to sea. The interior of London was not so riddled and its own canal systems were built later, being primarily for distribution and supply/service purposes; London was the consumer, the end of the line – not primarily a producer.

The railways, motor cars and highway design continued to overtake canal water transport and it had all but died out by the middle of the 20th century. However, it continues to have one singular advantage over all its successors: what it lacked in speed, it made up for in energy economy, as water travel substantially reduces friction, even for heavy loads. Capitalising on this advantage, there was one final idea, as original as it was probably infeasible, for a national canal system. JF Pownall's sought in 1942 to create a Grand Contour Canal that was to travel at a fixed natural contour of 95 metres (310 feet) across Britain, continuously connecting many parts of the country and linking to most river systems by boat lifts. The surface width of the canal would be an extraordinary 30.8 metres (100 feet) wide and 5.2 metres (17 feet) deep. The canal was not only to be used for shipping, but also for water transfer. This idea was never built, but if it had been it would have created another network on top of the canal systems, a radical 20th-century layer that would have turbocharged the aged declining network.

Tube-style map of waterways

One of the few attempts to apply the integrated mapping system of the London Underground to another movement system. If only it could be done as convincingly for the buses and mainline trains. This map includes canal and river systems, and the Thames is shown in green.

The London Canal Network

Within London, British Waterways has produced a most delightful map inspired by Harry Beck's tube map. Just as the underground railways evolved incrementally, so did the canal system, first as an intellectual idea and then with mapping, information and national controls to make it work as one. The core of London's network is the Regent's Canal, which is an essential part of two other systems. The first is the earlier Grand Junction Canal, known since 1929 as the Grand Union Canal, which was opened in 1800 as a through route from the Midlands via Watford and Uxbridge to west London, terminating at the Thames in Brentford. The second part is the Paddington Arm, opened in 1801, which linked the Grand Junction Canal to Paddington Basin.

The Regent's Canal, which was built by John Nash with the support of the Prince Regent between 1812 and 1820, joined the Paddington Arm to east London. A great looping arm was connected from Little Venice right round to Limehouse on the Thames, just before the river swerves around the Isle of Dogs. The core of the loop system and its 12 locks fed right across the north of London – indeed, it was also known as the North Metropolitan Canal – and featured, for industrial use, a collateral cut (now filled) between the Park Villages in Regent's Park. It also included several major basins: Paddington Basin, Cumberland Basin (to the east of Euston Station), St Pancras Basin in King's Cross and City Road Basin, which was significant for being closest to the City of London. The final loop ended at Regent's Canal Dock – now known as Limehouse Basin – where cargo could be transferred from barges to seafaring vessels on the Thames. What is really original about the Regent's Canal is that Nash, the ever inventive

and supreme urban planner, designed it as a multi-layered idea. Not only would it provide infrastructure (in the normal goods-delivery manner of all canals), it would also become part of the picturesque landscape scene of Regent's Park – the Prince's grand real-estate venture where the park and its landscape would help sell grand homes to the really rich and the aristocracy. This was a piece of place-making of which any modern developer would be proud and which anticipated by nearly two centuries the eventual primary role of all canals as environmental and lifestyle attractors.

At both ends of London, the Regent's Canal system links to two complex river systems: the 32-kilometre (20-mile) long Brent to the west and the 72-kilometre (45-mile) Lea to the east. Both are navigable systems that have long been canalised and were at the centre of much industrial innovation and activity during the 19th and 20th centuries. There are many other subsidiary canal systems going to Basingstoke, Guildford and down to Croydon, Gravesend and Chatham, but these were quite small and not part of any overall canal scheme. Rather, they serviced the Thames itself. How the Brent and Lea evolved is covered separately in the previous chapter, but it is fitting to mention here that these two tributary rivers form a ring called the London Cruising Ring, like a water version of the Circle Line or the M25, which runs round the Grand Union and Regent's canals. Only the very brave go out into the Thames to get from Brentford to Limehouse or vice versa because it is difficult to navigate, particularly for smaller boats, as the tidal range and ferocity of flow has been increased by the banks moving steadily inwards. The canal system provides a very quiet, elegant and secure method of going on a parallel urban route to the Thames. It is also a less swerving and more direct conduit through the action – London's urban scenery.

Tourist boat on Regent's Canal, 2006
John Nash's intention of the extension of the Regent's Canal to the north of London was to provide a setting for the sale of fine houses on the lands owned by the Prince Regent. Here, 200 years later, new houses are being built by Quinlan Terry facing the canal bank on the northern edges of Regent's Park.

Canalside Regeneration

The reincarnation today of the British canal system as a major environmental, urban, place-making asset more than makes up for its relatively short-lived supremacy before the days of the railway. People now live in pleasant houseboats in the very centre of London, in the quiet, peaceful and natural surroundings of the canal waterways. Tourist boats and barges rented out to holidaymakers provide the main activity on the water, while amenities such as cafés, restaurants and theatres are offered by vessels that are both travelling and moored. This continues a leisure tradition dating back to a time when the canals were in industrial use and many a London working man, from even the poorest areas, learnt fishing skills and had contact with nature along the canal banks.

Since the late 1960s when commercial traffic all but vanished on the Regent's Canal, towpaths have gradually opened up to the general public. Now, they have become a loved and integral part of the north London pedestrian network. The most dramatic and relatively recent change has been the way that the rural yet urban qualities of the canal have been capitalised for new developments of all kinds. Little Venice was an important early pioneer in this respect. It was developed in the 1840s at the junction of the Paddington Arm of the Grand Junction Canal and Regent's Canal. Its most imposing streets of stucco semi-detached villas, Blomfield Road and Maida Avenue, were designed to face each other on either side of Regent's Canal. Like Nash's plan for Regent's Park, the development of Little Venice aimed to appeal to the wealthy homeowner, recognising from the outset the potential to create a desirable location around water.

Previous page: Canal boats in Little Venice, 2005
The invention of the canals as a place to live and for recreation is shown very clearly here. There are now more canal boats than ever before – 35,000!

In contrast, Camden Town, north of Little Venice on the Regent's Canal, evolved in the late 19th century into a vibrant but gritty working-class area with a strong Irish community. Its busy high street was home to several popular music halls, but was also covered by layers of soot from the railway termini at King's Cross. In the 1950s and 1960s, Camden's commercial heart, which was centred round the railways and the canal, was brought into steep decline by the widespread adoption of road transport for goods. The catalyst for regeneration only came in the early 1970s with the creation of its market based around the canal. The original market buildings at Camden Lock were redundant warehouses and an old timber yard, leased from British Waterways. By the 1980s, the market had burgeoned into a phenomenal success. Having expanded to three further markets around Camden Town, it became a major destination for London's youth and foreign tourists alike. This upturn in Camden's fortunes coincided with our own design for the canal-side TV-AM Breakfast Studios (now home to MTV), completed in 1983; a landmark building, it was immediately identifiable locally and on TV by the giant eggcups on its roof. The building of these new studios provided an important precedent for the arrival of an increasing number of creative companies in the area that changed the commercial base of Camden for good, securing its transformation from a railway goods-yard backwater to one of inner London's most successfully regenerated areas.

The basins and locks have become urban magnets. This is most apparent at Paddington Basin, which has undergone a large-scale development, the size of Soho, since 1998. It typifies the potential for new place-making that is possible in these former backlands of the Industrial Revolution. Previously, rail

Narrowboats on the Grand Union Canal
The canal was for many people a complete
lifestyle. They lived, worked and brought
up families entirely on the boats. Note the
horses, in the background, which towed
the boats.

goods yards and canal basins formed large introverted, solid, inaccessible blocks, interrupting urban connectivity and the flow of streets and community relationships. These were also the focus of noise and pollution – timber yards, coal stores and manufacturing lined the banks – but much of this gradually faded from use during the late 20th century. Reconnecting these industrial islands (like Paddington Basin back to Paddington proper, Bayswater and Maida Vale) meant radically reinventing whole districts of metropolitan London, reversing the effect of the urban voids and proactively creating positive centres of animated urban life. But this has not proved easy or quick. London's heavy reliance on private enterprise has meant a stop-start pattern and some development failures mixed with some successes. For me, the most rewarding experience at Paddington now is to walk the towpath from Maida

Steamship advert, 1931
A telling advertisement of the relationship of London to the Rhine. The Thames was once a tributary of the Rhine and as they both face each other across the North Sea they form a direct connection from the heart of Europe to the heart of Britain, particularly once the canal systems had been built on both sides. Water travel enabled the industrial north and Midlands to connect to Europe. As the advert states, 'Birmingham to Duisburg, Dusseldorf, Cologne ... Mannheim, Frankfurt and Basle'. The canal system intensified the role of London's ports with Europe and the world.

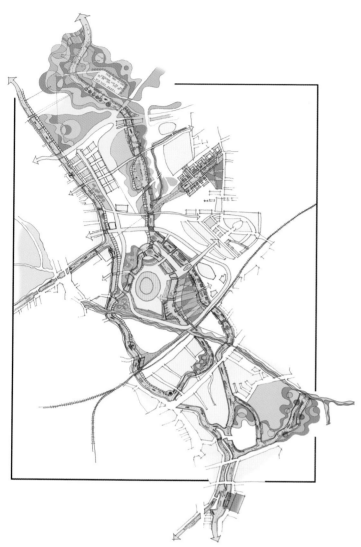

reopened territory its 'nowhere else in this world' feel, its highly theatrical, spectacularly original and unique sense of place.

There are many urban patterns that the canals helped shape which still prolong urban discontinuities that reinforce social and environmental disadvantage and problems. The industrial area created by a combination of the road bypass (the New Road of the mid 1750s, which became the Marylebone-Euston Roads to Smithfield), the mainline rail stations alongside Paddington to King's Cross and their associated industrial lands is a broad divisive swathe that runs east to west for two or three miles. The

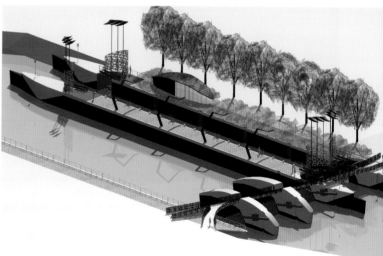

Vale to Paddington Station, passing under the hitherto hugely divisive 1960s-built elevated motorway of the Westway as it flies over the canal, to find a continuous, connected-up world with new bridges, bankside restaurants and squares and sculpture. The intensity of the collision of ad-hoc transport systems now gives this

Farrell, Possible future for the Lea Valley waterway, 2008

This post-Olympic plan for British Waterways shows that the canal system can add to the Olympic experience as well as being part of the legacy.

Farrell, Diagram of Prescott Lock, Lower Lea Valley, 2007

This new lock in the Lower Lea Valley is being constructed in time for the Olympics and will mean the whole of the Lea river navigation system is unaffected by tidal range and thus fully navigable.

LAND USE PATTERN

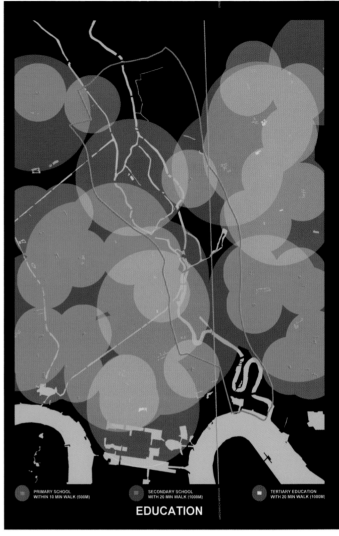

PRIMARY SCHOOL
WITHIN 10 MIN WALK (500M)

SECONDARY SCHOOL
WITH 20 MIN WALK (1000M)

TERTIARY EDUCATION
WITH 20 MIN WALK (1000M)

EDUCATION

Regent's Canal, due to water's particular abilities to separate and divide, forms a remarkable border or barrier in this area: to the north are the prosperous areas of St John's Wood, Maida Vale and Primrose Hill, while to the south there is the biggest contiguous group of large housing estates in central London. They house

250,000 people – a population the size of a large town or city such as Milton Keynes, Wolverhampton or Nottingham – in a kind of 'lost land' between the posh areas to the north and the similarly posh areas of Notting Hill, Bayswater, Marylebone and Bloomsbury to the south.

Farrell, Land-use pattern
Lower Lea Valley, 2006
The ability of mapping to express
the underlying patterns can be very
beautiful as illustrated in this land-use
pattern drawing of the Lea Valley.

Farrell, Education in the
Lower Lea Valley, 2006
Drawing showing schools
and their catchment areas.

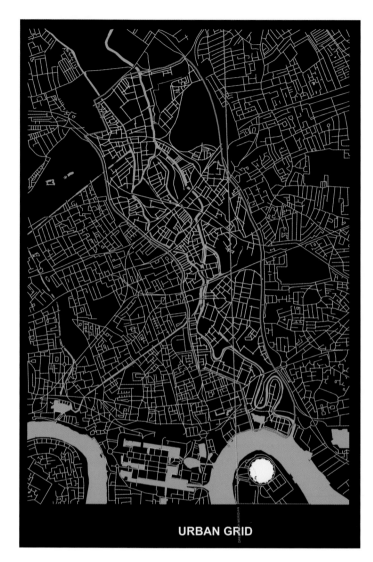

URBAN GRID

OPEN SPACES

The great urban planning potential of London's canal system is that it is owned and run by one body, British Waterways, which today recognises that the system's best future is in integrating with London's wider planning development. Unlike London's river, road and rail systems, which are so fragmented in their micro-compartmentalisation of ownerships and responsibility areas, the canals are one. They are linked in a discernible pattern with the river systems of the Brent and the Lea and the large docks in the East End. They have nothing but a positive, joined up, connecting contribution to offer to London's future planning.

Farrell, Urban grid of the Lower Lea Valley, 2006
Drawing showing the existing street pattern in the Lower Lea Valley area with the Millennium Dome in the lower right-hand corner and Canary Wharf and the Isle of Dogs clearly visible with the River Lea stretching across.

Farrell, Open spaces of the Lower Lea Valley, 2006
Drawing showing how the waterways join the open spaces of the Lower Lea Valley.

Railways

Pioneering Steps

So much of the present shape and form of London was a creation of the 19th century. No contributor to the city-making forces for good or ill, though, was more fundamental than the building of the railways in the middle and latter half of that century. It all began in 1808 when Richard Trevithick, the inventor and mining engineer, erected the world's very first passenger-carrying railway line, albeit one that was a funfair novelty ride. Fittingly, this was built in Euston Square, on the Euston Road (then still known as the New Road), where most of the mainline railways stations – Euston, King's Cross and St Pancras, and Marylebone in a direct line west on the Marylebone Road – were later built. Trevithick's 'Steam Circus' was located right in front of where the current Euston Station stands and more or less where the great Euston Arch by Philip Hardwick stood from 1837 to 1961; the arch served as a monumental portico or entrance to the original classical-style station that had an expansive wrought-iron and glass shed by engineer Charles Fox, until it was demolished by Dr Richard Beeching and his successors at British Rail in a misguided bid for modernisation in the 1960s.

The scale of urban reconstruction that accompanied the building of London's rail infrastructure in the mid to late 19th century was truly astonishing, involving a level of disruption and a scale of enterprise that no city in Britain will probably be able to contemplate ever again. Yet, in metropolitan terms, all this was done in an unplanned way, spurred on by the initiative of independent companies, each of which worked intensely and intro-vertedly on their own particular projects for their own benefit in a stand-alone, self-contained manner. Typical of just how singularly London did things, the city's railway-construction mania occurred at more or less the same time that Baron Haussmann and his emperor, Napoleon III, were in Paris rationalising, organising and laying out an ordered, centralist geometric plan of the great capital city of the country next door – what an astonishing contrast!

Perhaps it could be said in mitigation that proceeding without a plan – testing pragmatically how things went along the way – was perhaps inevitable for a country that was leading the

Dairy workers at Paddington, 1926
Milk arriving from the country and a busy scene of passengers arriving on the same platforms. Also apparent is the dark fume-filled environment with the ironwork covered in soot from the steam engines.

In order to understand the pattern of rail infrastructure in London, it is necessary to begin with the shape of the whole island of Britain and the origins of the goods and resources that the country has, and then, of course, to consider the capital city relationship to these factors. It is self-evident that London is located towards the bottom of the British Isles, and that the vast majority of people, as well the major sources of coal, food and other goods that were transported by rail, are all to the north of it; this is important to reflect on. The geographical position of London within Britain gave shape and urban form to its railway plan.

way with a completely new kind of urban infrastructure project. It is a simple fact that wherever else one goes in the world, it seems that railways and their stations have been integrated into the overall plan of cities in a more deliberate and planned way than London has ever managed. But then London was never a city in the first place: it was the world's first sprawling metropolis, made up of many individual towns and villages and nodal points, and, until the London County Council was created in 1889, there was no coordinating metropolitan government. Any new infrastructure systems were overlaid on top of this and were always layering the ad hoc and pragmatic on to the existing ad hoc and pragmatic. In the 18th and 19th centuries, every step of the creation of the canal, railway and tube systems was a pioneering one.

Model of Richard Trevithick's
Penydarren steam engine, 1804
This replica is on show outside Cyfarthfa Castle, Wales. The original made history by successfully pulling a 10-ton load of iron along a 15-kilometre (9.5-mile) stretch of tram road from Penydarren and Abercynon.

Trevithick's 'Steam Circus', 1808
The world's first ever passenger-carrying railway was the 'Catch-Me-Who-Can' engine which ran around a circular track at a 'Steam Circus' established by Richard Trevithick. Its location was probably close to the site of the great Euston Arch by Philip Hardwick which was the entrance to the future Euston Station. Tickets for this ride were sold to the public at a cost of one shilling.

The world's first railways began as on-site industrial working machines around and within mines – including the tin mines in Cornwall, with local man Richard Trevithick powering a road vehicle with steam in 1801 and inventing the first working railway steam locomotive in 1804 for the Penydarren Ironworks, near Merthyr Tydfil in Wales. They were then properly developed as a transport system in the northeast of England in 1825 with the Stockton and Darlington Railway, where George Stephenson developed wrought-iron rails and sleepers, as well as the universal gauge (based on the width of a pit pony!) which was to be established throughout the world. Central to the rail system of London was the presumption that the new infrastructure was to be focused on bringing coal and other goods to the metropolis –

the idea of the railway as primarily a passenger transport system was still some way off. Therefore, from the late 1830s onwards a great row of goods stations were arranged along the northern edge of London, built with large yards to accommodate the weight and cubic content of the loads arriving from the north and west to service London's industries.

The New Road – London's Railway Epicentre

The stations were located along the edge of the New Road, north London's mid-18th-century bypass, with Paddington Station in the west and Euston, King's Cross and, later, St Pancras towards the east. Somewhat fortuitously, John Nash and others had

Philip Hardwick's Euston Arch, 1837
The arch on its original site. It was
subsequently demolished in the 1960s as
part of the Euston Station improvements.

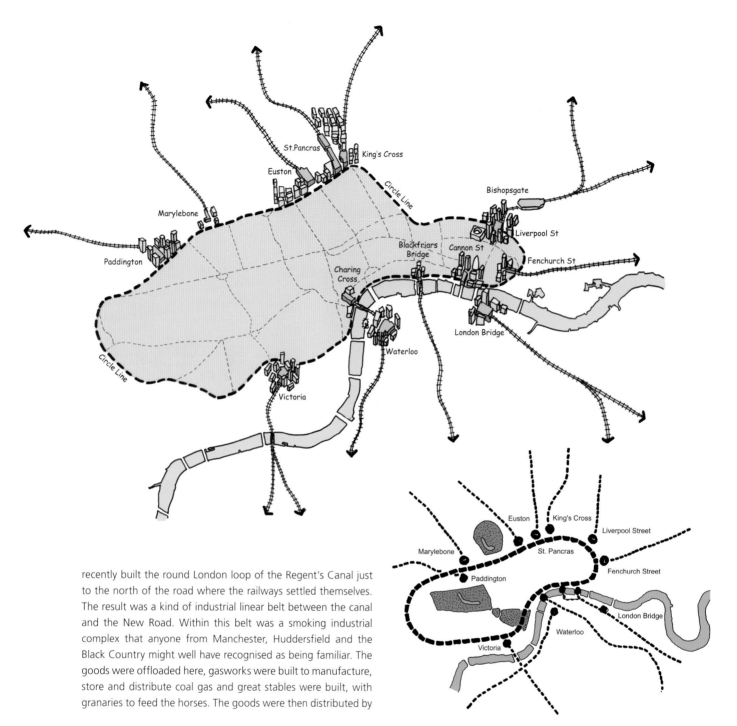

recently built the round London loop of the Regent's Canal just to the north of the road where the railways settled themselves. The result was a kind of industrial linear belt between the canal and the New Road. Within this belt was a smoking industrial complex that anyone from Manchester, Huddersfield and the Black Country might well have recognised as being familiar. The goods were offloaded here, gasworks were built to manufacture, store and distribute coal gas and great stables were built, with granaries to feed the horses. The goods were then distributed by

Farrell, Drawing showing the locations of London's great railway stations, 2004
It can clearly be seen that the railway stations have influenced the positions of high-density developments.

Farrell, Diagram of London's mainline stations, 1999
Goods arriving from the north and south of England to mainline stations, showing how those coming in from the north of England led to stations on the north bank of the Thames. These were set apart to the north of the developed urban area and linked to the canal for distribution. The stations to the south, however, with a limited land mass and no real resources, brought in people and set up a completely different kind of service and rationale. This drawing shows how they were first linked by the Circle Line: the world's first underground railway to connect it all as one.

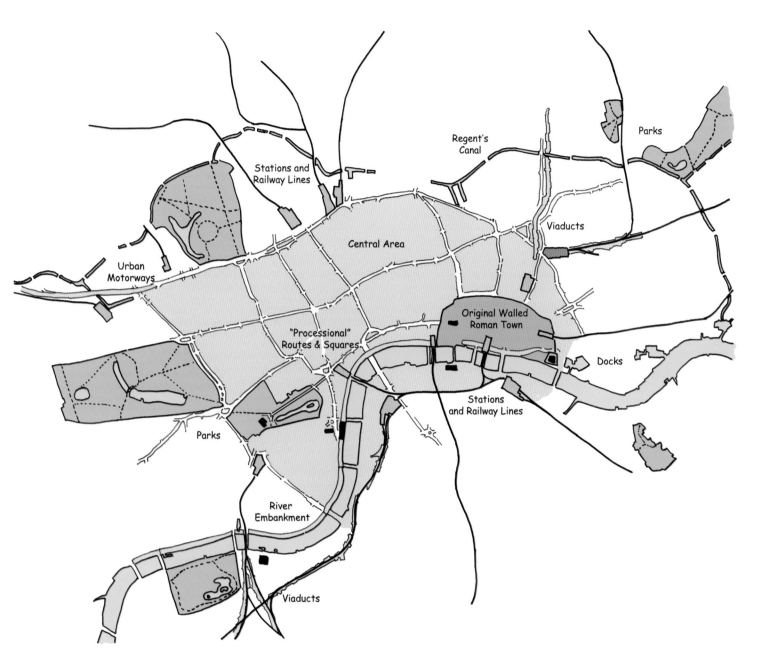

Urban
Motorways

Stations and
Railway Lines

Regent's
Canal

Parks

Central Area

Viaducts

Original Walled
Roman Town

"Processional"
Routes & Squares

Docks

Stations
and Railway Lines

Parks

River
Embankment

Viaducts

**Farrell, London's large-scale
engineering infrastructure, 2004**
Plan showing the core of London, the City
and West End and the urban infrastructure
that rings it, with canals and rail hardly
entering into the central area.

horse power via the New Road back into London or by canal in a great loop to supply London's burgeoning number of inhabitants. Great new docks were built next to the stations themselves, running from Brentford in the west right round to Limehouse in the east – including at Paddington Basin, and then Cumberland Basin next to Euston goods station, while a complex of docks and water facilities was built behind King's Cross and also adjacent at Battlebridge Basin. Paddington soon became the world's first modern transport interchange, with the railway, the canal and London's first horse-bus service all located there.

Between the stations, to the north of the New Road, terraces and tenements were built, in the same way that the colliery owners up in Northumberland accommodated the workers within walking distance of their particular industrial complexes. Right to this day, the area has the biggest collection of social housing anywhere in London, and within it, divided and chopped up in great land blocks, are the former large goods yards of the railways. Statistically, these housing estates formed the most deprived wards in the southeast of England. Unsurprisingly, though, as the metropolis was fuelled by the stations, both employment and the population of the area grew, with the homes of the workers ever expanding outwards and northwards.

'The Passenger Age'

People then started travelling from outside London in greater numbers to visit the city for pleasure and business, and so the railway companies began to realise that they could make as much or even more money from moving people to London as they could from goods. The speed and comfort of the new rolling stock and carriages improved and the whole system of stations and signalling grew and developed. It was a kind of simultaneous product development, with invention and application happening at the same time. As demand developed, more towns needed to connect to the capital so the system was extended and multiplied. However, unlike goods, the passengers needed to arrive closer to the centre of the city and did not want to be set down among all the industrial complexes. Consequently, the passenger stations were extended immediately southwards adjacent to the New Road so that passengers could step off Paddington Station at Paddington Green, Euston Station at Euston Square and King's Cross and St Pancras along the road, where the Gothic splendour of George Gilbert Scott's Midland Grand Hotel was revealed in 1868. With the construction of large-scale passenger termini, a new kind of civic architecture – grand entrances through which people would flow to and from the trains – was established as an urban pattern.

The world's first passenger railway station was opened at Liverpool Road in Manchester in 1830, and soon after the development of passenger stations in London continued apace. The new stations, which featured designs by some of the great Victorian architects, incorporated platforms, concourses, ticketing offices and waiting rooms, all under great metal and glass roofs. Euston opened in 1838 and expanded in 1849 to feature a new public facility – the dramatic, coffered Great Hall, designed by Philip Charles Hardwick (the son of the original architect Philip Hardwick). King's Cross, designed by Lewis Cubitt, opened in 1852, while the adjacent slums were cleared for the 1868 building of St Pancras, featuring a Gothic Revival facade by George Gilbert Scott, and a huge single span arch over the platforms. Paddington

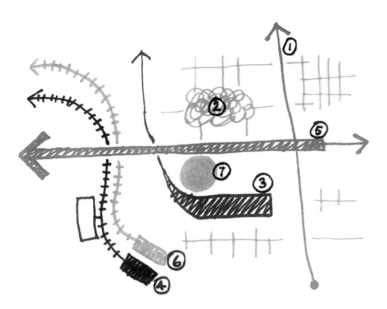

Station, with its three spans of wrought-iron arches and glazed roof designed by Isambard Kingdom Brunel, opened in 1853. Closer to the City, Fenchurch Street opened in 1841 and Liverpool Street in 1874, replacing the original station at Bishopsgate, which had been operating since the 1840s but was deemed too far from the City. Liverpool Street soon featured the Great Eastern Hotel, designed by the sons of Charles Barry. Marylebone Station was a somewhat late arrival, opening in 1899. Consequently a great fan of London railway stations was established from the west, northwest, north, northeast and east.

Following the building of the railways coming into London from the north and west, entrepreneurial rail companies and speculators soon began to assess how they could make money from the short section of England that remained still untapped –

Farrell, Historic arrival points at Paddington Basin, 2001

Paddington in particular, together with King's Cross/St Pancras, were extremely important nodal transport interchange points – transport being attracted to the same points because it could connect to other modes of transport. At Paddington the seven points, historically, are:

1. The Roman Empire arrival point (Watling Street arrives at Marble Arch: 1st century AD).
2. The village of Paddington emerges (centred around Paddington Green: 13th century to present).
3. The Grand Union Canal arrival point (Paddington Basin: 18th century).
4. Great Western Railway arrival point (Brunel's Paddington Station: 19th century).

5. Motorway network arrival point (A40 motorway and the Edgware Road flyover: mid 20th century).
6. Air travel arrival point (Heathrow Express: late 20th century)
7. Electronic satellite communication arrival point (Telecoms company headquarters: 21st century).

Railways from the south jockeyed for position to cross the river and often overlapped each other as separate railway companies built their viaducts, trapping land along the riverbanks where industry grew, creating a whole band and isolating a large swathe of south bank territory. In 2007 I suggested that this land (trapped between railway viaducts and the river) should today become a kind of 'third city', a south bank focus with status and function like the old cities of Westminster and the City (see diagram on p 137).

Breaking down the **'band of deprivation'** and creating balanced communities

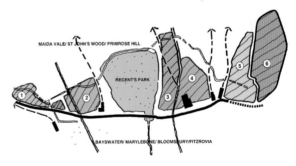

transform the estate 'monoculture' and create social and economic diversity

Farrell, Estates to the north of the Marylebone-Euston Roads, 2003

Railway, industry and the homes of the working classes have always interrelated. This diagram shows the six housing estates that run in and around north of the Marylebone-Euston Roads.

the land that lay between the metropolis and the south coast. Here, there were far fewer long-distance travellers and no significant resources like mineral mining or manufacturing goods, so rail companies came up with the ingenious solution of deliberately creating freight solely from the people themselves. They created the world of planned commuting, where house building and rail stations were established in tandem to feed London's voracious appetite for further workers. Central London, between the New Road and the Thames, was substantially made up of the great, high-value, settled estates that had been owned and run by the landed aristocracy since previous centuries, but to the south of the river, in the flat, marshy areas, there was land with low value with no significant urban communities. Therefore, the railways from the southeast had at least one advantage in that they could readily buy up land to get very close to London's centre and across the River Thames itself. The southeast railway companies fought each other to get land access right up to and over the Thames and into central London, creating an extraordinary, spaghetti-like maze of overlapping railway lines.

There are two additional characteristics that distinguish the southeast railways from the northern passenger ones. First, they were short-distance lines (the south coast being their limit), with many short stops, so the system became a truly small-scale regional commuter railway. Second, the land was immediately flat prior to arrival in central London, so unlike in north London less tunnelling was required and the trains invariably arrived on elevated viaducts – it was all the better for the lines to reach the Thames' edge at an elevated position, which they then maintained to sail across to the north bank on bridges. The competing rail systems criss-crossed and often paralleled one another as they

snaked along the south bank, looking for crossing points. Most southern lines managed to establish beach-head stations on the north bank, sometimes by using existing infrastructure (as at Victoria and Charing Cross), and other times by creating new routes (at Blackfriars and Cannon Street). The only two southern railways without land holdings on the north bank ended at the termini of Waterloo and London Bridge. Waterloo subsequently built its own underground rail system, the Waterloo & City Line – an extraordinary little shuttle system constructed in 1898 and popularly known as the 'Drain' – to take the workers directly to Bank in the heart of the City. London Bridge Station, meanwhile, was deemed to be close enough to the City that people could walk across London Bridge, and so there was no need to meet the huge cost of building a proper railway bridge and acquiring a land holding among the higher property values to the north.

There was considerable enterprise and ingenuity in all of this. For example, the line to Victoria used the Grosvenor Canal and its basin, while the Charing Cross line bought the old Hungerford

St Pancras Station, 1875
The hotel frontage by Sir George Gilbert Scott reflected the civic aspirations for railway stations that were no longer purely for goods but for passengers and became part of the embedded town planning of London.

Crowds of holidaymakers at Waterloo Station, 1912
An exodus of Londoners heading to the south coast for the day.

market buildings and re-engineered Isambard Kingdom Brunel's bridge; the original Hungerford Bridge, built in 1845, was a suspension footbridge, but was replaced in 1859 by the new railway bridge. The old bridge's chain links were sold for use on the Clifton Suspension Bridge in Bristol – completed by the Institute of Civil Engineers as a memorial to Brunel – while the stumps were reused to take the railway on to the site of the old north bank market building. Downstream, Blackfriars Bridge was built in incremental stages, with the first part completed on the south bank, followed by a station in the middle of the river and finally, when profits and passenger growth justified it, the bridge got a toe-hold for a new station on the north bank. If this all sounds utterly random, chaotic and opportunistic, it is because that is just how it was.

Almost any social price was paid, even if this meant that all known city-planning logic and traditional patterns of development were abandoned, and all environmental and civic qualities were ignored in the frantic pursuit of business and money. Considering how noisy and polluting these coal-fuelled enterprises were, it puts into perspective any criticism we in the Western world may have of the pollution that is currently being experienced in developing countries such as China or India while they pursue their stake in modern industrial society. During the mid to late 19th century, the metropolis abandoned wholesale most urban standards of convenience, comfort, general hygiene and quality of life; the railways themselves were mostly responsible for this.

The Underground Railway

Gradually, both during and after the 50-year period of mainline railway innovations in the mid 19th century, London set about putting the pieces back together again and making sense of what was done in all the rush and enterprise. Leading this was a great new technological development and an ingenious piece of town planning: the Underground. All these mainline stations, for good reasons at the time, were set in a great ring around the capital, all well back from the centre, but they needed to be connected

Euston Station, 1838
Open-topped trains carrying people almost as if they were cattle freight, in an adaptation of goods carriages in which people sat and were brought in as commuters. In the foreground is an early form of covered carriage.

Plebeian travel, 1865
The arrival of the workmen's Penny Train at Victoria at 6am. The idea of the working men arriving by train – with their picks and shovels – for an early start, paying only a penny, was a world away from the well-upholstered comfort of the first-class passengers.

to each other and to the urban centres to make one integrated transport system. So, in the 1850s – an extraordinarily early date considering when the mainline stations were built – the roads of London were being dug up in a great ring to create the Circle Line, which was finally completed in 1884. If anything captures the character and spirit of the essence of London, it is this great line that created what to this day is called Zone 1 (the very heart of London Transport). If you now live within walking distance of the Circle Line, or within the ring itself, you are in central London – to my mind this is the simplest and most singular definition of centrality that we have. Other cities may have their ring roads, giant loops and *périphériques*, but in London the defining perimeter of the inner centre is the Circle Line, the world's first underground railway system. It was steam driven, because it predated electrical railways, with vents at intervals along the lines and at stations to take the smoke away and bring fresh air to underground passengers just beneath the street level. It is an extraordinary enterprise and a great foundation for the mental map of London.

Following the Circle Line, other underground lines were introduced to traverse the centre of the city and to draw people in from London's outer regions, connecting passengers to the streets, neighbourhoods, workplaces, schools and shops. Of course, once the overground and underground systems were built and in place, they themselves provided the location of the new communities which trebled the population of London between 1800 and the early part of the 20th century. This is dealt with more fully when describing the development of the Underground and London Transport in the next chapter.

To understand the pattern of the railways, which are not based upon a preconceived plan but on a scrambling rush of uncoordinated opportunistic enterprises over a short period of time, is to understand so much about the shape and form of modern London. We continue to try to make sense of London by layering the underground railway network and the mainline network, which of course were themselves overlaid on a set of roads that had far less metropolitan logic than most other cities. There is something dynamic about all this. It is not that there was no planning, as every bit of it was planned discretely in its own terms – the regularity and the logic are in the individual components themselves. It is just that when we look at the whole we have such trouble seeing some order, yet somehow it is there. It is a counter-intuitive and illogical pattern held together by the ghosts of 19th-century entrepreneurial logic. It needs, of course, improvement; it needs interpreting and understanding to be made to work better, but it is well worth the effort as it all adds up to a unique dynamic.

Rail Development in the Age of Consensus

Today's rail enterprise continues this process of overlaying in a much more knowing way, as it is now much more concerned with the overall order, plan form and integration of the systems. This is for the good of the metropolis but – in an age that has much less courage, much more democratic answerability, and much more sensitive involvement with the people living in London – this overlaid patterning is also very much about consensus. Consequently, it is essential to understand people's perception of what is there, what it does, why it is there and its history. I believe passionately that this is the essence of what the London planner is faced with today: not only to understand the patterns but to communicate them to all levels of society, so that people can see and understand that something very worthwhile can continue to be done with London's public transport evolution.

Two further pressing logics have emerged in the late 20th century to initiate further development of the London rail system. The first of these was to connect all rail systems to air travel. It was a hundred years between the invention of Trevithick's passenger train and the first successful flight of the Wright brothers. By the mid 20th century airports were being built to service London's need to connect to the rest of the world with great speed and efficiency. Eventually Heathrow, Luton, Stansted, City Airport and Gatwick had all been built in a way that the railway entrepreneurs would recognise – in a pioneering, opportunistic fashion, all in positions that today we probably would not want them to be if we had known how air traffic would grow so exponentially and rapidly: the number of passengers at Heathrow alone has grown to 68 million in 2008. Nevertheless, the airports are there. They have eventually accumulated huge and entrenched investment in their planning and infrastructure, not only within their sites but in terms of road access, employee catchment areas and support services. So, new rail connections have been made from London to these airports, including the Victoria to Gatwick express service in 1984, the Heathrow Express from Paddington in 1998, the St Pancras to Luton service in 1999 and the Liverpool Street to Stansted service. Now, even the world's furthest points like New Zealand, Australia, Argentina and Japan are not much more than 24 hours from the centre of the metropolis.

The second logic has been the rail planners' dream of direct routes connecting up north, south, east and west London and at long last having train systems that actually run through the centre of the capital without having to change. The first of these is the Thameslink route, running north to south with Blackfriars Bridge as the crossing point. It grew in a rather ad hoc way but is now substantially in place. The second is the planned east to west system, called Crossrail, which will run from the Thames Valley to the west, through Paddington and down Oxford Street so that it goes through the very centre of the two old cities of Westminster and the City of London. It will then exit the city through the emerging communities along the new regeneration region of the Thames Gateway, with branches going both north and south of the river into Essex and Kent.

The meeting point where the Thameslink and Crossrail lines cross is right on the historic divide between London's two cities where the River Fleet separated the City and Westminster at Clerkenwell/Farringdon, at the point that the great Smithfield markets stand. This location is no accident of pattern and form: a major connection and central service point of London has always been here. This is where the New Road supplied livestock to Smithfield Market, which in turn supplied food back into London to the west and east. This is also where, to the west of the Roman city and to the east of the city of Westminster, the ancient cities were held together, but divided at the same time by the Fleet. It is typical of London that even now there is continuous uncertainty regarding the start and completion of the Crossrail project and, indeed, about what it means to Londoners. It is typical, too, that everyone is in a state of disbelief that it will ever happen in their lifetime, if it does at all. Therefore, rather than planning ahead, we will all wait until it is finished to see what it means to Farringdon, which will then undoubtedly become the most accessible place in London and potentially the very pulse at the centre of rail travel in the city.

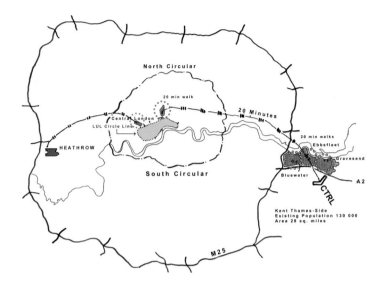

London and Britain were the great inventors of the railway system and pioneers of its integration within the urban realm – but they were not so for long. In the natural order of things the pioneer tends to have the lead for just a short time before others learn to capitalise upon their work, often without repeating the same mistakes. This is particularly true in terms of fast-speed rail travel; inhabitants of the whole of western Europe, Japan and very soon China are seeing the benefits of ultra high-speed rail services that have moved a very long way from the first British passenger steam cars, which originally were preceded by a man with a red flag to ensure that people and cattle got out of the way! Now, trains travelling to and linking the very centre of cities are seen as a viable alternative to air travel, partly because of their high speed and partly because airports are situated inconveniently outside urban centres for safety and operational reasons. The pioneers of these newer rail systems, the Japanese and the French, have criss-crossed their countries in a way that the British have never done. Rather ironically and predictably, the only fast system we have is one built in conjunction with the French – the so-called Eurostar that connects us to the western

Farrell, High-speed rail
connection diagram, 2001
The fast Channel Tunnel Rail Link to Europe dramatically affects rail travel times from parts of London to Stratford and Ebbsfleet, and transforms the time/distance map of London.

European system via a tunnel under the Channel, enabling London and the southeast of England to join up with all the major capitals at very high speed. London is now just over two hours from Paris which, in travel time, makes it as close as most major cities in the UK.

Like Japan, Britain is a long, linear island and a fast rail system is a logical and practical thing to have. However, the will and enterprise of the Victorians is now difficult to replicate and our increasingly sensitive democratic consultation systems have brought with them many difficulties that were non-existent when the Victorian entrepreneur crashed through all landowner rights and urban residents' sensibilities. However, the prospect of something happening surely must be there. With Glasgow and Edinburgh being potentially reached as quickly by rail as by air, and the possibility of Manchester, Liverpool and Birmingham being within fast, daily commuting distance of London, the mental map of London's relationship with the British Isles could be radically changed. Railways – the first mechanical transport system and the first to go faster than man or horse – have forever changed our mental map of places and their relationships. As the Victorians often said at the time of rail invention, 'space has been conquered by time' – a prophetic term in view of all transport inventions right through to air and then space travel.

Thoughts about future changes to rail, how they will affect London and their potential begin with the outer relationships with fast-speed trains, the way they come into stations and the way they link up with the rest of Britain and Continental Europe. This is all part of a new awakening of the understanding that the British Isles is part of Europe and that the great city of London could be a more significant major player in a united Europe.

capital?' This continues to be addressed by London mayors, politicians, local councillors and, of course, various affected local communities. Lately, much has been made of plans for new airports out in the Thames Estuary, at Manston in Kent or elsewhere, with the emphasis being on the east of London and the regeneration out there. The reality is that London's airports, like its railways, have grown and grown in an incremental and unplanned way – Heathrow is the best example of this, with each new terminal thought to be the last. When you try to make communication sense of Heathrow by linking the railway to the different terminals, it becomes something of a labyrinthine or problematic task, as getting from one terminal to another is not sensibly or conveniently possible. This does not compare favourably with projects in the Far East. For example, at the Integrated Transportation Centre at Inchon International Airport, in Seoul (2002), which my company designed, all rail passengers come to one point and access to the terminal buildings is all from a series of spokes radiating from this point – this is how you plan a proper 21st-century airport.

In London, there are two choices. One is to start again, as some propose, with a brand new major hub airport that leapfrogs the developments, capitalising on the experience of building and operating the latest international airports. The other choice, in true British style, is to continue the existing pattern of cobbling our short-term solutions together. The airports have their own kind of charm and some of their inefficiencies could be ameliorated, if not necessarily overcome, by a peripheral rail link, a grand Circle Line, which, just as the original was needed to connect the railways 150 years ago, would connect the airports. After all, with potential extra runways at Stansted and Heathrow, and

The question that hangs over all considerations of connections, balance and the rationalisation of all this pragmatic growth is: 'How will air travel and London's airports relate back to the

Farrell, Integrated Transportation
Centre, Inchon International Airport,
Seoul, Korea, 2002
An organic steel and glass structure that
forms a focus and gives identity to the
entire airport with the planning complexity
of an urban centre.

perhaps with the utilisation of the Manston and even Southend runways, there are probably more runways in total than there are in most other capital cities: it is just that they are all disconnected. However, just as London, the great metropolis, was never really one city, the airports were never a hub – there never was a big, grand plan. There is something in the British way of doing things that connects with its own particular dynamic logic, and so a ring railway that travels 32 kilometres (20 miles) out from the centre of London and picks up fast bullet-train rail links to elsewhere, including the Continent and north of England, might prove to have its own kind of efficiency in an interesting, idiosyncratic way.

Looking at the future of London's patterns of growth and form, and building on the railways to see if there is a clue in their particular shape as we find it today, I think there are some very interesting things emerging. First, there is a rationalisation going on at each of the stations, much more so than along the lines. Because there are so many lines, it is the stations themselves that bear the complexity. A recent group of railway specialists from China, who had visited Waterloo, asked myself and my colleagues, with a great deal of consternation and perplexity: 'Just how does Waterloo Station work? We couldn't see just how it worked'. We could not help but smile and be embarrassed at what our eccentric Britishness has produced in our railway stations in contrast to the Chinese state-driven, centralised, single-provider, single-operator railway system. Here we have tube lines, Continental railway lines, many different train operators, lines owned by a different body and the railway parcel system all working semi-independently of each other, yet all trying to connect. Even the ticketing system, we realised in conversation with the Chinese delegates, has its own peculiarities and in-built inefficiencies and oddities, with train

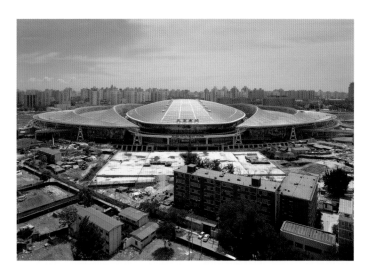

tickets sometimes collected at barriers, sometimes not, sometimes on the train and sometimes not, and so on.

However, the stations themselves have begun a period of modernisation and thankfully this is being done the right way, building on the character and presence of the original Victorian architectural achievements, such as at St Pancras. Here, the re-ordering and rethinking of the whole system has been partly inspired by Thameslink connecting north with south, partly by the fast rail links and the Channel Tunnel Rail Link arriving here in 2007, and partly by the terrible fire in the Underground at King's Cross in 1987 that made it necessary to rethink the whole of the tube connection – all of this has added up to an urgency to do something and make it all, as much as possible, one

Farrell, Beijing South Station, China, 2008
In the Far East it is possible to start afresh. Unlike British airports and railway stations, the new infrastructure can be a totally new kind of object that integrates with its surroundings. The new Beijing South Station serves high-speed and local trains. It is larger than three of London's mainline stations combined and has its own bus station and other linked networks.

Aerial photo of Waterloo Station

The new 1990s Eurostar station
snaking in at the bottom and the old
station, both mainline and suburban,
above. Over the years various decisions
and indecision meant that the Eurostar
came in for a mere 10 years; it was then
transferred to St Pancras making the
new building redundant.

system. The net result is something rather special, and the most remarkable experience I have had in railways in my life was the grand opening ceremony of the Eurostar terminal at St Pancras station in 2007, when current and previous prime ministers, senior leaders, the monarch and high-level representatives from France were entertained by a spectacular tableau of events while the first Eurostar trains arrived. I think a French minister was to publicly announce afterwards that he thought St Pancras was the finest railway station in the world. This integrated modernisation is continuing through all the stations, connecting and improving on the Victorian model, and is clearly a *'grand projet'*, albeit not in the French style, but by cobbling together all the bits, British style, making the picturesque work in a way that John Nash would have understood, but not Baron Haussmann.

The other thing, and the most important to my mind, about the future of the railways in London, is that having begun in the age of steam, with goods delivery and industrial complexes around the main stations, they have been landlocked within their own perimeters. In their relationships with the rest of the city,

the stations were essentially 'bad neighbours' and, indeed, they were bad for many, many decades. The net result has been that the stations are not part of the community and the integrated London plan, unlike, say, Grand Central Station which arrives right in the centre of New York and is a public grand hall, or the stations in Germany, Milan and Rome and elsewhere around the world. The new Chinese ones that I have been involved in are particularly integrated, including the airport rail link which arrives in the middle of new urban districts that have been specially planned. Our London main stations sit in a monocultural void in urban terms, for many hundreds of metres around them all life has been drained away, while all developments have turned their backs on the stations. From the middle of the 19th century, only the poorest people, who came to work in what were then heavily industrial areas, have lived close to the stations.

Today these stations are being rethought as potential new hubs, new nodal points in London, where new housing, offices and cultural centres can be added like new villages overlaid upon all the nodal points from earlier times. The idea that, instead of

St Pancras Station, 2007
The newly restored St Pancras Station, enclosed by the unique arch which forms the Barlow shed. The new roof contains 18,000 panes of self-cleaning glass. The station, which cost 1.2 billion euros to restore, has the longest champagne bar in Europe. This complete transformation has resulted in what has been described by many as the greatest train station in Europe.

Passenger trains at
St Pancras Station, 1868
The interior of St Pancras Station showing passenger trains on the platforms.

voids, the stations can become places of dense human urban activity 24/7 is a radically new concept for London's railways. It has begun already. I was involved with the redevelopment of Charing Cross in 1990. During the time of Charles Dickens, the area around the station was a slum and again during the 1980s, the Thatcher years, it was the place of soup kitchens and homelessness with cardboard shelters amassed under the arches of Hungerford Bridge. Now it is a lively, busy, theatre and shopping area with headquarter offices above. Likewise, Broadgate was developed as a new urban work district at a similar time, in the late 1980s and early 1990s. Currently, mixed communities are being planned for King's Cross/St Pancras – the no-man's land of backyards and goods yards will become a large new area, capitalising upon the great Victorian granaries and train sheds as primary historic place-making features of the new districts. Paddington Basin next to Paddington Station has already become a new area for

living and working. Fenchurch Street and Cannon Street stations have air rights and new office buildings which are economically fully feasible in the City where land prices and rents are so high.

There are also future plans to develop the station areas and the way they exist alongside their local communities at Victoria, Euston and Waterloo. The most spectacular is at London Bridge, where the proposal will involve the tallest building in Europe. This will hopefully bring the funding needed to rationalise the station complex which is one of the worst 'transportation slums' (as I have called it in the past) in Europe. In sheer intensity, it copes with more passengers in 60 minutes of rush hour than Heathrow Airport does in a whole day. A particular project of interest is the combined linear effect, east to west, of the two great arcs of railways. One arc is to the north along the Marylebone-Euston Roads, which is part of a major study about how this major communication link connects not only to the major rail and tube stations but also to the rail and air links to the Continent. The other great arc is the one to the south of the south bank, where the elevated viaducts criss-cross, as described above. The railways have isolated an area between the elevated viaducts and the river, a piece of territory that was once the pleasure ground of London. It is a short step to think of this area as not part of Southwark, Lambeth and Wandsworth, but as part of the central area, as a lot of it is within a short walking distance of Circle Line stations, and therefore it could be considered as a Zone 1 district.

The potential to layer new patterns and new interpretations of the urban opportunities upon the railway system continues to grow. There should be enormous future benefits in continuing to treat the railways as an extraordinary and positive key to London's shape and form.

Aerial view of St Pancras Station, 1989
The new British Library can be seen under
construction immediately to the left.

Charing Cross Station, 1992
Another version of retrofitting of a railway station, with an office building above the existing 1864 station. The 1990s project, with which Farrell was involved, included the total regeneration of the ground level and surrounding streets, helping to overcome the 19th-century associations of railway areas being ones of poverty and begging. Right up to the 1980s, the area beneath Charing Cross was one that Charles Dickens would have recognised, characterised by the slums and workshops that he wrote about in his time. Now, over 37 million people pass through Charing Cross every year.

The Tube – London Underground

London's Mind Map

Nowhere in this entire book is there a phenomenon that provides a better key to all of London's patterns than the London Underground – 'the tube'. What is it that makes it play such a key part in London's shape and form? Primarily, it is the fact it is a singular entity delivered in a remarkably short period of time – little more than four decades – between 1863 and 1906. The tube did not evolve over centuries. It had no predecessor. There was no equivalent of an underground railway system in Roman or medieval times! It came as its own unique phenomenon after most of the shaping and incremental growth of London had happened – after most roads, canals and the forces of the mainline railway stations had been laid and had established their impact. (The railways in particular brought massive activity and energy from the rest of the nation to London, but with virtually no regard for the planning and rationality of London's layout and overall order.)

The tube system is the rationalisation of London. It is a metropolitan, unifying system, whose *raison d'être* is to give order to disorder. It does this because it is a consumer-based passenger system. In public hands today, it is there to serve the people it transports. Unlike other urban developments it was not implemented for the aggrandisement of princes, nor for the benefit of the aristocracy, nor even for the self-interest of individual industrialists, driven by efficiency and profit. Instead, the tube is for everyone. It could be said to be wholly 'people-centric', if it were not for the innately hostile unnatural underground environment and subsequently the strenuous environmental demands it puts upon the commuting, shopping and moving mass population. In the end it enables Londoners and London's visitors to make necessary movements around the city, but also to take trips for social, cultural and leisure reasons that make living in the growing metropolis acceptable. The price, though, is that the tube moves in a way that is apart from nature and landscape, always away from the sunshine and light, and provides fundamentally unwelcome travelling conditions. Almost every other form of transport, from walking to horse-riding to sailing on a boat, even to riding in a bus, car or train, can have

Richard T Cooper, *The Business Man's London*, 1930
Designed for the Underground Electric Railway Company Ltd, this poster depicts the various commercial activities of Londoners through the ages matching them with tube stations.

SHIPPING · INSURANCE · NEWSPAPERS

GRESHAM · ANGERSTEIN

MARK LANE   BANK   MONUMENT   TEMPLE   BLACKFRIARS

DOMINE DIRIGE NOS

THE BUSINESS MAN'S LONDON
BY
UNDERGROUND

R.T. COOPER.

"The Efficient Way"

FILMS

PICCADILLY CIRCUS   LEICESTER SQ.RE

FOOD · DRINK · LEATHER

COUTTS · GLYN

ENT   POST OFFICE   COVENT G.DN   MONUMENT   MARK LANE   LONDON BRIDGE   BOROUGH

By the mid 19th century, the railways, roads and canals were each separately bringing such an overload of goods and distant visitors and commuters into the city that a new connecting system of order and efficiency was required to make the burgeoning metropolis work. The human environment was not a priority. It put people in unnatural conditions underground, so that they became like moles and cave tunnellers, having to contend with further factors such as rapid movement, claustrophobia and intense noise. It also took control out of passengers' own hands, placing them under the vicarious auspices of steam and, from 1890, electrical power; it required people to entrust their safety to hidden operators, signalmen, drivers, train operators and the

some association with land, nature and pleasurable pursuits such as leisure, tourism and holidays. You might take a coach tour or even hire a car when on a break to enjoy the scenery, but you never go for a holiday solely on the tube system. It is purely a means – an efficient and critical means – to an end. It is transport stripped of the joys of travel.

The tube made order out of London's chaos and disorder, and it did so for everybody, but with scant regard for comfort and enjoyment. It achieved its success with urgency because its need to exist was so great – all the other systems collectively had failed.

Gustave Doré, _Ludgate Hill_, 1872
Ludgate Hill with the London, Chatham, Dover Railway in the background and considerable congestion travelling up to St Paul's. The promise of London Underground was that it was going to greatly relieve the congestion. The transport planner's panacea, the politician's promise of ever evolving newer layered transport systems had begun. They continuously try to overcome the success of London in attracting people; inevitably the better the transport, the more people come and the more predictable the failure of the transport systems.

Construction of the District Line at Blackfriars, 1867–71
London's second underground railway was built as part of Queen Victoria Street by cutting through the densely built city streets between the Victoria Embankment and the Bank of England.

The first trial trip on the Metropolitan Railway, 1862

The open carriages, the obvious surface railway tradition, and the euphoria of a project that has been completed.

moving parts of 412 escalators and 122 lifts to take them first below then above ground again at their final destination. Yet it is a system. It is London's primary system – it is what we think of when thinking about how London works. Whether we use it or not, it is the very mental map of London that we all recognise.

How this came about, and what it means to London today, provides a fascinating example of how the form and pattern of this city has taken shape. The tube is without doubt London's best example of an incrementalist, self-ordering patterning of step by step bits, each with their own internally driven logic, each an addition to the step before, gradually becoming assimilated into the greater network through merger, through one connecting to the next, even though they were each meant to do their own independent things, until eventually a total unified pattern emerges. Though this process existed embryonically in the evolution of other forms of transport – the roads connect one to another and their very universality is their essence, and the same can be said of the railways and canals – nothing comes close to

the self-ordering connectivity of the underground rail system. Like so much of London's mechanised transport and town planning, much of the incrementalism came about because London was experimenting and inventing the processes and built product as it went along.

The tube was without precedent, and like so many other things during the industrial revolution in Britain, the prototype was the final product. It is still today the largest underground railway system in the world, with 268 stations covering not only the whole of Greater London but well beyond – five stations even lie outside the outer ring road, the M25. It is also the world's oldest underground railway and the oldest rapid public transit system. Its very name, the tube system, derives from the very deep bore tunnels – almost half of the network is below ground

Cross-section showing the junction at Hampstead Road, Euston Road and Tottenham Court Road, mid 19th century
The upper surfaces of both drawings here show interesting characterisations of road transport in the mid 19th century with (left) a coach and horse-drawn omnibus and (right) a steam-powered omnibus.

Pipes under London's streets, mid 19th century
The underground rail system completely reinvented the urban metropolis and its transport system. Quite subtly and importantly it also improved the sewers, water supply and drainage in London – in the words of Louis Kahn: 'making the streets a building'.

one billion passenger journeys were recorded. It is astonishing how soon after the invention of the railways that the tube came into being: George Stephenson and Edward Pease's Stockton–Darlington line of 1825 preceded the Act of Parliament to make the first underground railway by a mere 29 years, and the first section opened in 1863.

in varying lengths of tunnels (the longest continuous one, from East Finchley to Morden, is 27.8 kilometres (17.3 miles) long). It was originally entirely built by private companies, many different ones, even though it eventually became one system in 1933, first as the London Passenger Transport Board and now under the title of Transport for London. With 402 kilometres (249 miles) of track, it is also the longest underground system in the world. In 2007,

Twin entrances of the Thames Tunnel
The London Underground system began life capitalising on Marc Brunel and his son Isambard Kingdom's celebrated first tunnels for road and pedestrian traffic. These were later bought by the underground rail system and it was eventually realised that tunnelling was the way forward to avoid disruption to streets and the problems of land ownership.

Piccadilly Circus cross-section
The drawing now known as the 'stomach diagram', as it is like the intestines of an organism, no doubt human, shows the overlapping lines of the Piccadilly and Bakerloo underground systems, all united below ground on a common concourse. One of the most ordered rationalisations of pedestrian movement underground.

The Construction of the Underground

As happened with much of our public transportation, the tube began at Paddington, connecting passengers to the City to work at Bank, and was aptly called the Metropolitan Railway, perversely a name which provided the title of 'metro' for so many of its worldwide successors while Londoners continued to prefer the simply descriptive 'tube'. Sections were gradually added from Paddington to Farringdon and then extended from Hammersmith to the City, and then on to Moorgate, followed by connections to South Kensington and then Westminster, until in 1884 it almost 'incidentally' became a circle. The 22.5-kilometre (14-mile) Circle Line itself is the unifier, the definer, of central London; in ticketing terms, in its own mental mapping of passenger costings, it is Zone 1. Yet it did not originally set out to be a circle; afterwards there was for a long time an idea that having 'accidentally' built an inner circle, an outer one might be deliberately planned and built, but this never came to fruition. Such is the seemingly ad hoc, haphazard nature of how London's transport as we know it today was finally arrived at.

The first tunnels were cut from above; they were trenches dug under existing roads that were then covered in the 'cut and cover' method, and the resultant 'tunnels' were then ventilated directly to the surface for venting steam and smoke. So the pattern and geometry of the early network was inevitably road-based, following the path of the Marylebone-Euston Roads at one stage and also running along under the Embankment road next to the river. The connection back to the mapping or streets above is by its nature conjoined as it was the same, and short steps were all that was required to get back to the surface and the street pattern above. All the travelling passengers needed to know were the surface streets above their heads and they would know where they were. Then, in 1865, the expanding East London Railway Company purchased Marc Brunel and his son Isambard Kingdom's pedestrian tunnel, which went under the Thames from east London, with the intention of converting it into a railway tunnel. And so the idea was born that Marc Brunel's revolutionary tunnelling shield method could make it possible to do something quite spectacular, something that would change the mental map of London in a way that no one could have conceived of before: a transport system which could travel independently of surface landscape and its existing man-made urban terrain. It would be independent of the long historic patterns of roads developed by the Romans through to medieval and Victorian times, and independent of everything above one's head. Of course, it had to connect up key points in space to deliver and take on board passengers, but in-between these points the tubes could travel any way they wanted to, cutting linear paths independent of all existing urban planning patterns, and they did so, not only in plan, but in three dimensions too.

London Underground
publicity material, 1909
First attempts in 1909 to start the
Underground brand, to show it as
one system, with the invention of the
roundel that then became the London
Underground symbol.

The deep-level tunnels, of course, needed something more than Brunel's invention. They needed completely new smaller, more compact rolling stock than the heavy main rail stock to fit within the tunnels, and so the idea of 'light' rail on an intra-urban system was born. They also, in time, needed electric traction and power stations, and the application of the invention of electricity not just to traction, but to signalling, lighting, ventilation and escalators and lifts. The inventiveness of London's scientists went hand in hand with its growth. In 1821 Michael Faraday and the Royal Institution in Albemarle Street, Piccadilly, invented the electro-

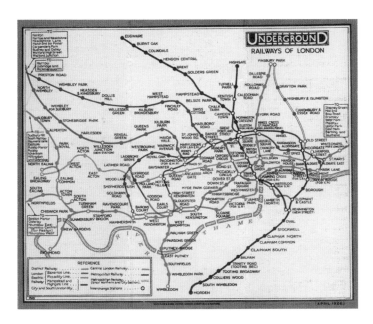

London Underground
Railways map, 1926

Before the revolutionary drawings of Harry Beck, this map shows the difficulty in branding, giving identity and mental mapping to a system that was inherently piecemeal and chaotic, with different ownerships in different colours and different lines that eventually became one.

magnetic motor. The public fascination with the importance of science resulted in Albemarle Street being made London's first one-way street to cope with the crowds and carriages attending Faraday's lectures. The first deep-level tube was the City and South London Railway, now part of the Northern Line, which was opened in 1890. It was followed within eight years by the Waterloo & City Line and within 10 years by the Central Line.

London Underground poster,
Edward McKnight Kauffer, 1931

The marketing, branding, engineering and expansion of the tube network as a complete system. This poster shows the world's longest running power station at Lots Road (built 1905 and closed in the early 1990s). Built by an American entrepreneur, it was the primary power source for the whole of London Underground, a dedicated power station all of its own, before it was closed when London Underground joined the National Grid.

London Underground
publicity material, 1909

This poster shows 'homelike and
weatherproof' as the roundel states.
People were being attracted away from
the buses and walking, to travel regardless
of the weather and with greater certainty
of arrival time.

A Unified, Metropolitan System

All the lines were originally named after the separate railway
companies that built them, such as the Central London Railway
or the Charing Cross Euston and Hampstead Railway. However, in
the early 20th century the problems of having many independent
operators running different underground lines was recognised
– this awareness incorporated a completely new idea that the
tube was for passengers, that the customer came first and
that its organisation and all its communications had to change.
Concomitant with this were the inefficiencies and costs of running
independent companies. Gradually, they merged and bought each
other out, creating larger and larger organisations, so that not
only did the lines join up, the companies did too. Even names
conjoined so that Baker Street and Waterloo became the Bakerloo
Line, the Great Northern, Piccadilly, and Brompton Railway Line
became the Piccadilly Line, and so on. By 1908 all the operators
combined to promote their services jointly as the Underground,
publishing adverts and giving out free maps of the network.
Marketing, branding and accessibility – all the things that identify
a modern, consumer-driven company today – were part of the
evolution of the tube in the early 20th century. The ubiquitous
logo, the red roundel, that is synonymous the world over with
the London tube first appeared in 1908 and was placed outside
the stations, on the tickets and on ticket-issuing machines. In
1933, as the development of the network continued to progress,
a self-funding public corporation, whose name was abbreviated
to London Transport, was created to run it and oversee it.

In a sense, these early 20th-century developments emphasised that the tube is primarily a brand system, superimposed

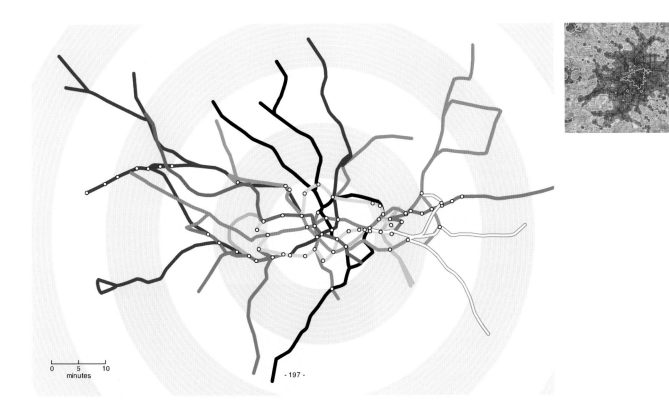

0 5 10
minutes

- 197 -

with an electrophonic, cartographic and ticketing system. Created incrementally and not as one system, it was not based originally on its common spatial, mechanical and technological characteristics. It was never built as an integrated system on any of these fronts. It was only conceived of as an organisational system post-construction, when it was then realised as a thing of the mind, a brand, a logo, a marketing device. This is a unique modern and London city-making phenomenon; it is a kind of post-rationalisation – planning backwards not just with what is there now pragmatically, but with an understanding of why it is there and what can best be done for the future.

An important part of the branding of the tube has been its map. Transport mapping reached its high point in 1933 when Harry Beck, an electrical engineer used to wiring diagrams, created the design classic of the tube map which showed how to get about London in such a clear way that it is still the best understood mental map of London. Even those moving by foot, car or bus today have some subconscious concept of London's form based primarily on an inherent grasp of Harry Beck's map and use it to orientate themselves whatever their transport mode.

Extensions and additions, including new sections of the Central Line, continued piecemeal after the Second World War,

Tom Carden, Travel-time map
The underground rail system is a closed system with predictable and measurable ticketing and customer movement. Passenger start points and destinations can be charted and timed. Explored here is an interactive map plotting the time to travel between stations; this example shows Piccadilly Circus.

Chris Lightfoot and Tom Steinberg, Travel-time map
Using travel time as the map's core value, Lightfoot and Steinberg produced maps using colours and contour lines to show how long it takes to travel from one place to every other place in the area using public transport.

HOMES IN METRO-LAND

the perceived distances of walking and orientation are skewed. Interesting pedestrian maps have been developed to try to help overcome this distortion and disorientation and to relate different mapping systems of different transport modes.

There is another extraordinary feature, which is that the tube is not just a system that moves people two-directionally on rails in trains; it is also a unique three-dimensional pedestrian walking system at the nodal points of intersection, both reaching

but completely new lines were also built later in the 20th century: the Victoria Line was completed in 1971 and the Jubilee Line opened in 1979, and was later extended in 1999.

It is the tube system, this metropolitan system, which has led to the integration of all aspects of public transport thinking, including united ticketing zones and combined ticketing for several modes of transport – tube, bus, rail etc. All London's conceptual transport thinking is based on the one system that was designed specifically to connect all of London, to make it one place. There are many today who seek to progress further this rationalisation process, to make sense of and to integrate all discrepancies in the patterns of London. One of these, for example, is the considerable difference between the real map and the perceived pictorial map, which has become distorted either because it is based on Harry Beck's abstraction or simply because the tube system exists independently of the map of the streets above. Consequently,

'Homes in Metro-land' poster
The Underground system was promoted as a way of expanding London. Along with house builders and developers, it enabled the metropolis to grow and extend beyond its Victorian core and out to suburbia and areas like Pinner, Kenton, Kingsbury, Watford and Amersham.

Farrell, Section through Kowloon Station masterplan, 1998
The realisation of these visions, with skyscrapers and underground rail systems linked with a complete integrated city.

above ground where its entrances meet the streets and buildings, and below, where there is an intersection with other tube systems, which can be particularly complex. At Bank and Monument, for example, there are several lines, including the recent Docklands Light Railway, which thread past and to each other and their independent platforms and stations which connect underground for system-to-system interchange purposes and then connect back to the streets and pavements at convenient points, next

to or within existing buildings or pavements. This in itself has its own ordering system which survives almost solely on signage as, being underground, there are no landscape features from which to orientate. A whole system of signs, steps and escalators creates a parallel world that is a small city or village existing both beneath the ground and in above-ground centres. This world, which lies beyond what is called the ticketing point, the other side of the barrier, can still be used for storage or war offices when lines or stations are

**Farrell, A vision for development
at Tottenham Court Road, 2005**

Cross-section of Oxford Street and
Tottenham Court Road station, showing
the new Crossrail station with much larger
tunnels and rolling stock arriving beneath the
redevelopment on the junction at Tottenham
Court Road. Pedestrian movement flows
from beneath ground to the topmost levels
as one internal escalator-connected world.

abandoned (over 40 stations have been abandoned or moved during the life of the Underground), or indeed for living in, for example during the air raids of the Second World War when people spent a large chunk of their lives there, particularly at night.

This system, being a controllable, measurable thing, makes it possible to know where people are coming from and where they are going to. In this world dominated by management and process, we can work out exactly where the demand is and understand mass movement in a more thorough way than we can for much surface activity, particularly car and pedestrian movement.

The tube was also part of another system, one that the suburban railways had been part of, to drive out the expansion of London to the Home Counties, to Middlesex, Hertfordshire, Sussex and Surrey. The tube became a method of taking people to new places to live, so it went hand in hand with the property and land development of many new suburbs. The first area to be developed by the Metropolitan Railway Company itself in the 1880s was the Willesden Park Estate, laid out near Willesden Green station. The company went on to develop areas such as Wembley Park, Harrow-on-the-Hill, Ruislip, Pinner, Chorleywood, Rickmansworth, Rayners Lane and Amersham. Dotted along the Metropolitan Line with their own stations, these new estates became known as Metro-land.

There is another pattern that can be seen as transport systems to the north and south of London developed in different ways. The south of London had already developed its own intricate overground passenger network system, distinct from the later tube/underground railways, and brought commuting passengers into the centre of London quickly. As a result the tube concentrated on expanding from the centre out towards the north, which did not have a suburban mainline network, with the Metropolitan Line serving stations far out on the outer edges of north and west London. The furthest southern station is Morden, 16 kilometres (9.9 miles) from central London, while the furthest northern station is 29 kilometres (18 miles) out at Epping, and the most westerly is fully 43 kilometres (26.7 miles) distant, at Amersham. The northern expansion bias was also influenced by the geological substrates in the north being more favourable than the south. This has resulted in quite a difference in commuting life, so that most people to the south of London travel in daylight on mainline and suburban trains, while those who live and move around in central and north London are the true underground 'moles'. The tube is geographically biased, it is more of a north bank phenomenon primarily because of the way that mainline stations evolved from the overall shape and form of the island Great Britain.

Continuous Development

So, where next? What now happens to this unique system? The later parts of the tube, such as the Jubilee Line extension in 1999, with its integrated platform doors, compare well technologically with the new generation of light-rail systems being built in Singapore, Hong Kong, China and Japan, with their fully air-conditioned carriages. But these East Asian systems are based on pre-planned integration, where all systems are conceived as connected from the very beginning, while London's creaking, archaic Underground shows all the characteristics of its birth and evolution. The tube was a pioneering product development, but being first meant it could never be the most modern or the best. So the biggest challenge is quite simply continuous refurbishment,

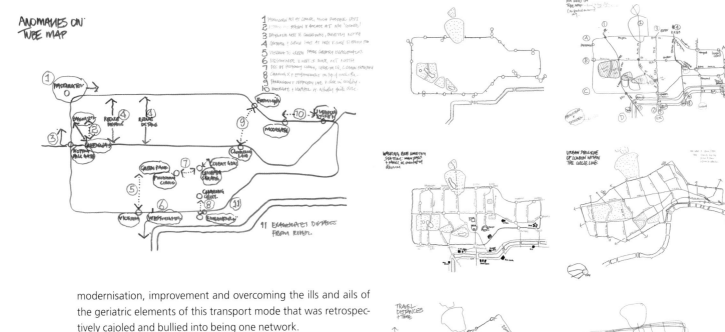

modernisation, improvement and overcoming the ills and ails of the geriatric elements of this transport mode that was retrospectively cajoled and bullied into being one network.

A second big challenge is to continue the integration beyond the tube system itself, to continue the connection to main lines and to lines with special transportation aims, such as connections to the airports, like the Heathrow Express, and also to improve connections to planned new hybrid underground/heavy-rail systems such as Crossrail and Thameslink.

The continued development of the tube should also be about the effects of London being rationalised. London is still evolving as a place, in its real estate and density awareness, but it is over tube stations and around them where land values are highest. Places like South Kensington, Earls Court and many others still have all the evidence of the old 'cut and cover' holes in the ground and suffer some urban chaos caused by the existence of the tube stations themselves. Some stations, though only a few, have inherent integrated and organised pedestrian movement – Piccadilly is one of the best, with its circular pedestrian distribution system, with the names of the streets above the exits giving added clarity and order to the terrain above (rather than diminishing clarity as most stations do).

Farrell, Anomalies on the Underground map, 2005

Harry Beck's Underground map is such an abstraction, it helps to clarify the system itself as a self-contained body though it does not match the overground reality.

The process of integration, connectivity and development continues. I have done some planning work recently for London's Mayor at Tottenham Court Road, looking at the effects of Crossrail. When Crossrail is built the pavements will simply not be big enough to take the increase in passengers. The effect on the buildings above and the road chaos – not just during construction, but after completion – need to be planned for now. The integration of public transport rail systems and the urban terrain is unending: it will never be perfect and will always be a challenge to property owners, local planners, politicians and others to continue to get it 'more right'.

Farrell, Sequence of six drawings, 2005

The Underground map was the inspiration for an overground map for central London, using the same iconography to create a base. These freehand sketches show the methodology by which the tube map system was developed to relate to all the overground systems.

London's Roads and Pavements: Emerging Conflicts

Inner Roads

Imposed and Intuitive Geometries

From the Greeks to the Romans, to the imperially dominated city of Beijing and the great American metropolises, many cities have been laid out in deliberate geometrical patterns, mostly based on a rectilinear grid. The grid plan, a rationalised system of streets running at right-angles to each other, is particularly suited to towns and cities being built from scratch. Not only was it adopted by the founding fathers in North America, most famously in New York, but it was also run out by the Spanish conquistadors throughout South and Central America. In Europe there have been far fewer opportunities for building entire cities afresh, but the grid plan has been favoured for modern extensions of medieval cities. Perhaps the most conspicuous examples are the airy, elegant Georgian streets of Edinburgh's New Town, initially designed by a 22-year-old James Craig in 1766, and the imposing late 19th and early 20th-century avenues of Ildefons Cerdà's Barcelona Eixample. It takes another order of rule and will, though, often only enforceable by autocratic power, to impose a new urban system on the core of an existing city.

The foundations for Rome's grandeur were laid by Sixtus VI who, though only pope for five years from 1585 to 1590, implemented an impressive programme of public works, which included the completion of St Peter's and the restoration of water with the rebuilding of the aqueduct of Septimus Severus. He introduced axial planning and a unified scheme into the holy city by opening up long and straight streets through the medieval slums that covered most of Rome's urban area. This created stately processional routes for the Papacy and their growing audience of pilgrims flocking to the city. Similarly almost three centuries later, when Baron Haussmann transformed Paris under Napoleon III between 1853 and 1870, he overlaid the medieval street pattern with a greater centralised geometry of boulevards, giving rise to the unique juxtaposition of medieval informality and formal 19th-century classicism that gives the city its extraordinarily dynamic character today. Since Roman times though, London, unlike Paris or Rome, has never succeeded in being supplicant

Previous page: Aerial view of Oxford Circus, 2005
It is at night by the lights that the primary and secondary routes can most easily be seen from this vantage point. It is quite an interesting way of showing the hierarchy, here you see Oxford Street intersecting with Nash's great route of Regent Street.

Piccadilly Circus, VE Day, 8 May 1945
Here the streets are used as a public theatre, for public celebrations. The statue of Eros was boarded up throughout the war for protection from bombs.

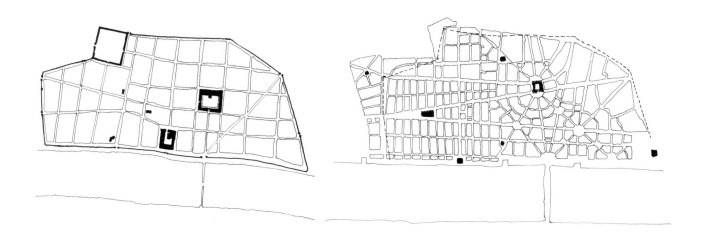

to a single monarch's or autocrat's rule nor has it even in part been developed from scratch – it has evolved in an altogether different manner.

When the Romans, as an occupying force in AD 60, laid out London as a typical Roman town with a regular grid of streets, they certainly had a lasting impact on its development. The true character, though, that the city has returned to ever since then is largely unplanned; it has an informal and almost organic nature. London's story and character is typified by the failure of the formal Baroque plans, proposed by Christopher Wren and others after the Great Fire of 1666, to gain any support; the city eventually regressed back to its pre-fire pattern, more dependent upon traditional streets and individual ownership. It has been almost knowingly unplanned and unpredictable – as Peter Ackroyd said, London has '... never followed a theory or an idea. It has never been driven by a coherent philosophy. It has simply grown in an organic fashion, opportunistic, haphazard and market-led. Yet every building seems part of a general pattern, of a general will to exist in this shape and in no other.'

Redrawn by Farrell, The first city, 2007
A Roman city military garrison, a form that
has endured for 2,000 years.

The West End 'Wobbly Grid' and the Four Great Routes

So what is the nature of this plan of London? How does it come to have its unique form and character? How do we make sense of it today, if it has a will to exist in a pattern that is all of its own? It is, in fact, not innately chaotic, and this is what particularly interests me about planning London today: it requires a skill in pattern divining, searching to see the underlying, intuitive geometries.

So what ordering is there beneath the surface? There is no doubt that roads are the critical public realm for any city; they are what give the city its mental map, its true identity. This identity is, of course, tied up with the natural landscape, as touched on earlier in the book; see 'The Urban Thames' chapter, for instance, where it was described how on the outside of the deep water bend of the Thames, the two initial towns that became the City of Westminster and the City of London grew to form one great arc which defined the core, the central organising idea behind the whole centre of the metropolis. Having started with the big river

Redrawn by Farrell, Christopher
Wren's Post Great Fire proposal, 2007
This 17th-century proposal is centralist,
monarchic, formal and autocratic, but
not London.

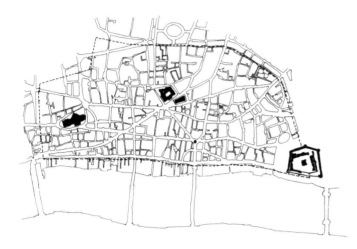

such a way that they form a pattern that, once grasped, provides a clue to seeing more clearly the organisation of London's central West End.

The Great Processional Route: The Strand and Whitehall

The first of these great routes begins with The Strand, which is set one block back from the river (see 'The Urban Thames' chapter, pp 42–3). The most obvious place to start a street was close to the river where London began. Running from Westminster

bend and the two cities, how were the roads then layered upon this? There are some surprisingly clear patterns – one part of which is a kind of 'wobbly grid' that has been drawn as though in casual freehand without reliance on set square or drawing board. This pattern has grown because layer upon layer has produced a certain kind of ordering.

When looking at London and its streets today, it is probably a sensible starting point to divide the centre into two areas: the City and West End, as they originated as two contrasting road and urban planning cultures – one Roman and formal and the other organic and British, which gradually enveloped and assimilated the Roman plan which today sits digested within the wider metropolitan plan form. London-wide, and particularly in the larger West End, it is clear that the road layout grows outwards as a kind of ripple pattern of parallel streets from the river and its first street, The Strand, like the annular rings of a tree. These parallel streets became the east–west components of a giant, wholly irregular grid. Today, four of these central streets predominate and they have each accreted activities, becoming specialised in

Redrawn by Farrell, The real City of London, 2007
As it eventually evolved: free market, democratic and based on private land ownership and parish boundaries.

Champs Élysées from the top of the Arc de Triomphe
It is worth comparing the roads of London with those of Paris. The Champs Élysées is several lanes wider and of a considerably larger scale in every sense than anything in London; London has nothing to equal its size. But in true French dirigiste manner, the side streets are more narrow and medieval, by and large, than anything in London. So the French have two systems, the grand routes and the narrow routes.

Traffic in Piccadilly, 1880
The dip in the road where the Tyburn crosses over to Green Park can clearly be seen (as in the photo on p 103 of 'The Tributaries' chapter). A horse-drawn bus is by the kerb on the north side, where ladders are casually leaning against buildings, reaching up to four storeys, which would contravene all 21st-century rules of access and safety.

Abbey to the Tower of London, the great arcing street was literally 'the shore' connecting the two historical first bridging points – the ancient London Bridge in the City and the new arrival, at Westminster, centuries later – providing an alternative route to the river. Before the banks were built up and the river was narrowed in the 19th century, and at the time when the water speed was slowed by the closeness of the piers at London Bridge, the Thames was a much more placid river that could be easily used as the primary route for getting about. Not only was the river used for crossing before the arrival of more bridges (for example, Wren lived on the south bank facing St Paul's and was

rowed across from his house there to see the work's progress), it was also, for a very long time, the quickest and most direct route from the City of Westminster to the City of London. The Lord Mayor's Parade was held along the Thames simply because it was accepted as the great water highway – London's primary 'high street'.

Typical buildings along the first of the parallel central streets included the great palaces and houses of nobility and bishops such as Somerset House, Savoy Palace and Hungerford House. Each would have had a doorway to the road and a doorway to the river, such as York's Water Gate, which is the surviving 17th-century

The Banqueting House, Whitehall, 1815
The Banqueting House, on one of the
finest wide roads in central London.

The great central street through London:

1   Notting Hill
2   Bayswater
3   Oxford Street
4   New Oxford Street
5   Holborn
6   Holborn Viaduct
7   Newgate Street
8   Cheapside
9   Poultry
10   Leadenhall Street
11   Whitechapel High Street
12   Mile End Road

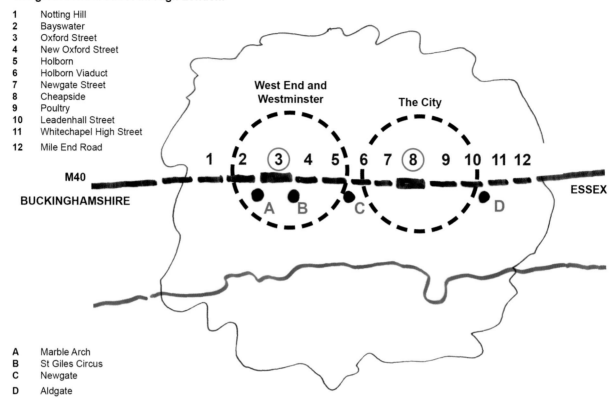

A   Marble Arch
B   St Giles Circus
C   Newgate
D   Aldgate

water entrance to the Duke of Buckingham's York House (see p 37 and 43 of 'The Urban Thames' chapter). These were akin to the wharfs of later centuries on the river's industrial banks, where goods were offloaded on one side directly from boats and then craned on to vehicles that ran along the road behind. Along this route Whitehall, St Paul's and the Tower are gathered as a set piece of state and civic buildings, housing the seats of monarchy, government, church and law – the four pillars of British society. This is where you feel you are in London, the capital city of a nation. The Houses of Parliament face Westminster Abbey while along Whitehall, jostling for proximity to power, are the great buildings of governance – the Treasury gets pole position but right next to it, shoulder to shoulder, is the Foreign Office.

Farrell, The great central street through London, 2009
London does have one great linking street. A connecting steet linking east to west and incorporating the two major 'high streets' – Oxford Street and Cheapside.

Halfway along this street is the military; through William Kent's imposing 18th-century archway is the great parade ground of Horse Guards, facing Buckingham Palace, from which the monarch (not only as a head of state; the Queen and her family also head up all sections of the military) comes to take the Trooping the Colour. At the centre of Whitehall is Edwin Lutyens's Cenotaph erected in 1921 to commemorate the military war dead and for parades. Trafalgar Square, dedicated to the defeat of Napoleon and our great naval battles, has over time become the place where people meet, debate, have festivals and jostle with tourists. They have this one space to attend – this is their one seat on the great route. Further along, the law courts on The Strand and the lawyers at the Great Inns were followed by the Fourth

Estate, the press, until the printing revolution moved them out to the suburbs.

After the valley of the River Fleet, the great route splits, with one leg going up the hill to the great steps of Wren's St Paul's Cathedral, thereby linking it to Westminster Abbey and Buckingham Palace for great state events such as royal marriages and coronations. The other secular section leads around St Paul's (the precincts of which were closed to traffic during the hours of worship) and along the rear of the bankside buildings to the Tower, the fortified prison and gateway to London, passing on the way the two great monuments to trade and the sea: the Custom House overlooking London's trading harbour and Billingsgate Fish Market – sadly neither are any longer operational as such. This is the great route of state which has superseded the river for parades of national and civic significance.

The Aristocratic Route: Kensington High Street, Knightsbridge and Piccadilly

The next 'ripple effect' route runs parallel to The Strand, but much further west. It is to the north of Buckingham Palace and south of Hyde Park. It is London's aristocratic thoroughfare and represents the next closest tier of power, influence and affluence to royalty. It runs from Kensington in the west along the bottom of Hyde Park, adjacent to London's finest residential districts of Knightsbridge, London's wealthiest borough, and links embassies and palaces en route – Kensington Palace to the west and St James's Palace further east. After Hyde Park Corner it enters the land of gentlemen's clubs as Piccadilly, with its tailors, shirt-makers, gun-makers, fine shops, hotels and art galleries. This

poshest of streets dies in the rambling chaos of the 17th-century grid developments of Soho and Covent Garden after it has passed Piccadilly and Leicester Square.

The Route of Everyday Commerce: Oxford Street, High Holborn, Newgate Street and Cheapside

One giant grid/step further north is the third of these parallel roads. This is the street of the ordinary people, the street of markets and everyday trade, with its centre being London's two high streets of Oxford Street in the West End and Cheapside in the City to the east, with the large meat markets of Smithfield in-between. This great

Hyde Park Corner (postcard), 1907–15
Photo showing horse-drawn and motor vehicles and buses. This was before the creation of the current gyratory roundabout, and shows a complete confusion of roads and intersections at this nodal point. Decimus Burton's arch is in the distance and Number One London, the home of the Duke of Wellington, is to the right.

The Great Connector: The Marylebone, Euston and Pentonville Roads

The fourth road on our giant wobbly grid is the one street that could truly be said to unify London, the West End and the City. Its problem has always been its success, its ability to attract activity and therefore congestion. The New Road from Paddington to Islington was built in 1756, sanctioned by an Act of Parliament. The world's first bypass, it was a singular invention to take animals and their drovers away from Oxford Street so that they could arrive at Smithfield without going through the centre of town. But this road never was a true bypass; it rapidly attracted settlements and became a significant urban street in its own right, with a series of real places that gave new separate names to what had been simply the 'New Road' – Marylebone, Euston, Pentonville roads – while four parishes grew and consolidated all along it.

But in our time, for traffic planning convenience, it is designated a 'through road', a 1960s invention; a non-place which on motoring maps appears as 'the inner ring road' though in truth no such ring exists. That this road, which among the many other activities has four major churches and many urban communities living in over 3,000 homes along it, should be called a 'through road' is a complete denial of what is actually happening on the ground. It is a great street of communication. Although it was built as a bypass and attracted traffic from east to west in a more free-flowing way than further south in the urban terrain, it also became the place where the major railway stations terminate and where there are more tube stations than on any street in Europe. To the back of it, to the north, there is the Regent's Canal which connected to the railway stations to extend their distributive

route is a very long one, connecting outwards to the countryside – it originates in Middlesex and Berkshire to the west, once bringing in farmers and shepherds to London's markets. They would travel through Shepherd's Bush to Bayswater where the cattle would drink before continuing down Oxford Street on their way to Smithfield, or they would be pastured in the flat eastern fields of Hyde Park or Green Park. After St Giles in the Fields, the street takes in Holborn on its route from Oxford Street to Smithfield, and then enters the city through Newgate to Cheapside, becoming a continuous link which connects the two great high streets, each a centre of twin-citied London. The City, of course, has its own agricultural hinterland in the fields and farms of Essex, which are directly connected as the route travels out along the old main road to Colchester (the Roman capital of Britain), leaving the City through Aldgate and along the Mile End Road.

Piccadilly street scene
Looking towards Piccadilly Circus: with
its one-way street and a counter-flow bus
lane, all the congestion of modern London.

Top: Thomas Shepherd, Lithograph of Regent Street, c 1850

A horse-drawn world of people riding individually as well as being driven in traps. The backdrop is of original Nash buildings with the wonderful arcades and controlled facades that made Regent Street one of the great streets of Europe, almost in the European style.

Horse-driven carriages on Regent Street, 1900s

Horses in a much less free-spirited and individualistic sense. Although primarily horse-driven, there is a noticeable increase in the amount of wheeled traffic. The new architecture of Victorian/Edwardian facades after the demolition of all Nash buildings is visible.

Traffic jam in Regent Street, 1929

Initially motor cars and buses eased the traffic problems as they were faster and took up less room than horse-drawn vehicles, but with the sheer numbers on the roads the old road networks quickly became congested. Seen here are double-deckers with open tops, and old-fashioned taxi cabs, almost all motor powered.

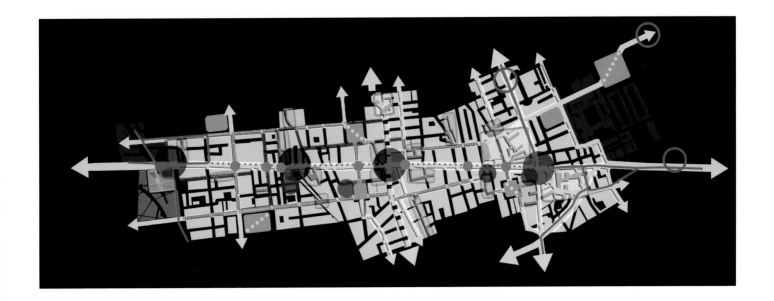

benefits to all of London from here. It is where George Shillibeer ran the first bus service from Paddington to Bank from 1829. It is also where you connect to the Continent through the Channel Tunnel Rail Link at St Pancras and to the world via Heathrow international airport's link at the Paddington end. This is truly the best connected street and the best for communication, not only in Britain, but probably in the whole of Europe. This fact is reflected in the sheer density of pedestrian movement along it. The very rail, bus, tube and centres attract passengers and also urban intensity of gathered activities that seek to benefit from the connectivity – originally most of this activity was industrial but in time academic, industrial, commercial and civic tourist facilities also found a home here.

In road traffic terms, the new Marylebone Road now brings vehicles into London along the M40/A40 Westway, built amid much local protest between 1966 and 1970. This is the only elevated road in the entire inner part of the central metropolis, in extraordinary contrast to the elevated freeways of cities like Hong Kong, Seoul, Shanghai and, of course, many if not most American cities. A distinctive part of mid-20th-century road engineering, such freeways provide a three-dimensional road network/grid in the air, where invariably massive intersections have to be designed to connect between each of these road systems and the smaller grained urban street terrain below.

In London, we just have the Westway which dives down to its exit point where the New Road begins at Paddington Green, eliminating the old town centre of Paddington in the process as well as most of Paddington Green. It travels eastwards to meet John Nash's great early 19th-century route at Park Square and dips into the only underpass on this road built at Tottenham Court Road before it then runs in front of the railway stations at Euston, St Pancras and King's Cross. It then travels along Pentonville Road and City Road to arrive at the City at Old Street roundabout. As a road it is the result of pragmatic bits of planning. Some of the old road itself still exists but it is mostly a 20th-century patchwork of road improvement inventions – some parts, such as the overpass and underpass, are grand pieces of 20th-century road engineering and some parts are cobbled together from ordinary urban streets. Each junction along its way creates serious havoc for local pedestrians, buses and cyclists as well as a significant loss of urban fabric and urban identity. It has become one of the most polluted, congested and ugly roads in London.

Opposite: Automobiles on Kingsway
Taxis can be seen stationary in the centre of the road waiting for custom. Kingsway is a very generous boulevard, one of the few in London that was laid out as a very deliberate piece of planning.

Above: Farrell, Eight main design principles for the general improvement of Oxford Street, 2006
The unique qualities of the great high streets are that they are social places. Oxford Street is not just London's high street, it is one of the great high streets of the world: a gathering place for events, car-free shopping days, Christmas fairs etc. This shows how it could be transformed into a real place, echoing historic gatherings such as Bartholomew Fair and even the great squares of Italy. It is not just a monocultural shopping street, it is London's high street.

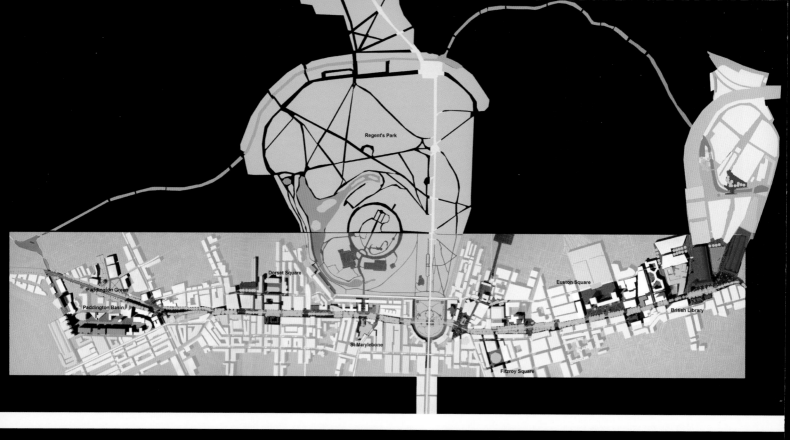

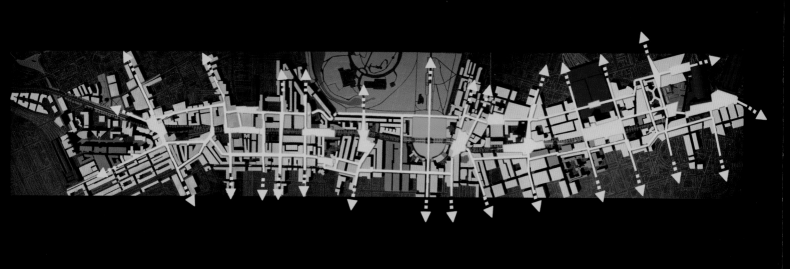

Top: Farrell, Plan of Marylebone-Euston Roads, 2002

By the end of the 19th century the roads ceased to form London's outside edge. They became the New Road, the bypass, and a series of places that by the late 20th century made up the best connected street in London, Britain or even Europe. They also became a place of large new developments on station land, at Paddington, Marylebone and King's Cross. They contain 3,000 homes and two universities. A modern version of the New Road links all the major rail and tube stations on what has been designated as a through road to show it as a place, something positive, rather than a negative non-place.

Above: Pedestrian links and parallel routes take the priority away from the Marylebone-Euston Roads.

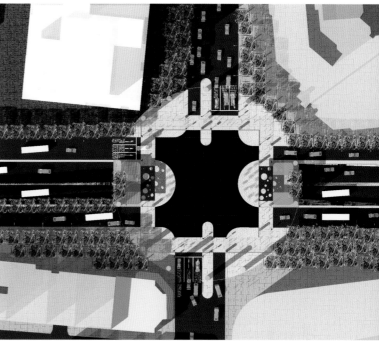

The Roman City of London

The street plan of the City of London is much easier to read than that of the West End. It has been overlaid so many times that it is much less legible now than it was in Roman times, but the real key to understanding the City today remains the Roman plan. It is a plan that still survives even as a defensible concept – it readily returned, in a geometry close to the shape that the Romans endowed, to being a fortified city in the late 20th century when the 'ring of steel' gates or checkpoints surrounded it to protect against IRA bombers. In-between, until well after medieval times, it was contained as a walled city with curfews and controlled gates, with most of the latter surviving into the 18th century. This meant that within the City there was an intensity and bustle, and a network of little streets that were all based upon close-knit pedestrian movement. It echoes the kind of pedestrianised, centralised areas familiar to us still in Mediterranean towns and cities. The success of today's banking city relies upon this very Roman, Mediterranean, defensible compactness. It is an extraordinarily small city compared with Westminster and the West End, which is spread out, informal and in parts almost suburban or even rural, with its Royal Parks. In fact, the whole City of London could fit within Hyde Park. This walkability means that the modern world's leading banking and financial services, established here during the last few centuries, were so compact and centred that familiarity with the alleyways and the coffee houses encouraged the culture of marketplace exchange that the stock exchange and the banks benefited from.

The most emphatic geographical reference to the Roman plan today is provided by the historic bridge-crossing point over the Thames. The modern London Bridge sits very close to the site of the Roman bridge which came into the walled city (and travelled right across the city to Bishopsgate on the far side). On that axis were the basilica and the forum, the heart of the Roman town.

Euston Circus today
The so-called traffic improvements of the mid to late 20th century are nowhere better caught than at the intersection of Euston Road and Tottenham Court Road. The present intersection is laid out solely for the benefit of the traffic.

Farrell, Euston Circus proposal, 2003
How the junction could be rethought as an integrated system of pedestrian movement and traffic, bringing about a vast improvement to the pedestrian realm without harming the movement of the vehicles.

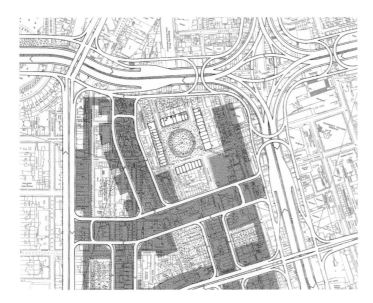

Of course, the Roman town of London was a clone of repeated DNA of all Roman fortified garrison towns; it was a military town, a conqueror's town. Having conquered, the Romans did not just house the military here, but brought a whole culture, an urban civilisation with them. As well as the basilica and forum there would have been an equivalent to a coliseum – remains of the amphitheatre were discovered in 1988 when the Guildhall Art Gallery site was excavated – and there would have been temples, along with the beautiful house plans and villas. Today, Pompeii provides us with a vivid picture of Roman urban life and its plan-form arrangements; it is a powerful and memorable idea that London began as a city that was not unlike Pompeii.

Centred between the bridge point and Bishopsgate, as the road runs north, is the main east–west street, with its barracks and markets, which ran through to Newgate. It is worth remembering that the Roman riverbank was much further north, before successive generations moved the bank southwards; it was probably a soft-edged, natural water line, much more so than today, as it has been built out in Viking, medieval and Victorian times, with new roads and warehouses built along it to form Upper and Lower Thames Street.

The midway street was the heart of the City of London and has been ever since. Today, it is still called Cheapside, from the Old English word for market, and is the descendant of the medieval market street from Newgate on the west side to Aldgate on the east. Of course, as in most defensive towns, the City's premier defensive position is river based at the Tower and located at the furthest 'gateway' downstream corner. With these simple historical elements in place, most of today's city plan has evolved and endured. It is very noticeable how there is an underlying grid: to the south of Cheapside runs Cannon Street, right through to Great Tower Street at one end and Ludgate at the other, while Upper and Lower Thames Street are built on the base of the extended Victorian waterfront. To the north is London Wall, a modern street which is the outer limit, as the name suggests, of the original fortified town and has been the most redeveloped part of the City of London in recent times, primarily due to the bombing of the Second World War and subsequent demolition of damaged buildings.

Like the Marylebone-Euston Roads, London Wall is a new road, built in the 20th century. With it came a whole postwar vision for London, a piece of town-planning utopia of the kind rarely seen

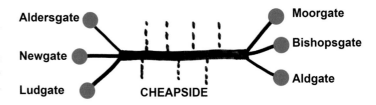

Colin Buchanan, Traffic In Towns, 1963
Euston Circus featured in the Buchanan Report (see p 195) which demonstrates the serious implications of designing for redevelopment and increased car use. It is a wonderful illustration that to meet car demand would be utterly futile and devastating; in the end there would be no London left. To me this is one of the most evocative town-planning drawings for London of the 20th century, an enormous contribution by Buchanan demonstrating that it was not simply a matter of meeting car usage; there had to be a balance, choices had to be made, and Buchanan indirectly became a pioneer in planning through consultation and choice.

Farrell, City of London diagram, 2009
Diagrammatically there is a simple driving pattern to the City's streets. Cheapside, the ancient high street, has subsidiary small specialised market streets (Bread Street, Milk Street etc) at right-angles along its length. At each end, west and east, the streets fan out to the City's gates creating interesting triangulations of the urban geometry.

A pile-up on the Finchley Road, 1924
With the arrival of the motor car in London came a great increase in road accidents, which peaked in the 1930s prior to the legal requirement of passing a driving test from 1935.

in the city. The Barbican Centre, first conceived by Chamberlin, Powell & Bon in 1959 but not completed until 1982, was built on a bombsite outside the area of the original Roman wall, to the north of the city, as an experimental plan with emphasis upon freeing up the ground level and eroding the original road map with traffic segregation and upper-level walkways.

Cheapside is the most interesting street in the City. It was and is the City's heart and leading off it are all the little streets and sub-markets of Wood Street, Milk Street and Bread Street, which self-evidently describe themselves as secondary roads supplying specialised products to those who shop in the main street. The gates and the enclosing wall have shaped the ends of Cheapside in a very clear pattern. The streets start to fan out on the west side, immediately after St Paul's Cathedral, to Newgate in one direction and to Ludgate in the other. The other end of Cheapside is a mirror-image bookend, where the roads fan eastwards down to the Tower, down King Street and Leadenhall Street to Aldgate, and then north to Bishopsgate at Threadneedle Street.

The 20th century saw two big schemes at Cheapside. The first of these is Paternoster Square which, at the western end of the St Paul's complex, has been the subject of great controversy. It has been rebuilt twice since it was bombed in 1942: first to a design by William Holford in 1961 and then most recently to a design by William Whitfield in 1996, which was completed in 2003. It first became a centre of debate in the 1980s with the very apparent failure of Holford's Modernist scheme, which was no longer able to attract tenants to its monolithic buildings in its unwelcoming windswept square. Several changes in the site's ownership and the currently raging style, which involved the Prince of Wales, brought to the table a whole series of different schemes, most notably by Arup Associates and John Simpson. In 1990, I was brought in as masterplanner. By the mid 1990s, though, the site had again changed hands and the commercial parameters for the scheme shifted. The masterplan was passed over to Whitfield, who rallied a group of architects together and divided up the buildings between them. The current square is evidently an improvement on the Holford scheme. The fact, though, that office workers still prefer to spend their lunch hours in the adjacent St Paul's churchyard suggests that it has been difficult to knit seamlessly into the fabric of the city. With few immediate precedents in the City, the design of this sort of urban set piece remains an elusive goal.

The site of James Stirling's Number One Poultry across the street from the City's major institutions – Mansion House, the Royal Exchange and the Bank of England – proved equally contentious. Lord Palumbo, property developer and former Arts Council chairman, had tried to rebuild on the site since 1968, first inviting Mies van der Rohe to design a great tower and piazza there. This was superseded by the Stirling design in 1988, which outlived the architect, and took a decade in its planning and development to get to completion.

Critically for London, it did not build upon the classical Roman city plan and, unlike most European cities, it never went through a stage of unification. This was partly because it evolved from two main centres and many sub-centres and partly because its growth was so rapid in the 19th century that it became a different kind of place – a multi-nodal metropolis without the intervening stages of being a centred and structured, European-style city. As a result the City of London, in terms of layout, solidified and stayed in its medieval phase with a relatively light overlay in the 19th and 20th centuries. Apart from the peripheral Barbican and London Wall, the only large-scale street changes have been King William Street (laid out in 1829–35 as an approach to the new London Bridge) and Queen Victoria Street, cut through in 1867–71 as a diagonal connecting Blackfriars to Bishopsgate and along Threadneedle Street, crossing over Cheapside at Bank; otherwise the city's evolution in plan form stopped some time ago.

South of the River

The big bend in the Thames between the cities of London and Westminster leaves the south bank as a rather low, flat peninsula. The roads all converge upon the Elephant & Castle in a very singular pattern, quite different from the north bank. The overall influence of the railways is dealt with separately, but here they arrive at the riverbank in elevated viaducts and have all but obliterated the earlier road system, together with its legibility and mental mapping, alongside the river edges. Further inland, the radial nature of roads from Elephant & Castle, the central focus point on the arc, provides a simple urban pattern by which to navigate. The inside bend of the river turns the south side into a great shortcut and the quickest way to travel from east to west. Many a taxi driver and mini-cab driver takes advantage of this. If one stands on Chelsea or Lambeth Bridge, the towers of Canary Wharf appear well over to the right in a location one would never expect to find them. Most Londoners have the simple idea of a north bank and a south bank, and in general terminology this is the way they refer to them, even if these banks often travel due north–south, vertically up the map, as it were.

London traffic jam
Contemporary picture of Oxford Street, a bus and taxi only route. Bus managers use it as a depot, a shortcut, and as a route to manage the bus empire, thus the two sides of the street are often separated by a wall of red and cannot relate to each other.

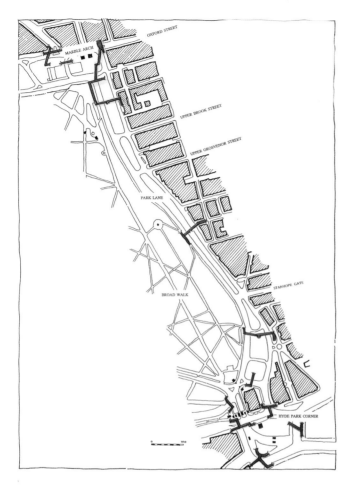

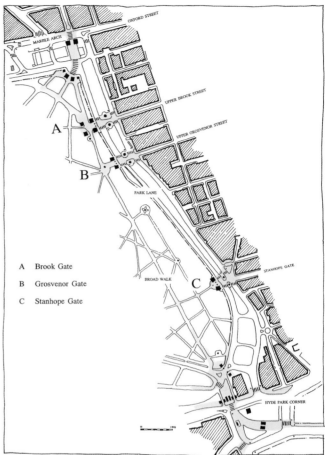

A   Brook Gate
B   Grosvenor Gate
C   Stanhope Gate

The Outer Edge of the Growth Rings

There is a final observation here to make about the sequenced evolution of London's east–west roads: if the analogy of London's roads is to be extended as one of annular rings found in a sliced-through tree trunk. This pattern can be perceived as one of waves and ripples growing outwards as expansion is followed by consolidation, followed by further expansion and consolidation again. On each road can be recognised both an edge – a boundary defining a new growth ring – and also an attractor for

new growth beyond it at either side. For example, The Strand has along the south of it one type of land condition (riverside houses, palaces) while to the north there is another band quite different from the other side of the road but consistent to itself (newer palaces and institutions relating to the monarch or civic life etc). Piccadilly divides the monarch, the higher-level aristocracy and the establishment (from Buckingham Palace to St James's) to the south from a lesser order to the north (Mayfair). Oxford Street clearly shows this sort of banding in its shops – all the big department stores (Selfridges, John Lewis, Debenhams and House of Fraser)

Marble Arch, Park Lane and Hyde Park Corner
Above left: Pedestrian underpasses were built in the 1960s to speed up traffic, but severed the urban territory to the east side of the park itself.
Above right: Farrell's 1990s proposals, much of it now implemented for surface crossings replacing most of the underpasses, giving priority to pedestrians.

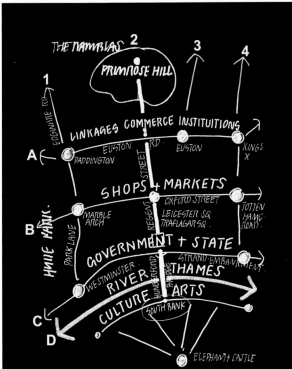

Farrell, London's Layers, 2002
London's main east-west streets can be seen as layers that, over time, have evolved specialist functions.

are on the north side, partly because this is the sunny side of the street, but mainly because this level of growth was permitted more readily on the slightly less well-off and keener north-side estates than the more conservative Grosvenor Estate to the south side of the street. And so the banding continues northward; the Marylebone-Euston Roads represent a particularly severe demarcation as to the south are the landed estates for the middle classes (Portman, Harley and Cavendish) while on the north side sit the railways and social housing estates. The canal further north then divides these social housing estates from the middle class of the first layer of suburbs in St John's Wood, Maida Vale, Primrose Hill and Canonbury. These are clear patterns dug deep in London's shape and form; emphatic in their seemingly gentle manner, but unmistakable and the key underlying structure that makes London a legible, clearly shaped place (see diagram on page 19).

Pedestrian priority
Eliminating dark and gloomy underpasses (top left) and dangerous jay walking (top right) by prioritising pedestrians at street level as shown here in Park Lane. Introducing a new crossing at the Animals in War memorial on Park Lane (bottom right) leads to clearer wayfinding and orientation.

Outer Roads

The Radial Pattern

The greater roads that extend out beyond London, connecting the city centre outwards to the southeast and to the rest of Britain need to be looked at separately from the inner roads, such as the central east–west roads, and the high streets, which serve the core and inner neighbourhoods and villages within the metropolis. Many of the inner roads are the 'annular ring' type that were laid as London grew, organically, and can be dated and aged in archaeological terms, just like dating the rings of a tree. However, there is also a set of radial roads, which stem from Roman times and led from the ancient gates out to the countryside, that by their very nature predate most inner roads and the urban expansion of the metropolis and, in fact, have quite different characteristics.

The radial roads really begin with the Roman London Bridge, the first crossing point of the Thames – traffic would cross the bridge and radiate southwards and northwards from the banks. The pattern of these roads is still reflected today and they continue to do the same job they have always done, of leading traffic directly towards or away from this central focus, although with ever increasing traffic over time. The radial pattern reflects the Roman understanding of road building as a key part of empire building. The roads enabled the management of a conquest through the rapid, continuous supply of troops and provisions to the camps in the outlying areas. The successful maintenance of the empire was partly founded on the Roman ability to create engineering infrastructure, such as city walls, aqueducts and particularly the roads, which were built for longevity with proper foundations. As a result we continue to recognise their infra-structural alignments today. We all know when we come across Roman roads because of their extraordinary directness as they cut through the land, and this very directness is part of what has helped them endure.

Radiating out from London in both directions was the Roman road of Watling Street. It rose up from Dover in the south, through London and out to Shrewsbury and beyond to Chester, then a large city on the Welsh borders. It came in to London

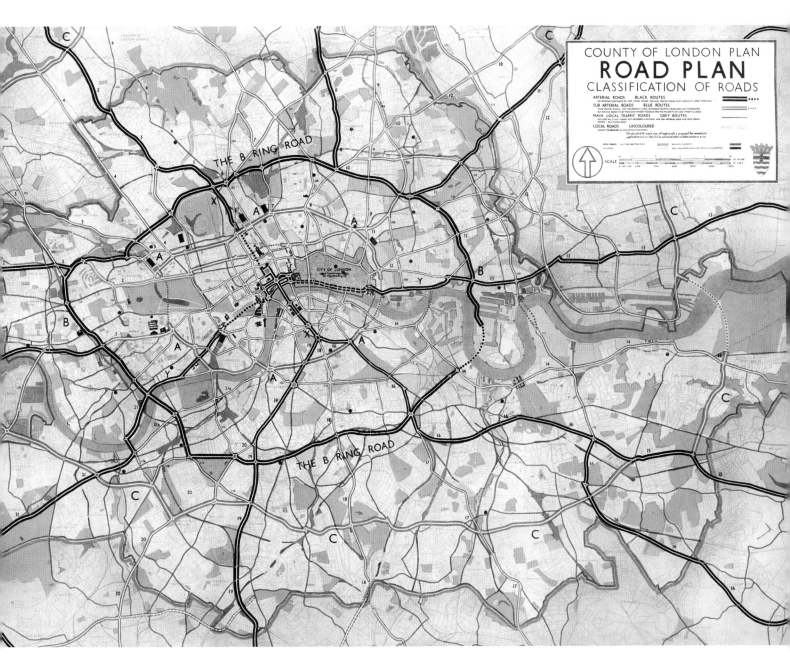

COUNTY OF LONDON PLAN
ROAD PLAN
CLASSIFICATION OF ROADS

Sir Patrick Abercrombie,
County of London Plan, 1943

The Abercrombie Plan of 1943 suggested
a series of eight-lane motorways (black)
through the centre of London. Only parts
of this proposal were implemented. Many
places within London would have been
lost: Camden Town, Primrose Hill, Maida
Vale, Earls Court, Clapham, Kensington
and Highbury & Islington.

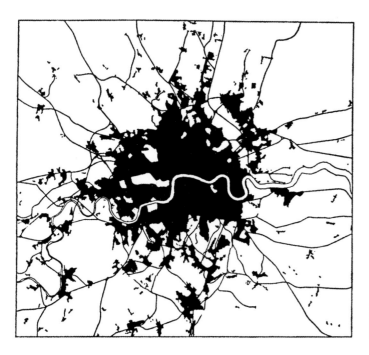 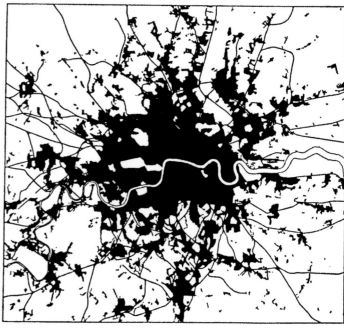

from the south through Rochester in present-day Kent and from the north through St Albans in Hertfordshire. Watling Street may be the most well known of the Roman roads, but London was also served by several others, including Portway, which went southwest to Silchester and Weymouth, and Stane Street which ran from London to Chichester in the south. Ermine Street ran along the alignment of the current A1 road for much of its route from London to York, and went out due north from the city through Edmonton. There were other Romano-British roads that are well known, such as Akeman Street and the Fosse Way, but these were country routes that did not pass through London.

The pattern of streets in Saxon and medieval times tended to grow for different reasons. For example, ancient droveways, often excavated with banks on either side so that cattle could be herded within the built-up walls, were established to supply

London with produce. Many Saxon villages were not placed on Roman roads, but well to one side, because their very efficiency made them the preferred routes for invading troops and therefore dangerous to be on or close to.

Even prior to modern times, the movement of produce and livestock caused congestion in the centre of London, as the only available route from the west before the creation of the New Road bypass in the 1750s was via Oxford Street and Holborn. The advent of the railways, allowing people to flood into London, escalated the supply problem in the 19th century, so an inner system of roads was developed to cater for the masses. However, it was in the 20th century that everything changed drastically, with the arrival of the motor car. The ultimate form of democratic transport, which became increasingly available to everyone through the course of the 20th century, brought about both an intensity

Redrawn by Farrell, The growth of London's outer suburbs (1901-11), 2000
Growth occurred along the rail and tube routes coming out of London.

of traffic and a hitherto unknown freedom of movement. Unlike public transport, which followed predictable lines so that the travelling public knew the timetables and routes, the motor car had great appeal due to its ability to transport anyone to anywhere in a completely personalised route.

The car made quite different and particular demands upon the radial road system that had been established for nearly 2,000 years. The system had to cope with the speed of these new vehicles and their size, including where to store them, but the biggest problem was the sheer volume of ever increasing traffic to, from and through London. It was not that traffic congestion was new – in the 17th century Samuel Pepys recorded being stuck in a traffic jam for an hour-and-half in a hackney coach – but it was hugely increased in the course of the century. The problem was obvious by the Second World War – in 1938 it was estimated that vehicles were increasing at the rate of over 500 per day – and accelerated considerably in the following decades. In the UK in 1951, there were 4.2 million licensed vehicles, and only 14 per cent of households had the regular use of one or more cars. By 2006, there were over 33 million licensed vehicles, and 75 per cent of households had cars. Car ownership in London has always been lower than in rural areas, but even in this most urban of settings, the number of households with cars rose from 58 per cent in 1985 to 65 per cent in 2005.

A Grand Plan?

Naturally enough, the rapid growth of car ownership in the mid 20th century was met with considerable alarm. Commissions, boards and study groups, which characterised so much of London's

planning during the last century, were established to meet the demands. It is surprising how much energy and time was spent on these studies and how little was actually implemented. The net result was that by and large most of the grand plans failed, which is probably just as well as many of the plans were so drastic that they would have damaged London irreparably. Right at the beginning of the 20th century, in 1905, the Royal Commission on London Traffic reported on obstructions to road plans such as road widening, in terms of ownership, bylaws and so on. It saw its role as extraordinarily draconian and wide-sweeping, recommending 43-metre (140-foot) wide main avenues and 30-metre (100-foot) wide first-class arterial roads, all laid out on a grid system. Two major avenues would quarter the central area, with one running from east to west along the old high streets of Bayswater, through Oxford Street and Whitechapel via the City, and the other north to south roughly on the line of the A1 from Holloway right down to

Kingston Bypass, 1938
Although central London was already congested, these were the days of clear suburban roads.

always the places where people lived and where the high streets were, and were consequently the busiest human interchanges on the ground. London's orbital routes came very much more into focus at this time, ring roads were beginning to be proposed, which laid the basis for the North and South Circular roads and the M25.

War once again intervened, allowing a further opportunity to reconsider how the major roads could be developed. An important figure emerged in the form of Patrick Abercrombie, the Professor of Town Planning at University College London, who was asked to prepare plans for what the new postwar Labour government perceived as a 'brave new world', offering a chance to wipe the slate clean and to begin to rethink London more fundamentally. Abercrombie had already outlined his thoughts in the County of London Plan of 1943, co-authored by JH Forshaw, which designated London's major defects as traffic congestion, depressed housing, maldistribution and inadequacy of open space and the non-zoning of housing and industry. In a nice, clean, rational way there was a hierarchy of three road classifications proposed: arterial, sub-arterial and local – rather like the branches of a tree. Theoretically, this was quite a promising start, except for the fact that they were simply superimposing an ideal, desirable order upon a network of roads that already existed.

Throughout the 1950s, the excitement of the postwar new world was typified by the building of new motorways through the cities of Britain. In Newcastle, where I grew up, the whole of the east side was demolished to make way for an inner motorway, but in London the excitement was seldom made concrete – plans stalled because of the sheer complexity and density of the city and in the end central London was spared. Car ownership and

Elephant & Castle. It was proposed that these avenues would have tramways on the surface and underground rail lines beneath.

One of the characteristics of 20th-century road planning, however, is how it was disturbed by the interventions of each of the world wars: the Royal Commission did virtually nothing due to the outbreak of the First World War and a further phase of planning was disrupted by the Second World War before the grand plans gave way to a more pragmatic and commonsensical approach. The phase between the wars was particularly distinguished by the involvement of the architect Edwin Lutyens and the engineer Charles Bressey, who began their work for the Ministry of Transport in 1934. They were asked to prepare a new highway development plan for London. Typical of all these early plans for London, the proposals were so radical that they would have eliminated all the places that the highways were supposed to serve – after all, the (so-called) centres of congestion were

Traffic roundabout at Gants
Hill on Eastern Avenue, 1933
Although in this photograph space is plentiful, the subsequent colonisation of these arterial roads, built between the wars, by 'ribbon development' housing and factories would later cause problems.

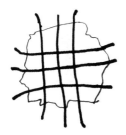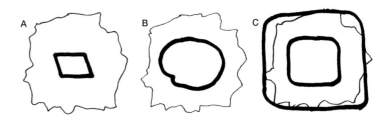

usage was escalating beyond all expectations, though. Forshaw and Abercrombie had felt it was 'perhaps doubtful' that the ratio of cars to population – then 1:22 – would ever equal the American figures (then at about 1:6). In fact, the ratio of population to all vehicles (not just cars) reached 1:12 in 1951; 1:4 in 1971; and is now less than 1:2. It was finally beginning to be perceived that whatever was done to London would be inadequate. There was a dawning realisation, in our post-modern era, that the scale of road improvement merely increased the scale of road usage, so there was not a simple functionalist relationship between supply and demand. The Modernist idea of analysis leading directly to a hypothesis and then to application was recognised as inappropriate as, in reality, what was there already had to take precedence.

Another factor that gradually prevented London from falling in line with these grand plans was the growth of political awareness of the broad population – the 1960s was a new age of wider democratisation, with student revolts and the rise of neighbourhood groups and the conservation movement. In the 1970s, the latter led to the protection of Covent Garden from inner ring roads, while in Highgate and Haringey locals and councillors became intensely politicised over the proposed road widening at Archway. Many politicians, like Nicky Gavron, the former Deputy Mayor of London, began their political careers by opposing some of the ambitious motorway schemes of the 1960s and 1970s.

During this era, the London County Council and its successor, the Greater London Council (GLC) tried to develop plans to bring radial motorways right into the city to link up with a huge

'Ringway', also called the London Motorway Box, which would be accompanied by several outer-ring motorways. The GLC believed its prerogative was to solve the problems in a didactic, paternalistic way and resorted to attempting to hide its motorway plans from the public by burying them in an overarching Greater London Development Plan. Its plans, just like those of Lutyens and Abercrombie, look absolutely appalling in retrospect as they would have demolished so much of London, making it a completely different place with little benefit. A singular figure, not typical of this era, was Colin Buchanan, whose 1963 study *Traffic in Towns* looked at balancing the demands of increasing car ownership and the inherent qualities of the towns; at last 'place' was on the agenda. He studied regional places like Bath (which I was involved with briefly when I worked in his office), with some sensitivity, and also looked at inner London. Instead of offering solutions that merely met growth, he presented a series of choices, ranging from meeting the demands of traffic growth and congestion at the expense of the urban fabric, to keeping the urban fabric but paying the price of the anticipated increase in congestion. Again Buchanan was ahead of the times, with choice and consultation part of his concept of the planning process.

Initially though, the GLC looked more towards the once aborted plans of Abercrombie than to Buchanan for guidance. So inevitably the 1970s was a time of considerable controversy over the proposed new radial roads and the detailed inner-city motorway plans and their effect upon the reality on the ground – the communities and places that existed. The resolution of the conflict set the future for planning in London; ironically the

Redrawn by Farrell, A E Matthews'
1966 proposals for 'underways', 2009
Six tunnels combining all through traffic
under London: road, heavy rail, monorail,
light rail, pedestrians and main services
all within one giant (18 metres/59 feet)
diameter ring/tube, all 25 metres (82 feet)
below ground.

Redrawn by Farrell,
London's outer roads, 2009
The Motorway Box (Ringway 1):
The largest inner ring road the world
had ever seen (A).
Ringway 2: Proposal to replace the
North and South Circular Roads (B).
As built: the M25, North and South
Circular Roads (C).

Highway overpass
under construction, 1969
Building work at the Latimer Road
interchange with the Western Avenue
extension and the proposed West Cross
Route. This section of elevated motorway
links Marylebone Road with Western
Avenue at the Westway. The old White
City Stadium (venue for the first London
Olympics, 1908) can be seen top left.

result set a pattern for a future with less planning. Plans for the new roads went from committees and departments of the GLC to the national government and eventually landed on the desks of Cabinet ministers, all the time accompanied by intense public debate and intense lobbying by objectors. As a result it was politically expedient not to initiate any overall plan and renege on any that had already been agreed. In 1973, the Treasury declared that the road plan was dead: 'The Inner Motorway Box will never be implemented. We are no longer living in an environment where any government can displace thousands of people from their homes. I am sorry that ... Cabinet should have endorsed another project which is socially and financially out of the question.' Buchanan's thoughtful work setting out ranges of choices and possibilities had been too sophisticated for the crudity, the coarse-grainedness of British politics in his time.

The M25

It would be untrue to say that every plan came to nothing. Building a new road system beyond the suburbs and outer suburbs of London, on the far distant edge of the 'green belt', was eventually seen as less controversial than bringing radial motorways right into a central ring, and so the M25 was born. Finally realised in 1985, when the final stretch was opened, it encircles the far periphery of the city, much further out than anyone had ever envisaged in the era of the London Motorway Box. The M25 does not necessarily follow the most desirable route, but in effect it follows the only one possible, having been built by default as a result of our democratic processes and our attitude to urban form. Instead of continuing to an inner ringway, more or less all

of the major radial motorways that converge upon London – the M1, M40, M11, A13, M4, M3, M23, M26, M20 and A2 – peter out gradually as they enter the city, with most of them beginning to diminish as they meet the north and south circular rings, the latter an extraordinary mixture of local roads and almost mini-motorways with grade-separated intersections. In a way these

M1 and A1 roads, London, 1995
These major highways split apart residential areas and marooned them in disconnected islands. An extraordinary juxtaposition with the enormous scale of the roads dwarfing the little village-sized houses that had originally fulfilled the dream of suburbia, but which now sit beside major, noisy, polluted roads.

circular rings are the only surviving remnants, a shadow of the Abercrombie Plan. For many they represent the worst of all possible worlds; in some places, streets have been torn in two and whole houses have been cut in half, leaving a lobotomised semi, to let dual carriageways thunder through; in other places, full motorway standards have been achieved. London's ugliest journey by far is to travel in a ring around the north and south circulars and witness the shocking results of cobbling together non-plans, half-plans and part-plans, mile after mile of muddled highway, all non-designed and unplanned at any scale.

All in all, London's major outer road systems did not adjust to demand but to pragmatism and leadership convenience, simply because to meet demand would have meant demolishing so much of London – there would be no 'there' when you got there! The 1970s objections to road improvements began a deep and growing suspicion of all town planning, which grew to include social housing, town centre redevelopment, New Towns and green-field universities. The pendulum swung to the other extreme and by the era of the Thatcher government most state planning had been abandoned in favour of 'deregulation'. For

the British, the period of nationalisation in the mid 20th century was followed by a return to Victorian levels of deregulation which affected the financial markets, banks and other enterprises, and also the planning of the public realm, rail, airport and bus transport systems.

In order to plan roads properly, and how the city can relate to new major radial roads, there has to be some commonly agreed sense of what the real identity of London is, balancing improvements against what Londoners value of what is already there. This has always been one of the problems with London because its sense of its own identity has been so poor, especially if compared with Paris. Sitting across the Channel from each other, London and Paris are almost alter egos. The great radials and diagonals created by Baron Haussmann in the 19th century ensured that Paris did not have to face the same congestion problems as London in the early 20th century. It was later able to adopt a 'Périphérique', Paris's clear zoning of transport and travel, developed on the site of the Thiers ring of fortifications, to cope with car ownership – there is a clear understanding of the system of the city and how to develop that system, which

M25 motorway, 2005
Traffic moving on the M25 London Orbital motorway near junction 22 in Hertfordshire. The government is considering scrapping fuel tax and replacing it with a new road charge based on the distance and length of time motorists travel.

is passed from era to era. By contrast, London has no agreed consensus about the civic, the *civitas*, the public realm: there is still no common agreement about what is of value and therefore what needs protecting or enhancing. For instance, in recent times the Congestion Zone created by Mayor Livingstone as a 'popular measure', was aimed at enhancing the quality of life in central London and he consequently extended the zone to include Kensington and Chelsea. On election his successor, Boris Johnson, immediately scrapped the extension, as a 'popular measure', again

to enhance yet another view of the quality of life in London. This seesawing of public opinion, so complex and divided in so many areas, with so many different interest groups vying against each other, is what has distinguished so much of the planning that exists in London today.

With the collapse of the big plans, the rise of local community power, consultation and consensus planning came another kind of tyranny: the tyranny of the traffic bureaucrat. Having failed to introduce the major ring roads and inner radial motorways, traffic

M25 motorway

A Chiltern turbo-diesel multiple unit travels across the M25. This relatively new outer ring of London attracts huge densities of traffic and is now being substantially widened.

Northwest London from the air, 1997
The A40 connects to the M40 further
out of London. It divides hitherto
connected parts of traditional urban
street scenes, in particular Maida Vale,
Bayswater and Notting Hill. The elevated
roadway continues and drops down at the
Roman road of Watling Street, now the
Edgware Road.

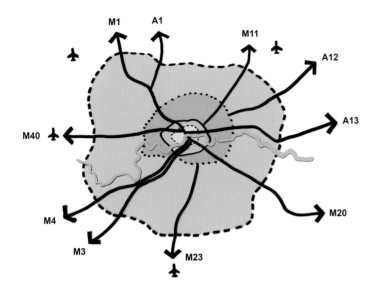

planners then concentrated on meeting car growth by stealth at a smaller scale with one-way systems and gyratories. On paper these plans often appear to be based on the abandoned grand plans, but down on the ground they were achieved by simply redesignating existing roads and pretending that they formed some kind of overall system by labelling them in different ways, and applying traffic management to make them work. This can be deciphered

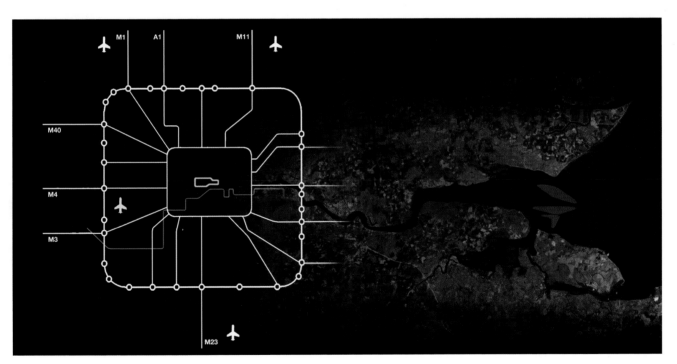

Top: Farrell, The major roads of outer London, 2006

In 1958 the first motorway was opened as the Preston Bypass (now part of the M6). In 1959 the first section of the M1 was finished. By 1972 the first 1,000 miles (1,609 kilometres) of motorway had been built.

Above: Farrell, Mind map over London, 2007

Junctions with the M25 and surrounding area.

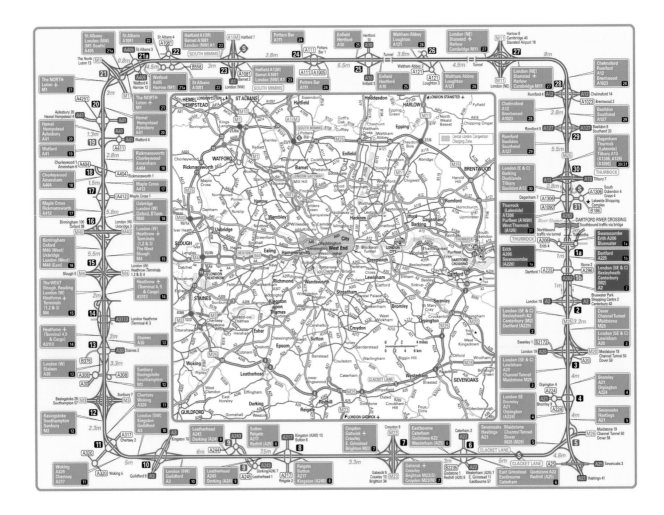

when looking at car users' maps such as the large-scale *A to Z* maps and particularly the AA and RAC maps of London. There is, for example, a hypothetical ring road that runs along the Marylebone-Euston Roads and down Park Lane to Elephant & Castle, and back north again up the far east side of London. In some of these maps, the roads are distinguished by coded colours to collectively designate them as part of an aspiration to a pattern of notional ring roads. In reality, though, when you are on them there is no evidence of them being different from most other large urban streets. The idea that these streets actually form part of a big system is made ridiculous by their different A-road designations: Marylebone Road is the A501, Park Lane is the A4202, Victoria Street is the A302 and so on. This, to my mind, is a kind of fantasy arterial road system existing only in the mind of the map-makers and the traffic bureaucrats.

Just as Christopher Wren's Baroque plan, with its great boulevards and axial planning, never succeeded after the Great Fire of London in 1666, neither did the plans of Lutyens, Abercrombie

AA map of the M25
London Orbital motorway

This 188-kilometre (117-mile) road which surrounds greater London was completed in 1986 and is often informally considered as a boundary marking the edges of the city. © AA Media Limited 2009
© Crown copyright 2009. All rights reserved.
Licence number 100021153.

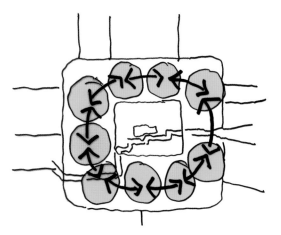

Improve connectivity between Outer Boroughs

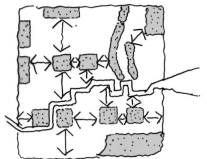

A London-wide 'Green Grid'
Connect major landscapes to one another

Outer London to be managed as a
metropolitan forest

and the GLC survive. They all failed for the same reasons. In this 'nation of shopkeepers', as Napoleon called the British, there is such diverse land ownership, property interests and local power. We are governed by vested interests, economic imperatives, pragmatism and, above all, a suspicion of all kinds of centralised planning. When it comes to the ultimate in democratic transport movement – the motor car – we are repeatedly in favour of deregulation and the non-plan. In the great debate, as the philosopher Isaiah Berlin would have put it, between a negative liberty and positive liberty: the freedom of the individual and the marketplace is always seen as the London way of doing things.

Positive planning can, however, create a kind of liberty, just as a constitution can, and this came often to my mind during a recent public enquiry on the future of planning part of the City of London itself. One of the senior principals in the planning department of the City – that great planned Roman complex which continues to benefit London today – said that he did not believe in masterplans, that proactive planning inhibits flexibility and reduces the options, and that it imposes an order that one may not wish to have at a future date! That, in essence, is what has happened to London roads since Roman times. One can only speculate what the Romans would make of London if they were to return now and see how for the last 2,000 years the British have muddled through. They would see a city of congested high streets and roads that have, underlying their busyness, tremendous picturesque charm and their own innate quirky order. But they would also see that

lack of resolve and common shared vision for the future has led to the 20th-century history of London's road planning being pretty unsatisfactory. Perhaps, just perhaps, there is a need to consolidate all roads just as London Underground post-rationalised the seemingly chaotic tube system. In the spirit of my plans for Euston Road, I have been continuing with ideas in outer London – 'urbanising' parts of the North Circular Road at Brent Cross. Perhaps the Harry Beck model can now be applied to our London roads of the 20th century; bringing integrated order retrospectively to disorder is a particular genius of London it seems.

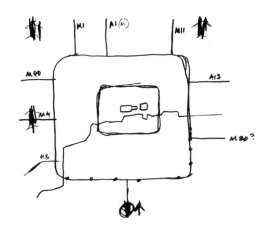

Farrell, Proposals for outer London, 2009
Part of Farrell's work for the Outer London Commission – thoughts on the large-scale structure of outer London.

Farrell, Mind map sketch, 2005
Farrell's sketch showing ways of rationalising and bringing order to the new outer road systems.

Pedestrians, Cyclists and Buses

On Foot

Walking is the most fundamental mode of transport – yet in town plan formation it is often the least understood, the least recorded and, in modern times, the least respected and planned for. Logically, walking patterns must have been a fundamental city form maker, but because of its small scale and its inherent adaptability its record is invariably quieter and less forceful than wheeled transport. Part of the explanation comes from the association with wealth and privilege – those who could afford to do so were carried and did not walk, only the poor did. Horse power (riding or in carriages) and, before wheels, people power (by litters – light carriages on shafts), were London elites' transport. Sedan chairs, patented in 1634, monopolised the rental of 'hackney chairs' and were popular because of the increasing elaboration of costumes coupled with filthy streets and bad weather.

There is one inherent pattern to walking which is its scale; a 15- to 20-minute walk – about 1.6 kilometres (1 mile) at average walking speed – is seen as quite a different thing from a one-hour or a one-day walk. The 15- to 20-minute walk is a purposeful, neighbourhood thing: the distance from one's home to a bus or tube stop is the distance for a Roman soldier to get to the gates of the city, or a banker to go across town for a business meeting. A one-hour walk (4.8 to 6.4 kilometres (3 to 4 miles)) is something that can be done across a park reasonably spontaneously and casually according to weather and social opportunity, but there are also many one-day walks across London that are defined and planned like the Metropolitan Walks in outer London, planned for the rambler, for those walking as a leisure or tourist entertainment.

Officials, politicians and planners are increasingly interested in the world of pedestrians, but it is still very underfunded. Looking at the budget of Transport for London in recent years (now £4.8 billion), one can see that the money spent on this most primary of human transport methods is quite derisory compared with the money spent on wheels, whether public transport or private car use. How can one really say that the streets and the map of London are primarily vehicle based? Clearly, the roads were

Pedestrian concourse in Canary Wharf, 2007
In the late 20th and early 21st centuries, pedestrian areas have been designed into shopping centres and new districts of London.

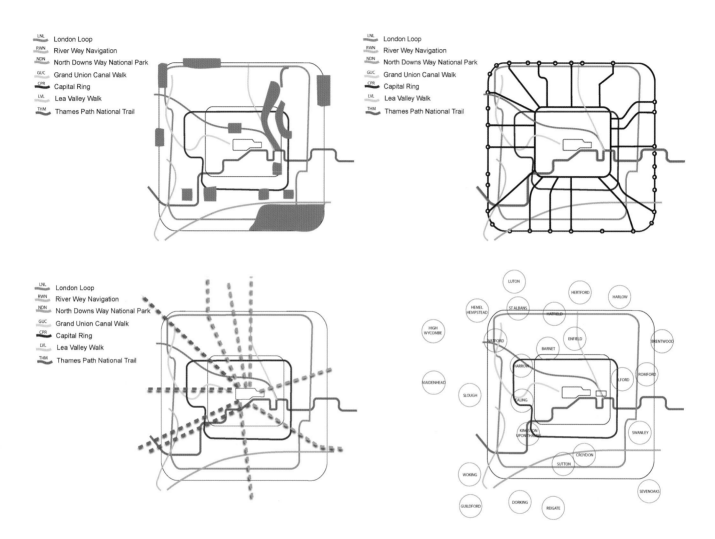

LNL London Loop
RWN River Wey Navigation
NDN North Downs Way National Park
GUC Grand Union Canal Walk
CPR Capital Ring
LVL Lea Valley Walk
THM Thames Path National Trail

LNL London Loop
RWN River Wey Navigation
NDN North Downs Way National Park
GUC Grand Union Canal Walk
CPR Capital Ring
LVL Lea Valley Walk
THM Thames Path National Trail

LNL London Loop
RWN River Wey Navigation
NDN North Downs Way National Park
GUC Grand Union Canal Walk
CPR Capital Ring
LVL Lea Valley Walk
THM Thames Path National Trail

originally for foot – the Roman army did not travel by car or train, it marched and laid out the straightest roads, the first proper ones, primarily for travelling by foot. The inability to measure walking has limited its modern-day influence on the form and pattern of London.

The space between villages and hamlets often emerged because of walking times: villages are often 15 minutes apart, towns maybe an hour or more apart, and cities perhaps a day apart. (These walking scales come purely from personal observation rather than academic scientific research.) I am certain that the whole map

Farrell, Sequence of diagrams, 2004
Top left: Metropolitan walks overlaid on metropolitan open space
Above left: Metropolitan walks linking into bus and train lines
Top right: Metropolitan walks linking into main roads
Above right: Metropolitan walks linking into satellite towns
A sequence of diagrams using Farrell's

Mind Map of the Greater London overground map as a base for a system of overlays to understand the main walks. Walking is not simply confined to local neighbourhoods for journeys to work and school, it is an enrichment to modern urban life.

Scene along Rotten Row in London's Hyde Park, 1899
People gather in anticipation of an event: cyclists, pedestrians, horses and carriages. This is a park and pedestrian path system that still exists today, having become a series of thoroughfares for commuters as well as being used for the original Victorian design purpose: for recreation and ambulation.

of London has, inherent within it, time/distance features that are based upon walking. The hamlets of Tower Hamlets supplied the Tower, as the name suggests, with each of them no more than an hour or so's walk away from the town that they supplied (even Hackney, Bromley-by-Bow and Poplar are only around 5 kilometres/3.1 miles from central London), while they were a day's walk to the fields in Essex where the produce came from. And so the centres, the settlements and all of London's multi-centred, dispersed nature began its layout with walking distances.

It was the urban pavement or sidewalk that first began to give solid planned benefit to the pedestrian, but at first these were found only in the good streets. Up until the 18th century London, like other cities, was a walking city. But pedestrians had to share narrow streets with animals on their way to market or to slaughterhouses, with the different forms of carriage used by the wealthy, and with a wide variety of wagons and carts transporting goods. The world of the urban pedestrian was inconvenient, dirty and dangerous.

Pavements/sidewalks first appeared in the early 1700s and the first recorded use in the *Oxford English Dictionary* of 'pavement' (from the Latin *pavire*, to ram down to make a flat surface), when referring to a footpath at the side of a road, was in 1716 (John Gay, 'There may'st thou pass, with safe unmiry feet, where the raised pavement leads athwart the street').

Servants and merchants kept these new pavements clean, but later a rate was levied by estate owners and developers. Non-pavemented streets had sweepers to clear walkable passages on demand. Pavements were clearly a notable feature in 1739 when included in the design for Westminster Bridge ('The side-walks for foot passengers are raised about a foot above the carriageway'). They were mentioned as being a feature of a few city streets in 1754 ('The fine pattern of pavement for foot passengers, to be seen in some parts of Cornhill, Cheapside, Ludgate Hill and the Strand').

Of course, much of the new road and bridge infrastructure, particularly Westminster Bridge (1739–50) and Blackfriars Bridge (1769) if anything benefited the ordinary (pedestrian) Londoner as much as the wheeled traffic, and today walkers, particularly during rush hour, dominate the scene on London's bridges.

Even English Heritage has acknowledged that street surfaces such as paving are an 'under-researched aspect of the historic environment'. Paved stones, then cobbles, were introduced, then woodblocks from the 1830s onwards. Modern street lighting began with the UK's first gas lamps at Pall Mall in 1816, and the country's first proper electric street lights numbered 40 in 1879, and were between Westminster and Waterloo.

Streetlighting transformed the experience and safety of the public realm, extending urban activity by making evenings in winter busier and more conducive to social life, entertainment, fun and leisure. Street signs, signposts, milestones are all still part of English Heritage's preservation domain and in the 20th century formalised, mechanised and visually signalled pedestrian crossings became part of the urban landscape with Belisha beacons and striped surfaces.

The world of the pedestrian is one that very much interacts with street furniture. So much of the Victorian and Edwardian eras and the early 20th century was composed in an elegant way, in a less crowded world. The postbox, the street sign, the milestone, the horse-drinking fountain, the taxi-cab shelter and, in particular, the telephone box were all part of the landscape,

the urban scene, which is suitably called, in town-hall jargon 'street furniture'. In a very fitting British tradition of layering, the telephone box has a fascinating history, having been designed in 1924 in a competition that came about after the London boroughs refused to accept the Post Office's original concrete version on their streets. It was designed by the great architect Giles Gilbert

Scott who was less heralded than he should have been because he was not a Modernist and did not fit within the modern view of architectural history, even though he was the architect for Bankside and Battersea power stations, two of London's most distinguished and prominent 20th-century buildings. The telephone box design is based on the monument/tomb above

Tour de France, London, 2007
In 2007, the Tour de France was held for the first time in London, with stage one passing across Westminster Bridge in front of the Houses of Parliament as the peloton took the start. With the bridge closed to traffic this becomes another piece of dramatic street theatre.

the family vault that was designed in the early part of the 19th century by the renowned architect John Soane. The shape and form of the red telephone box became a recognisable British icon along with the similarly red post-box (the colour was introduced in 1874), the red bus and the black taxi.

It is interesting that so many of these London icons were produced in public service for the pedestrian on the street; it is also interesting that the landmark objects/icons of the metropolis of London are of such a small, utilitarian scale. While the Eiffel Tower in Paris, the Opera House in Sydney and the Empire State Building in New York so readily define their cities and form part of their brand, for London it is these small, familiar street objects that set this metropolis apart and give it its signature. This perhaps points to a traditional concern for the design of the pedestrian world, for the street utilities that surround the people in their place. That there has been a shift away from such considerations is typified by the fact that the modern world of traffic management has made London recognisable by another feature, eclipsing most others, and that is the charmless pedestrian railings that the nanny state has provided to pen the pedestrians back in order to allow the traffic to move more quickly.

In contrast to car drivers, people on foot or cycling have a limitless number of choices in terms of the routes they can take and the type of journeys they can make. Once on the street, a walker or a cyclist can twist and turn responding to any sponta-neous change of mind or external stimuli, whether it be traffic or a sudden downpour. This makes them highly unpredictable and much less manageable from a systems point of view. So how can they be planned for in the modern city? In city planning there never was a truer application of Einstein's observation that

**Pietro Dorando at the
London Olympics, 1908**
Here the Italian marathon runner
appears, just before he arrived at the
Gates of White City Stadium. This tradition
of using the streets as theatre, closing
them for big events, is very much part
of the urban pattern of London.

**Funeral Procession of King
George V, Piccadilly, 1936 (opposite)
and Communist march, Victoria
Park, 1936 (above)**

Two events when the streets were used for
ceremonies and protests: the royal funeral
passing down Piccadilly at about the point
where the river Tyburn flows under Green
Park, and Communists marching in the East
End after fascist riots the previous weekend.

(to paraphrase): 'Everything that can be counted does not necessarily count; everything that counts cannot necessarily be counted', than in the world of the pedestrian and the pedestrian planner. Quite simply the pedestrian has suffered abysmally at the hands of those who measure and count, because the dictates of measuring and counting as the primary basis of planning meant that only the wheels on their defined lines of tarmac, or travelling on railway lines, were countable and therefore could be planned. Pedestrians were perceived as not countable and therefore did not count.

Walkers, by their very nature, have no combined agency or voice; after all they seem anonymous, who are they? The car owner registers, has a tax disc and a licence, has a recognisable vehicle with a number plate, takes out insurance in his/her name – and is an eminently measurable, countable and recorded entity.

Drivers are invariably going about their business in London for a predetermined purpose on a fixed journey, usually intending to go from A to B to do a particular thing. But how do you measure pedestrians who, on any one pavement, are a mixture of those going for a walk, or going on a regular daily journey to work, perhaps, or school, or could be lost, or up to no good, or combining several tasks? They go from A to B to C to D with the ever available opportunity to change their minds according to whether the shops are shut, or the groceries are too heavy, it starts to rain, or the children are tired – so the possibilities can open up endlessly as amendments to their plans are spontaneously made.

In the late 20th and early 21st centuries, there have been dramatic improvements in measuring, organising and predicting pedestrian movement. Serious research studies, such as those by

Modelled pedestrian flow diagrams from the Atkins Intelligent Space 2005 'Walking in London' report for the Central London Partnership
The accessibility model (above left) shows how well connected each street is within the surrounding street network, highlighting the major thoroughfares for pedestrian flow; red indicating the most accessible through the spectral range to the least in blue. The visibility model (above right) shows the most visible areas in red indicating those which provide the clearest local connections for walking, with blue being the most secluded routes.

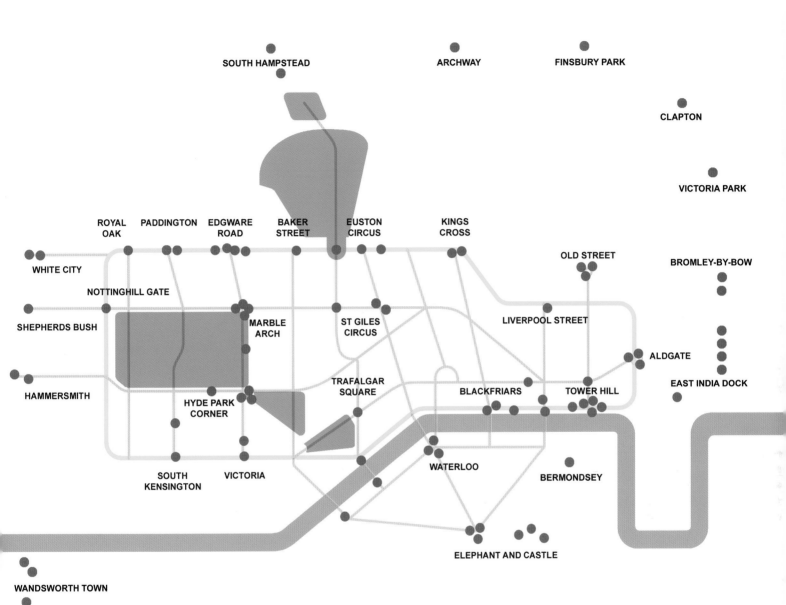

SOUTH HAMPSTEAD

ARCHWAY

FINSBURY PARK

CLAPTON

VICTORIA PARK

ROYAL OAK

PADDINGTON

EDGWARE ROAD

BAKER STREET

EUSTON CIRCUS

KINGS CROSS

OLD STREET

BROMLEY-BY-BOW

WHITE CITY

NOTTINGHILL GATE

LIVERPOOL STREET

SHEPHERDS BUSH

MARBLE ARCH

ST GILES CIRCUS

ALDGATE

HAMMERSMITH

HYDE PARK CORNER

TRAFALGAR SQUARE

BLACKFRIARS

TOWER HILL

EAST INDIA DOCK

SOUTH KENSINGTON

VICTORIA

WATERLOO

BERMONDSEY

ELEPHANT AND CASTLE

WANDSWORTH TOWN

Farrell, Central London pedestrian underpasses plan, 2007
Plan of central London showing the 84 principal locations where there are pedestrian underpasses at traffic junctions and major roads. Pedestrian underpasses are sited where there is the greatest conflict of traffic and pedestrian intensity.

Suffragette march, London, May 1911

Not confined to the great streets and the wide boulevards of the city, here in the East End the Suffragettes march by the National Federation of Women Workers in Bermondsey.

Dr Bill Hillier and his Space Syntax Laboratory at University College London have for 20 years conducted a computer-based analysis of pedestrian movement. A culture of knowledge has developed for new projects – like shopping centres, airports, railway stations and sports stadiums – where there is a commercial need to know mass pedestrian movement and this is being applied to wider town-planning areas. Now, how people walk and how they move has become clearer and even if there is not yet a full science, then at least pedestrian movement has become countable and has started to be calculated and analysed.

We certainly live in different times compared with the 1950s and 1960s when it was assumed that it was acceptable to push the pedestrians underground in underpasses or up in raised walkways to get them out of the way, to ignore their existence, so that wheels could become king. The supremacy of the pedestrian and the degree to which urban life is dependent on the feet, though, has still yet to be fully absorbed. Everybody on wheels always ends up on foot; the purpose of any journey is eventually to walk upon arrival, to get out, to walk around the shops, to walk into the office, to walk into the school or museum. This is why we are in vehicles in the first place, and this is what cities are about; bringing people together, talking, meeting, playing, shopping and always eventually doing so on foot. It is walking that truly defines a city, and yet for the most part, today, the world of pedestrians has been defined for them by other movement systems and their self-orientated priorities.

As the modern planning, organisation and systematisation of car transport preceded those of pedestrian movement, it remains inherently a process of post-rationalisation. So-called pedestrianisation schemes would have seemed extraordinary to

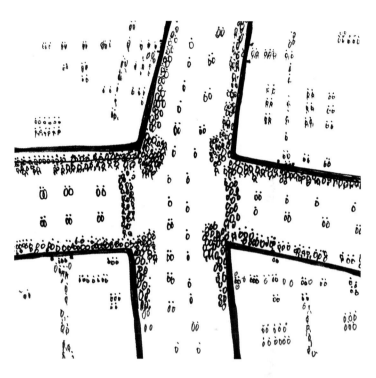

our ancestors, moving about pre-18th century, when just about the whole world lived and walked in pedestrian zones and only a minority travelled by horse or coach. Modern pedestrianisation is a term of reversal, looking back to what could be termed more 'natural' times, but it is often achieved as an amendment to the status quo of wheels and ironically has always to justify itself as a kind of 'newer' order.

Terry Farrell, Sketch, 1963
My student drawing, while at Penn University: stripping back the urban intersection to reveal only the people, in cars, walking and enclosed in buildings.

There are, of course, some enduring pedestrian domains in London, and there always were – street markets, enclosed markets, very narrow lanes and alleys. There are also pedestrian-managed domains available for certain periods of time. For instance, it is seen as increasingly possible to turn over public realm areas, such

Farrell, Paddington, 2003
During the 1960s, traffic flow took precedence and destroyed many town centres. After much campaigning here at the Paddington/Marylebone Flyover, the underpasses (top) have been superceded by surface pedestrian crossings (bottom) which have completely changed the relationships along this former Roman road (Watling Street).

as Oxford Street, solely to pedestrians for limited periods, even for a whole weekend. This can happen at certain times of the day for singular events, or monthly or annually for festivals such as the Notting Hill Carnival or the London Marathon. Time-managed, periodic pedestrianisation is a growing urban pattern that has spread everywhere in the world, and London is increasingly taking advantage of this spontaneous, small-scale planning reversal.

It is generally taken as read that walking is a pleasurable activity; some London walks, both long distance and short, are officially declared as such, including the Jubilee Walk, the Diana Walk and others through parks, woods and along river edges, while organisations such as Sustrans are establishing the Thames Path right out to the Estuary. Walking in itself is a joy and a pleasure, whether alongside canal banks or rivers, and it is increasingly made easier and more accessible through better mapping and signage.

With the aid of emerging digital technology with its innate ability to cope with great complexities, we will now begin to understand walking. The dynamic of walking lends itself to the sort of patterns reproduced by computer technology, helping to predict and manage a better quality of life for the pedestrian and therefore our cities. We can start to rebalance the perception of our streets with their actual use. As I describe more fully when discussing traffic management in the 'Inner Roads' chapter, a good example of the planning misconception of an area is the Marylebone-Euston Roads, which were declared to be a through-road in 1960 despite being residential in places and place-based with public buildings and amenities and tourist attractions. It has thus been defined as a wheel-based entity – an architecture of wheels. Yet the road plainly is not just this. The through-road

GLC housing project, Thamesmead, 1972
The experiments of the 1960s separating pedestrians from traffic resulted in many fantasy, modish schemes where people were placed up in the air and freed from imaginary traffic below (as you can see, none existed). They were built all over London, many with integrated walkways that were to be part of a city-wide system that never actually materialised. These isolated high-level street walks were subsequently proved to be dangerously anti-social.

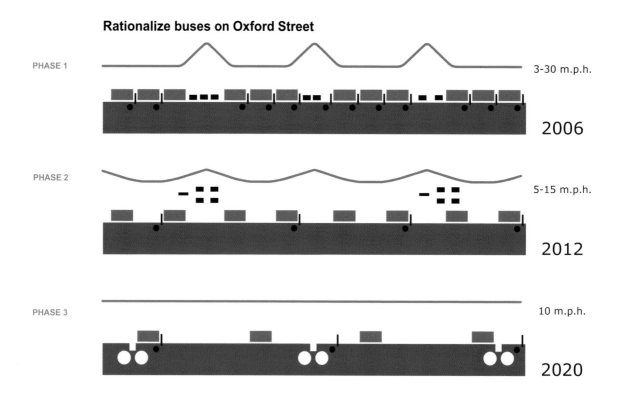

Rationalize buses on Oxford Street

PHASE 1 — 3-30 m.p.h. — 2006

PHASE 2 — 5-15 m.p.h. — 2012

PHASE 3 — 10 m.p.h. — 2020

Farrell, Rationalisation of
buses along Oxford Street, 2007
A plan in three phases to achieve
a constant flow of 10 miles
(16 kilometres) per hour.

was able to come into being simply because of the innate flexibility and single-minded determination of pedestrians to overcome whatever obstacle is in their way, because of the sheer diffuseness of the pedestrian voices, so that they never spoke as one, and also because of the immeasurability of the pedestrian so that nobody actually knew what they were doing collectively.

On the Euston Road, and indeed on any of London's other major roads, such as the Cromwell Road, Edgware Road, Tottenham Court Road or High Holborn – one sees people attempting to cross, dodging and jumping over the railings and through the holding pens on central islands. The term 'pen' comes from livestock management – the pedestrians are held in the middle of the road, while the lights work primarily for the benefit of the wheels. Pedestrians stand there, trapped, in all weathers, unprotected from the elements and indeed from the

pollution emitted by cars. While the driver is sheltered in his car and privileged by the traffic system, it is the pedestrians, with their limited range in distance and scale of movement, who are really of this place, who are located here. To the London pedestrian, a street is not a through-road – it cannot be: their business is on the street, they are here because of an office, home, shop, school or university. This is a place to the pedestrian; it is a non-place to the wheeled vehicle, yet everything on the road has been designed for the comfort, speed and convenience of the latter. The solution is to rebalance, not to prefer one over the other but to make the streets, the roads, work in harmony, to design for both.

There are now positive plans emerging from a better appreciation of the roles of pedestrians. The mayor's office has revealed that 50 per cent of tube journeys in central London would be quicker on foot. To this end, a new 'Legible London' signage

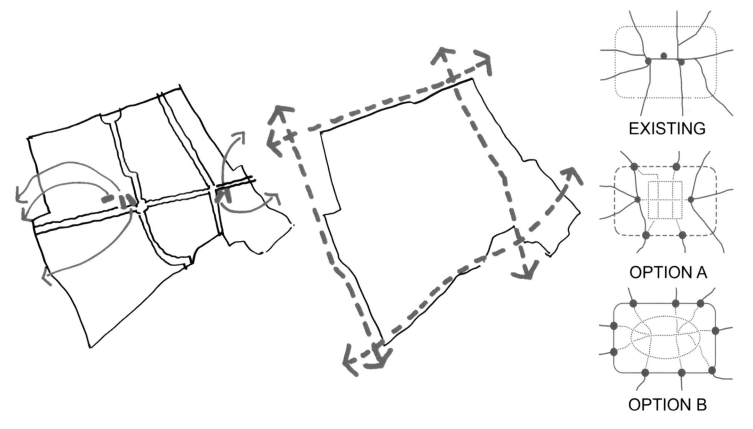

EXISTING

OPTION A

OPTION B

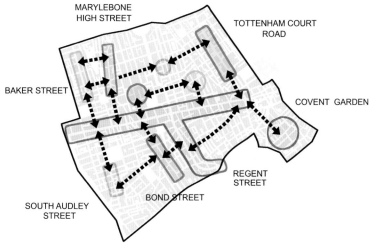

system will help people find their way on foot to counter the fact that comprehension of movement by foot is more hazy than the comprehension of movement by Underground. The campaign will include a walkable tube map which will help people to judge whether walking would be easier than going by tube.

Another map that has arisen from studies on walkability is the 'London Walking Distance', showing how a zone/pattern can be set up around tube stations that connects the tube 'villages' – tube stations become the village centres, 12 to 15 minutes around which there is a community of travellers. There is also a completely different kind of walking map, focusing on healthier places to walk by denoting less polluted areas. Interrelated with the physical health of the individual from exercise is the fact that

Top: Farrell, Further rationalisation, 2007
There is a need to further rationalise bus routes in central London, to minimise bus parking within the West End, minimise through routes, and rationalise route overlaps and duplications where possible.

Above: Farrell, Wayfinding diagram, 2007
It is necessary to improve wayfinding between existing retail destinations in Oxford Street to reveal hidden retail assets.

overall emissions and pollution will decrease if fewer people use cars. However, currently there is no doubt that there is a coincidence of walking and pollution. Along the busiest roads like the Marylebone-Euston Roads and Oxford Street, there is not only more traffic and more pollution next to more walkers, the traffic is also moving slower or standing still, leading to an accumulation of pollution at the points where there are more pedestrians.

Just as the tube's maps began to integrate and post-rationalise, in a reactive way, its own inner system, so city-wide it is becoming possible to correlate pollution maps, vehicle-traffic maps and people-moving maps to start drawing conclusions that are wide-reaching and fundamental to the health, happiness and welfare of those who live in London.

By Bike

Like the pedestrian, the cyclist has great flexibility of movement, but over a much wider range. By and large, although cycling is a pleasurable experience, most London cyclists, like everyone else on wheels, are pursuing an urban purpose, invariably going from A to B. They have the universal advantage that they can readily share all surfaces – roads, taxi lanes, pavements, one-way streets. Cycling has a flexibility and speed that makes it a very attractive option as a method for getting around town – and in my own office I have always made provision for a bicycle store, as it gives office workers a real option of a low-cost, quick and predictable method of transport. It is safer than other modes of transport in that it is less susceptible to terrorist attack, mechanical and electrical failures and so on, but at a price of constant exposure to the elements and the substantial dangers of not being in a

Rental bicycles in Place de la Bastille, Paris, 2007
A self-service kiosk for Vélib, the bicycle rental system in Paris. Ever inventive in public-service provision, the French have provided inspiration for London's recent mayors on ways of improving cycling as a means of transport within London.

London delivery boy on his bicycle, 1930
The bicycle has always been used as a service transport method, and continues to be a useful delivery vehicle around London today, for example where sandwiches arrive at the office via tricycles.

metal container when travelling at speed, so that any accidents, collisions or falls will have a far more serious outcome for cyclists than the vehicle they come up against.

Have cyclists influenced the patterns of London? Their little green lanes of tarmac have certainly affected the eye but, I suspect, very little of the patterns of movement, since cyclists view all surfaces as universally theirs, and rarely keep to their designated lanes. So do they really influence the public realm and the shape of our cities? Bicycle ranks and bicycle parks would, potentially, and so would hire bikes, Paris style, which could start to establish bike stations. Cycle stations, whether on the street or in office bike stores, provide safe and secure tethering space, and would make it easier to go shopping or get to the office by bike.

There has always been interchange between 'near neighbours' Paris and London on metropolitan developments. The ability of Paris to see the bigger, top-down benefits of larger ordering, with a more centralised, more powerful mayor, means that it leads London on ideas, such as centralised bike hire – just as it did earlier with the systemisation of coaches into the first omnibus service. London led more from the bottom up, for example with its pioneering engineering.

In Beijing, 10 to 15 years ago, I saw the impact of mass cycling upon road usage, but when I went there in spring 2008 it was noticeable how much of that cycle culture had disappeared. In Europe – particularly Copenhagen and Amsterdam – there is a strong cyclist presence, but mostly they behave quite similarly to pedestrians. The London cyclist – perhaps because of the greater commuting distances and the lack of pleasurable movement eliminating all those who are older or cycling for the purposes of leisure – is invariably travelling at speed on a set journey with crash helmet and lightweight bike. Whereas a continental European cyclist is closer to a walker, a London cyclist is closer to a car; the latter often seem to be focused on emulating the Tour de France and invariably are kitted out in a way that the Europeans and the Chinese have never taken to so much, with high-visibility outerwear, lights, 'Olympic velodrome' headgear, lycra leggings and reflectors on their cycling shoes and pedals, looking for all the world like spotted, luminous fish. The outfits speak volumes about the essential dangers of cycling and the lack of concern by the broader population driving cars, buses and lorries, or the managers of traffic. Until there is more planned provision for cyclists – dedicated routes through parks and primarily cycle-only tarmac streets – until there is a coherent strategy for all this then cycling in London will always be limited by the dangers caused by the bias towards other forms of traffic.

Ken Livingstone, during his term as Mayor of London, aimed to bring about new initiatives to aid cyclists and pedestrians, and these are being continued by his successor, Mayor Boris Johnson. In terms of bike stations, Livingstone aimed to introduce an organisational and spatial pattern through which 6,000 bikes would be available every 300 metres (984 feet). The current mayor also talks about a dozen radial cycling corridors, which are high-profile, easy-to-follow cycling streams into central London; of bike zones for shoppers and school runs; of cycle priority streets; and of 'streets of gold' by which key local destinations such as stations, schools and shops would be better linked for cycling and walking.

All of this is related to other organisational concepts, particularly to energy and green issues. Twenty per cent of the carbon emission savings that can be made by transport in London by 2025 will come from changing the way individuals travel – it is about getting more people to walk and cycle. For example, the mayor aims to have one in 10 Londoners making a round trip by bike per day, thereby saving some 1.6 million tonnes of CO_2 emissions, which is the equivalent of driving around the M25 55 million times per year – an interesting spatial equivalent to help conceptualise what this means. There is no doubt that this flexible low-energy, healthy movement mode is on a resurgent path. The balance – the tipping point in allowing for a more important role in urban planning – is, one feels, rather imminent.

On the Buses

The origin of buses begins with horse-drawn vehicles and also with road improvements. The first horse-drawn coach of any description was built for the Earl of Rutland in 1555 by Walter Rippon and was based on Continental models, as a four-wheeled coach with roof and some side protection. The first hackney coach was from 1625 (from the French *haquenée,* meaning an ambling horse), and was a one-horse chaise for hire from an inn. It was a springless box on wheels and the horse was driven by a seated rider. London's first 'coach stand' in the street was a rank for six hackney coaches at the Maypole in The Strand. By 1823 there were 1,200 hackney coach licences but these were soon followed in 1829 by Shillibeer's omnibus – about which more later.

To make sense of this urbanisation of horse travel for hire, the roads had to be improved in parallel. London's roads were largely unmaintained until the Highways Acts of 1555 which placed the responsibilities upon parishes. Longer distances between London's villages and parishes were addressed by the Highways Act of 1663 which led to the formation of turnpikes – literally controlled gates

giving access on payment of a toll or charge to improved sections of roads. By 1821, 28,968 kilometres (18,000 miles) of turnpike road had been established in England; and then eventually by 1878 all turnpike trusts were closed and responsibilities for road maintenance passed over to local government councils.

'The Railways' and 'The Tube – London Underground' chapters covered public transport systems that run on rails – the Underground system or tube and, of course, the mainline railways, both of which have had a fundamental effect on the invention and design of London as the great modern metropolis. It is somewhat debatable whether one could really put buses in the same category because they do a different thing: they are much freer spirits, operating with a greater fluidity as they are not restricted entirely to fixed lines in quite the same way. The modern bus map is a complete maze of densely packed routes, which are all subject to change if there are roadworks or changes

London stables, May 1911
Up to the mid 1920s, horse-drawn transport was still very dominant. Horses required stabling down mews and side roads. These small lanes were the predecessors to the car garaging and car servicing that exists today, continuing the tradition of the mews as a back-street transport servicing world.

of operational policies and planning. So they are somewhat of a hybrid between the freewheeling cyclists and motor cars, and the trains that are committed to travelling on rails. Of course, in the same category as the Underground, but on the surface of our roads, are trolley-buses and trams. As a principal form of transport in the capital, these came and went, although there are thoughts of bringing them back and there is a restricted tramline service running from Croydon to Wimbledon. By contrast, though, London's bus service has become so emblematic of the city that for many the single most iconic image of London is not a building, but a red bus. This was highlighted at the Beijing Olympics in 2008 when the most astonishing display of the Chinese national identity, expressed in a controlled exhibition of gymnastics, fireworks and lighting effects on a scale never seen before on global media, was followed by London's receipt of the Olympic torch for the 2012 Olympics in a solitary, modest red double-decker London bus!

In January 2009, I helped to judge a competition for the design of a symbolic gateway to London. The judges' final choice was a triumphal arch based on Edwin Lutyens's Thiepval Memorial on the Somme, built in 1932 to commemorate First World War soldiers missing in action, but here the arch was made up of Routemaster buses. The new Mayor, Boris Johnson, has made himself very popular by declaring that he wishes to replace the new Continental-style 'bendy buses' and bring back this particular double-decker bus that so iconically represents London.

The two things that the birth of the bus as a transport system depended upon were the evolution of the vehicle itself and the development of good road systems, with permission to operate in a certain way along these routes. Credit for much of what we have today belongs to George Shillibeer. He was originally a coach builder, which underlines that it was the invention of the vehicle that launched the system which has become a London-wide facility of widespread capability. The effectiveness and popularity of London buses continues to increase (6.4 million passenger journeys per weekday and around 2.2 billion annually), partly as a result of the former Mayor Ken Livingstone's initiatives and also partly due to the general public's recognition of their greater safety and reliability, compared with the Underground and rail systems which have been very slow to modernise and are more obvious terrorist targets.

A crowded horse-drawn bus, 1865

The first omnibuses which followed the Shillibeer pattern were the horse-drawn double-deckers. The knifeboard omnibus was one with a thin platform and seating on the roof, and was much like sitting outside up a ladder!

London omnibus, 1927

The motorised vehicle went through various phases: steam powered, electric powered and eventually settling into the petrol-driven, internal combustion engine. Seen here at Piccadilly Circus is a double-decker with an enclosed top.

London Transport bogie tram, 1920–6
Bearing an advert for Guinness, with an
overhead trolley pole, the tram is bound
for Tooting Broadway via Clapham. The
brief life of trams was eventually much
regretted and is now being reintroduced
in many British cities such as Edinburgh,
Nottingham, Sheffield and Manchester.
Unlike European cities like Prague and
some northern German towns that have
continued their use right through to the
present day, in Britain only Blackpool
continued using trams without interruption.

Before Shillibeer invented the bus and began his bus operation, he helped build horse-drawn coaches that operated separately between stages, usually over long distances and invariably pre-booked. On a trip to Paris in the 1820s he was struck by the way the French were developing extra-large buses, which they called omnibuses, and a network of new routes. The French really should be credited with the birth of the modern omnibus system, where a coach ran on a fixed route but passengers could board and alight anywhere along it. The word 'omnibus' is reputed to have derived from a business slogan – 'Omnes omnibus' – from the terminus at Mr Omnes's shop in Nantes where the idea originated before it was brought to Paris. By 1828 the Parisian system was carrying 300 paying passengers a day. Shillibeer came back to London and built a giant coach, a 20-seater with the name 'omnibus' on the side panel. Prevented from running it on the hackney coach routes, he then took advantage of the New Road that ran from Paddington to the City, where he was free to operate. Paddington has long been a very important transport node, with the Roman Watling Street, the canal basin, the train station, the Westway motorway and the high-speed rail link to Heathrow all becoming established there at various points in history.

On 4 July 1829, Shillibeer began a service that ran from the Yorkshire Stingo Inn in Paddington to the Bank of England, with four services in each direction daily. The vehicle was extra wide for stability and to accommodate a large number of passengers, and was drawn by three horses. Rival companies began to compete along the New Road so that, by the early 1830s, 90 omnibuses were running up and down the road at three-minute intervals. The need for a system and some control was gradually realised

and so inspectors were placed at key locations along the route to prevent total chaos. Within only five years there were 620 horse-drawn buses licensed in London, which doubled again by 1850. Their progress was aided by the lifting of restrictive practices, the building of new bridges across the Thames at Waterloo, Southwark and Vauxhall, and the widening of new thoroughfares, allowing greater access. An omnibus guide published at the time of the Great Exhibition in 1851 shows 150 different routes serving the capital. Four years later, the London General Omnibus Company was founded to amalgamate many of the London services.

A Routemaster bus on route 159
Driving over Westminster Bridge in London. The last journey of a scheduled crew-operated Routemaster on route 159 was in December 2005, terminating at Brixton Garage. This was the iconic bus that became the premier symbol for London eclipsing even Big Ben, Tower Bridge and other 'building' icons.

There were experiments with steam buses which went on for quite some time and continued right up until the invention of the internal combustion engine, but probably the most important early development that had a permanent long-term effect on the evolution of the buses was the birth of the double-decker in the 1840s. The practice of virtually climbing on to the roofs of busy buses was institutionalised in the redesign of the vehicles, with proper upstairs seating and metal rungs, which were followed by primitive staircases. Thus, the essential characteristic of the London double-decker bus, which London has somehow hung on to for nearly two centuries, was born.

With railways bringing increasing numbers of people into the centre at the mainline stations, the demand for a network of distributive roads to get travellers to their final destination on buses increased throughout the 19th century. The nature of the roads themselves changed, with tolls and gates gradually eliminated under the wave of mobile humanity. Buses got bigger, taking 26 passengers, with 12 on the bottom and 14 on top. At the horse-coach's peak, about 50,000 horses were being used in London's transport system, but inventiveness moved on to look at the horseless bus, including electric and steam-powered alternatives. By 1914, the National Steam Car Company was running 184 steam-powered buses in London, but their day was already nearly done. The London General Omnibus Company began using motor buses in 1902, phasing out their horse-coaches by 1911, and reached an agreement with the National Steam Car Company to put an end to steam buses in 1919. Meanwhile, London's first fully operational electric tram service began in 1901 and within a couple of years about 300 trams were operating in the capital.

This evolutionary sequence of vehicle inventiveness was accompanied by a fresh rationalising process of management and organisation. In 1933 the London General Omnibus Company and various independent organisations were brought together under the control of the London Passenger Transport Board, known as London Transport, as one overall unified company which coordinated services and fares, routes, ticketing and so on for all rail and road services. This coordination was led by figures such as Lord Ashfield and Frank Pick, who were both members of the London Transport Board, and Herbert Morrison, the former Labour transport minister who, in 1934, became leader of the London County Council. In 1934 there were 6,000 buses being run by London Transport, carrying two million passengers in a network of 4,023 kilometres (2,500 miles) of bus and coach routes in over 5,180 sqaure kilometres (2,000 square miles) of territory. By contrast, London Transport decided to phase out the more inflexible and expensive-to-maintain electric tram service.

The extent to which the bus system became incrementally more logical and integrated was demonstrated by the fact that, although the buses ran on fixed routes before the 1930s, it was not until then that the idea of fixed bus stops became universally adopted. Until then a bus would pick up passengers and set them down anywhere along the route. Step by step, bus shelters, unified ticketing, standardised vehicles and overall unity gradually coalesced into a metropolitan service.

Today, the bus service is a tremendously important part of London's efficiency and the mobility of its people. Bus stops have progressed to become points of electronic information. Ticketing has become unified across not only the bus networks; Oyster cards have linked them with other forms of transport such as the tube

Traffic in Regent Street, 1900

At the turn of the 20th century, traffic was primarily horse-drawn. This being Regent Street, people were in fairly formal dress. In the distance is a horse-drawn bus, and there are also delivery and private carriages, along with a cyclist. The street benefits from street lighting and is paved, albeit cobbled!

and mainline rail. Plastic cards have overtaken cash payment and buses operate without conductors, with one person driving and in control of the entire vehicle. The great appeal of the bus, and the reason it survived while the life of trams and trolley-buses was relatively short, is its great flexibility. No doubt, with the arrival of low-energy electric vehicles and improvements in integrating all the systems, particularly passenger information, the future of the bus will continue to improve and consolidate itself. But if the vehicles have continuously advanced and progressed, there has been much controversy over the management and organisation of the routes themselves.

The bus garages and stations, in both their location and purpose, seem to have driven the perspective of the managers in such a way that some, including myself, see the system as a fundamentally supply-led operation. Due to its considerable flexibility, the bus can arrive and depart in a variety of ways in a variety of locations and change from time to time. However, the so-called Shillibeer routes principle which has been adopted is, in its basic simplicity, one where the major routes cross London from an outer point, right through the centre to another outer point on the opposite side, so the north connects to south and the east to west and so on. Consequently, the great bus-station heritage of London lies on the outer perimeter, where depots are all set in a necklace around the city. There are depots at Epping, Peckham, Camberwell, Harrow, Hackney, Romford and Mortlake, with the most glorious of them all – a 59-metre (194-foot) concrete-spanned bus garage – at Stockwell.

The radiality of these routes creates an inherent inflexibility, as does the congestion at the centre. Recent studies in Oxford Street have shown that the amount of buses far exceeds the actual demand for travelling short distances in the centre, and the number of buses on the streets is causing considerable congestion as they travel through the centre outwards to some far distant place at the opposite side of London to where they began their journey. There have been arguments that the buses should form loop routes, leaving the centre free from the long-distance buses, while inner roads like Oxford Street would be served by smaller shuttle buses or trams providing a local city-centre-only service. This would mirror London's adoption of congestion charging and the treatment of the centre as being 'different'.

One thing that has always surprised me is the inherent flexibility of bus stations along the route. In the 1980s, I was involved in planning the bus station at Hammersmith for the Greater London Council (GLC), which could either consolidate all the buses in one mega-station or disperse them into lots of stops around the edge. The precise niceties of length of travel set against inspectors, surveillance and monitoring made for a fascinating interchange between the town centre of Hammersmith, the arrangements of its shopping, offices, tube station and buses and pedestrian movement itself. What was always apparent was that while the underground lines were inflexible, the buses were almost as flexible as pedestrians themselves and many different permutations of the arrangement were perceived. The positioning of stations and garages is a bone of contention in many urban centres. It was a short time ago that I was involved in the redesign of Preston town centre, a relatively small Lancastrian town with a population of a mere 130,000, which managed to have the largest bus station in Europe! This was because the managers, operators and inspectors perceived that they wanted the system to work from one place, with all the buses brought back to one point. There is such a range of organisational models for this most flexible of public transport modes.

Throughout the bus service nationally, there has to be a rethinking and rebalancing of the desires of bus management teams and the logic of the system. In London, we need to reassess the relationship of bus routes to the central shopping streets, particularly along Oxford Street right through to Holborn and the City. Recent studies of Oxford Street/Tottenham Court Road have shown that with the arrival of the new Crossrail train system there is going to be a degree of pedestrian congestion that nullifies all additional public transport improvements, simply because the pavements and the streets are not big enough. The surface streets of London cannot contain the number of people that will be brought in. It is clear that something has to give and, as it should be inherently more flexible than other transport infrastructures, the bus system is likely to be one of the components that will have to adjust and change in the way it operates.

In my home town of Newcastle, road transport remains one of the most unresolved areas of modern urban planning. I arrived in Newcastle in the 1940s and the city's transport system was substantially based on trams, as it was in London, with tramlines in the streets, cables in the air and an efficient infrastructure in place. In the 1950s, in virtually all British cities, traffic engineers decided to modernise by replacing trams with trolley-buses, which are really trams on fixed lines with overhead cables, but with rubber tyres – indeed, they were at first called 'trackless trams'. These seemed to last a relatively short time: trolley-buses disappeared from London in 1962, just 10 years after trams had been removed, and were succeeded by the universal adoption of motorised buses.

In so many British cities of late, the tram has begun to have a revival, with services returning to Manchester, Sheffield and Nottingham. The only British town that has continually had trams is Blackpool, but throughout Europe, in cities like Prague, the tram service has been unbroken despite motorisation. There have been plans for tram routes to be reintroduced to London, but they come and go, ebb and fade. In 2003 the then Mayor of London, Ken Livingstone, pioneered a plan for a tram running 21 kilometres (13 miles) up the Uxbridge Road, linking Shepherd's Bush with

Traffic on a London street, 1912
A typical secondary London street of the time with motor cars mingling with an open-topped double-decker bus, horse traffic, a bicycle and pedestrian; a properly laid-out road with clear pavements and kerbs.

Uxbridge. It was, however, met with resounding local protest in areas such as Acton and Ealing, as it was feared that road traffic would be pushed further into the residential side roads. Such was the weight of public opposition that it was eventually quashed in August 2007. A tram service may benefit from its ability to be adapted or reintroduced without huge infrastructural turmoil and disruption, but there are many problems with bringing trams back. Congestion is now much greater, while health and safety requirements for platforms and the visual intrusion of overhead poles and cables in areas of enhanced awareness of conservation all diminish the prospect of it ever taking place in the metropolis.

In conclusion, the pattern, the distribution and the workings of London's buses have interacted with the historical and modern shape of London in a fascinating, layered way. The tube and mainline railways have by definition run in linear paths of limited and specialised routing systems. If one were to liken the plan of London to a tree, they form the trunk and the branches. But the finer twigs, leaves and minute details of London at a local level have been developed, based on and absolutely integrated with the bus system, which is the public transport lifeblood for the city's corners, neighbourhoods, hamlets and local streets. It is the system that has the closest affinity with the pedestrian, who often uses it to reach tube and rail stations as well as final destinations. The bus system grew with the 19th-century need to move the mass, the bulk, the extraordinary growth of people, and continues to provide the bulk of the hydraulics for the overall transport system.

Once again, the unique character of London's early emergence as a metropolis is imbued in its transport system, and vice versa. Cities such as Hong Kong had a different progression – the linear path of its Mass Transit Railway system (developed 150 years after the London bus) follows the line of development, so it is possible for most people to be able to walk to it from their flats in the high-density buildings above and around the metro stations. Other cities such as Los Angeles and Houston developed hand in hand with the motor car, and with that went multi-lane freeways, underpasses, vast parking spaces at the point of destination and, of course, plenty of garage space at home. None of this balance was developed in 19th-century London. Unlike in Hong Kong, the streets of outer London spread out over a vast field like a micro-maze; without the bus the typical London suburban house and garden arrangement could not have emerged. The kind of streets we have, and the way we relate to corner shops, pubs and high streets is very much a bus-based system.

The bus has a universality of distribution across the pattern field of the whole of the metropolis, while there is also some universality in class, social status and age range of its passengers – if you look at a bus stop, you see schoolchildren, students, old-age pensioners. However, poorer people, of course, tend to outnumber the middle classes who travel by tube, taxi and private car. It is this ability to scoop in and liberate the mobility of those with limited means and less central locations that led to the 1980s' Thatcherite suggestion, sometimes mistakenly attributed to Margaret Thatcher herself, that anybody who uses the bus after the age of 26 is a failure in life. All cities need the masses to be mobile and none needs them more than the wealthy businesspeople who want their staff to get to work on time, to the factory, desk and dealing-room floor. For 180 years, the bus has played its part in creating an economic powerhouse and has made an enormous and formative contribution to London's shape and form.

Commuters on London Bridge, 1993
With London Bridge Station on the wrong side of the river, pedestrian traffic flows through during the rush hour. The pedestrians on the pavements flood towards the station that carries more passengers in one hour than Heathrow Airport does in a day. They are segregated on the pavement in all weathers with the buses and cars stacked right beside them.

Occupying the Land

Landscapes, Parks and Gardens

The Great Rural Metropolis

It is impossible to examine the current condition of London's landscape and the patterns that inform it without reflecting first on Britain's particular cultural relationship with its natural setting: landscape being deeply rooted in the British individual and collective sense of place. Fortuitously positioned on an island, Britain has not suffered invasion for almost a thousand years and has been relatively peaceful internally for many hundreds of years. This has enabled a way of life, or rather a manner of human settlement, to develop here that incorporates an open and welcoming attitude to nature, the elements and wilderness. This has been further shored up by the fact that as an island race the British have had to have a very positive attitude towards the seas, the oceans and exploration.

Britain's status as pioneers in the natural sciences, particularly the scientific study of plant and animal life, coincided with the height of the British Empire in the 18th and 19th centuries, as epitomised by scientists like Joseph Banks (1743–1820), the British explorer and naturalist, who was for many years the president of the Royal Society. In 1768 Banks joined the expedition led by Captain James Cook to explore the South Pacific in the *Endeavour* (1769–71) and *HMS Resolution* (1772–5 and 1776–9), and in the next century his explorations were followed by Charles Darwin in the *HMS Beagle* (1831–6). There has also long been an internal British interest in nature and wildlife, typified not only by the popularity of plant collecting in the 16th and 17th centuries and the establishment of botanical gardens, but also by the various voluntary bodies protecting and studying birds, beasts, parklands and forests.

The British have a passionate, intense, scientific and romantic love of the countryside and nature, and the relationship is one of openness and inclusiveness with the natural world. This to a large degree has been influenced by Britain's long-term status as a single political unit, as a nation state encompassing town and countryside; the landed gentry, the second tier of power from the medieval to the 19th century, governing through their great country estates.

Previous page: Aerial photo showing the centre of power in London
Whitehall and Trafalgar Square (out of picture) to the right and Parliament Square to the left. In the immediate foreground are the Treasury, Foreign Office, Ministry of Defense and Horse Guards' Parade. In the mid distance is Buckingham Palace with the parklands of St James's and Green Park.

Blackheath Common, 1993
This fine open space sits partially within the UNESCO World Heritage Site of Greenwich (top right).

Until the 19th century, many of the countries of Continental Europe, such as Italy and Germany, remained divided up into city states, subject to invasion, and their fortifications reflected these civic boundaries. The enduring consequence of this political difference is that the instability of the European urban condition created a defensive relationship to what lies beyond the city walls; even the smallest villages in France have a fortified attitude and mentality, each with a clear physical perimeter that is overseen politically by its own individual commune led by a mayor. This is countered culturally in Europe by a greater sense of collective togetherness, a foundation for the cultures of urbanity, making it stronger for that – the Vienna of Mozart was laid siege by the Turks, while the Paris of the Impressionist painters was at war with Germany and, later, that of Picasso and Le Corbusier was conquered by Germany in the 1940s. For mainland Europeans, the town square and their art and culture have developed in intense consolidation, so that an essentially urban character underlies their creativity.

One only has to compare the typical French country village with an English one to see the difference between the compactness of the former and the open-endedness of the latter, where the fields come right up to and merge with the village, where the street itself is the open meandering marketplace, and where the focus is often a crossroads, where the roads lead straight through

Johannes Kip, after Leonard Knyff, Garden design of Kensington Palace, 18th century
Showing the formal layout of the gardens for the royal palace. Connected near gardens, far gardens and avenues – one total composition.

and onwards, in a way that many a resident of suburbia would recognise today. This historical blurring of the built environment and the landscape is what led us to the Garden Cities movement in the early 20th century and the postwar New Towns. It is what has led us to believe that making a pact with the countryside, to bring the countryside into the town, is a necessity of urban life.

The British relationship with the landscape is also a key to understanding the value that the British have placed on the garden that goes with the house; as well as the very high regard within which the British people hold the house as their castle – over the town or village. The independence of the individual can be conceived as being attached to his or her natural setting rather than the community. This idea flows down as a cultural pattern from the top echelons of society. Even today we can see the long tradition of English monarchs regarding their town life as an exception – Buckingham Palace is only occupied for a small part of the year by the royal family, who prefer to live at Windsor, Balmoral or Sandringham. For the aristocracy, who set the pace of culture for so long, 'home' was the great country house. They only came to town for 'the season' and, to some extent, they still behave like that. Therefore, it is not surprising that, while they were living in London, they wanted elements of the country there as well. So the royal family established hunting grounds right in what is now the centre and hunted where Hyde and Regent's parks now are, while deer herds continue today to roam in Richmond Park, within the walled enclosure of its wide space. The idea that the monarch could be out and about chasing wild animals with horse and hounds right next to Hyde Park Corner was a surprisingly real one for the British. The urban aristocracy continued this relationship to nature when they developed their great urban estates with squares and gardens.

London itself grew from villages and rural hamlets. It rapidly became a metropolis in the 19th century, without going through the normal evolutionary stage of being a city. All the elements of villages such as Barnes, Hampstead, Highgate, Richmond and Wimbledon are still there and the commons and woodlands of these places are all part of what some might think of today as a fantasy of countryside. London is very different from Paris or New York and indeed is half the density of those two cities. While

Hyde Park Corner, 1985
The nodal point where Buckingham Palace, Green Park and Hyde Park all meet. For many decades, until the end of the 20th century, connection was impossible but, with advocacy and argument to promote surface connections, it is now possible to travel through the great arch (Wellington Arch) and link all these parks back together again.

Paris's Luxembourg Gardens and New York's Central Park are designed, geometric and proudly 'man-made', the Royal Parks of London, the commons, the woodlands and even the communal gardens of Maida Vale and Ladbroke Grove are for all the world like pieces of trapped countryside. With or without deer, they have a rambling, naturalistic look, suggesting that village life dominates London. A corollary of this is that London does not have a formal public realm: it does not have paved squares of the quantity and sort that you expect to see in the rest of Europe, and it does not have the boulevards of Paris or Berlin. Indeed, the only indications of a clearly connected-up public realm are these trapped pieces of countryside.

Hampstead Ponds and South Hill Park, 1991

The landscape of Hampstead is dominated by Hampstead Heath, Hampstead Ponds and South Hill Park. The surrounding residential areas take advantage of the characteristics of this landscape. Recognised for centuries as a healthy respite from the dirt and pollution of London.

It is one of the extraordinary contradictions and great joys of London that this, the first great metropolis, is dedicated to making itself allied to countryside and nature rather than to man and the manufactured. The fact that the Royal Parks and the commons and woods are the public realm makes our way of life as a civil society different in so many ways, including how we regard ourselves as urbanists. Even the word 'urban' has a negativity in London that I do not believe is found in the rest of Europe. Once, when I was talking about urban design at a presentation in Cambridge, the leader of the council asked me not to use the term 'urban' as it brings up ideas of crime, hooligans, pollution and traffic jams! The very idea of a city being linked to the word

Aerial view of Kensington Gardens, 1993

The more formal layout of Kensington Gardens and its relationship with Kensington Palace, now walled in and enclosed as a semi-private group of residences with limited access for the public. It needs to be opened up, much like Hampton Court, to once again make it one fine, total composition.

Greenwich Park, 1993

Part of the great Greenwich Palace
complex showing the parklands beyond
the collection of buildings, often called
Britain's Versailles.

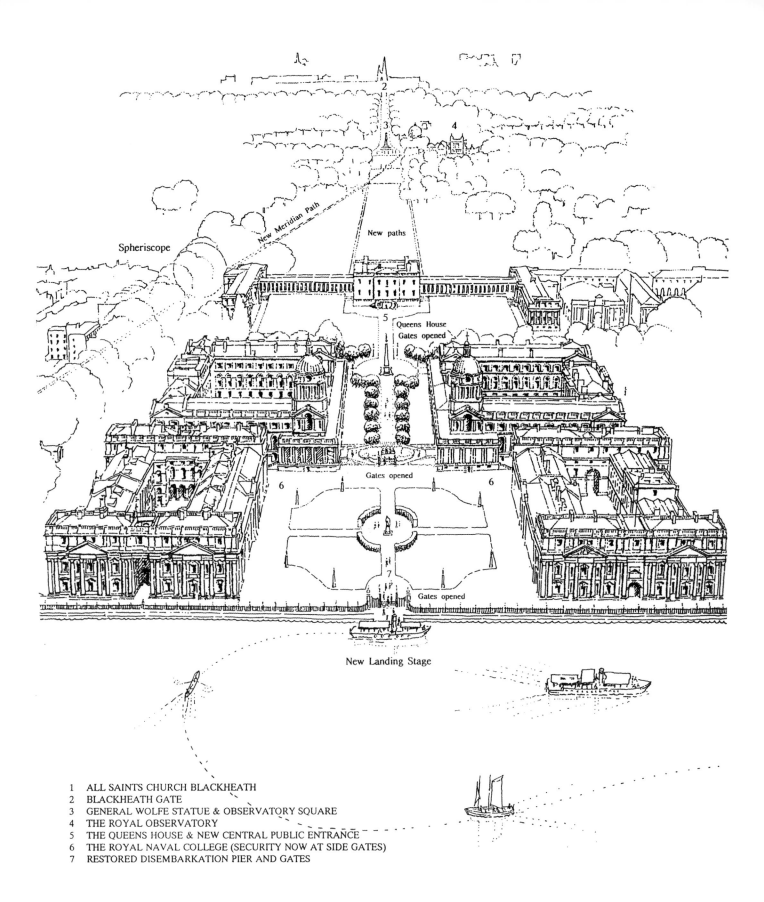

Spheriscope

New Meridian Path

New paths

Queens House
Gates opened

5

Gates opened

6   6

Gates opened

7

New Landing Stage

1   ALL SAINTS CHURCH BLACKHEATH
2   BLACKHEATH GATE
3   GENERAL WOLFE STATUE & OBSERVATORY SQUARE
4   THE ROYAL OBSERVATORY
5   THE QUEENS HOUSE & NEW CENTRAL PUBLIC ENTRANCE
6   THE ROYAL NAVAL COLLEGE (SECURITY NOW AT SIDE GATES)
7   RESTORED DISEMBARKATION PIER AND GATES

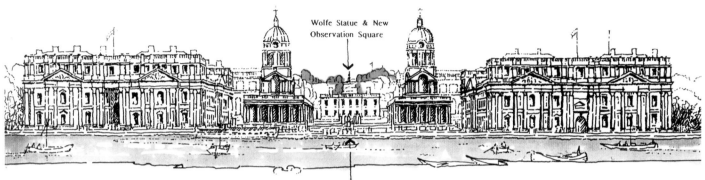

Wolfe Statue & New
Observation Square

New restored Disembarkation Pier, Landing Stage
and gates on Axial Vista.

'garden', as in Ebenezer Howard's early 20th-century 'Garden Cities' of Letchworth and Welwyn, could only have emanated, I think, from a British mind.

Reconnecting the Landscape

Inevitably, of course, there are contradictions in all of this, including within the manner that Londoners perceive themselves and use the city. London is a vast metropolis of eight million people (and growing) and it is full of cars, underground trains, office towers and large housing estates – there is no getting away from the fact that it is urban. Within this setting, the parks have transformed themselves but in a very gradual, evolutionary way. Britain does not have a taste for revolution, so unlike Versailles and the great gardens of Paris or the royal and aristocratic lands of Russia, such as at St Petersburg, the Royal Parks were not transferred to public ownership in a sudden historical moment.

Here, the monarch still reigns and there is some continuous idea that somehow the Queen, her predecessors and successors have some residual rights and can ride through Regent's Park and Hyde Park with a degree of implied ownership. In fact, the transfer of the Royal Parks to public ownership reveals a kind of limbo state, neither public nor the Crown palaces fully resolve their layouts. Many of the great houses and palaces of the Crown, such as Hampton Court, Kensington Palace, St James's Palace, Buckingham Palace and the assorted palaces of Greenwich, were laid out with a wonderful continuity between residence and landscape, with formal avenues leading to paved entry courts, and through great halls to great state rooms and apartments that then led outside to private gardens that gradually increased in size until they came to the openness of the park itself, with paths leading outwards into the more rural countryside beyond. However, with the gradual transference of all these parks to the commoner, palaces have walled themselves in: the connectivity between street, palace and park has been interrupted so that all these buildings sit in a semi-fortified way, protected by the array of modern security methods. For instance, the perimeter of Buckingham Palace, with its high walls, barbed wire, metal railings, etc, leads one to ask who is besieging whom? Who is free and who is imprisoned? The great set pieces of the designer/ architect/landscape planner are reduced in grandeur and vision to a much more impoverished level.

Opposite: Farrell, Proposed
axial progression at Greenwich
Palace and Park, 1994
Above: Farrell, Proposed views
from the River Thames, 1994
Restoring the original vista through
the Royal Naval College to the
Queen's House.

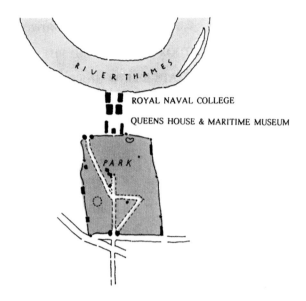

It is not so much a matter of whether the monarch should or would want to get the grounds back, it is more a matter of calling into question an unsatisfactory lack of continuity. Hampton Court is fully public, managed by the charitable foundation Historic Royal Palaces, and of all the palaces remains the best connected to wider landscape and its closer gardens, but even so, it is now a separate entity from its former parkland of Bushy Park. The buildings at Greenwich once formed a wonderfully composed integrated set piece featuring the work of all the great architects of the 17th century – Christopher Wren, Nicholas Hawksmoor and Inigo Jones – but there is no obvious continuity to Greenwich Park, which was also planted out in the early 1600s by James I in a French style with many trees. There is today a degree of gated separateness to the component elements, with the busy Woolwich Road interrupting everything. It would be wonderful to land at a pier at Greenwich again and walk through all the great buildings and the avenues, through Inigo Jones's Queen's House (1614–17) and up the hill to Wren's Observatory (1675) and the great avenue beyond it, which is one of the most wonderful axes in Britain. But bureaucracy, limited vision and demarcations of management have separated and compartmentalised the whole composition.

The monarch's grasp may have been prised away from the parks but we are in a halfway state in which no one can really enjoy the glory of all of it. Their fragmented handover to public bodies has resulted in a half-hearted, poorly appreciated inhabitation by the common man. During the early 1990s I wrote various papers on how these parks could be reconnected for greater enjoyment and successfully campaigned for the parks themselves to be joined up with the rest of London. Their edges may not always be fortified by walls, but perversely their enclosure-like feel led them to be bordered by highways – the roads and pedestrian underpasses of Park Lane, Hyde Park Corner and Marble Arch, which physically encroached upon the former parkland, making the parks as inaccessible as any wall could do. Now, with the introduction of surface crossings within these streets, the parks are beginning to be understood as part of the public realm and seen as part of connected set pieces.

The desire to re-establish these connections has led me of late to develop a plan to restore and improve the accessibility of John Nash's great route up the West End. Nash, sponsored by the Prince Regent (later King George IV) in the early 19th century, masterplanned a route all the way from St James's Park, right up Regent's Street to Regent's Park. Its most visible manifestation can be seen today in Nash's masterful All Souls Church, Langham Place (1822–5), that with its circular portico and elegant spire enables the termination of the north–south axis up Regent's Street while swinging around the boot leg into Portland Place that leads to Park Crescent and Regent's Park.

Above and opposite: Farrell, Proposed axis re-linking the grand architectural composition of river, palace and park at Greenwich, 1994 Gated and separate today, the plan restores the axial progression from river pier through the palace grounds to the park and up to the grand axial avenue at Blackheath.

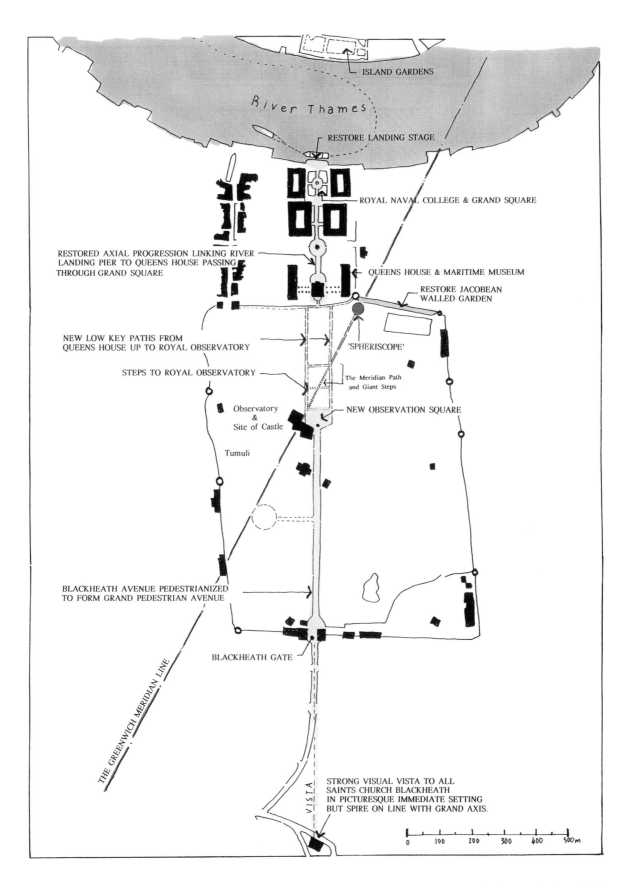

ISLAND GARDENS

River Thames

RESTORE LANDING STAGE

ROYAL NAVAL COLLEGE & GRAND SQUARE

RESTORED AXIAL PROGRESSION LINKING RIVER
LANDING PIER TO QUEENS HOUSE PASSING
THROUGH GRAND SQUARE

QUEENS HOUSE & MARITIME MUSEUM

RESTORE JACOBEAN
WALLED GARDEN

NEW LOW KEY PATHS FROM
QUEENS HOUSE UP TO ROYAL OBSERVATORY

'SPHERISCOPE'

STEPS TO ROYAL OBSERVATORY

The Meridian Path
and Giant Steps

NEW OBSERVATION SQUARE

Observatory
&
Site of Castle

Tumuli

BLACKHEATH AVENUE PEDESTRIANIZED
TO FORM GRAND PEDESTRIAN AVENUE

THE GREENWICH MERIDIAN LINE

BLACKHEATH GATE

VISTA

STRONG VISUAL VISTA TO ALL
SAINTS CHURCH BLACKHEATH
IN PICTURESQUE IMMEDIATE SETTING
BUT SPIRE ON LINE WITH GRAND AXIS.

0   100   200   300   400   500m

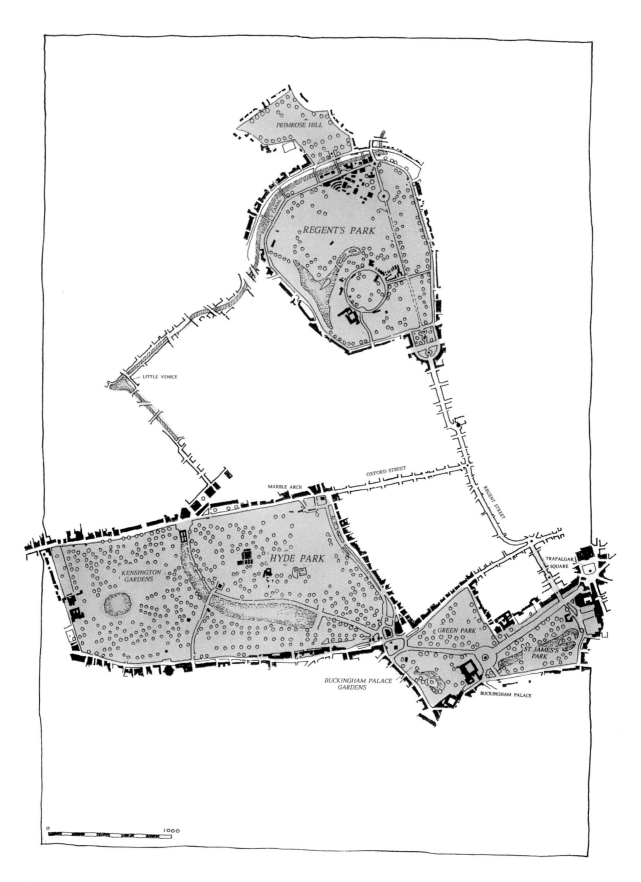

PRIMROSE HILL

REGENT'S PARK

REGENTS CANAL

LITTLE VENICE

OXFORD STREET

MARBLE ARCH

REGENT STREET

TRAFALGAR SQUARE

HYDE PARK

KENSINGTON GARDENS

GREEN PARK

ST JAMES'S PARK

BUCKINGHAM PALACE GARDENS

BUCKINGHAM PALACE

0   1000

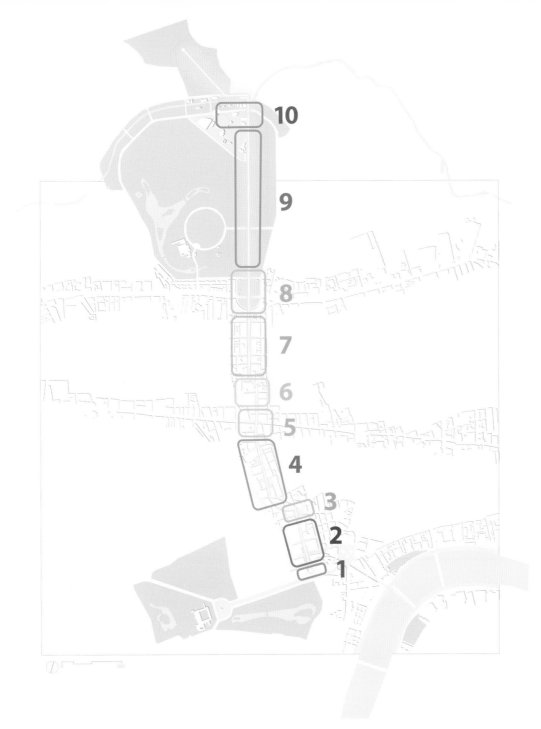

10 **9** **8** **7** **6** **5** **4** **3** **2** **1**

3. Piccadilly Circus. Studies are in progress to turn this landmark and meeting point into a real place for people.

4. Regent Street. Public realm improvements arising from a partnership of the Crown Estate and the City of Westminster to improve the quality of the environment.

5. Oxford Circus. Through the Oxford, Regent and Bond Street (ORB) Action Plan in partnership with Transport for London, the City of Westminster and the New West End Commission, Oxford Circus is to be made a pedestrian-friendly environment with diagonal crossings on all red traffic light phase.

6. BBC. Investment in the public realm by local stakeholders, including the BBC, University of Westminster and the Langham Hotel together with public-sector initiatives on wayfinding and public art will transform this section of the Nash Ramblas.

7. Portland Place. To create a new pedestrian walk down the centre of Portland Place, to once again make it one of the West End's grandest and loveliest avenues.

8. Park Crescent/Park Square. To create a new pedestrian route through Park Crescent and Park Square and across the Euston Road to form a new entrance to Regent's Park, and to connect the park, tube station, Euston Road and Portland Place.

9. Regent's Park. Reinforce the strength and significance of Nash's masterplan by improving north–south links. To enable cyclists to share part of the route, road crossings and facilities should also be transformed.

10. London Zoo. New masterplan will move the entrance to 'New Square' sites on the Broadwalk, giving direct access to the zoo from the Nash Ramblas.

Opposite: Farrell, Proposal for pedestrian links between Regent's Park, Kensington Gardens, Hyde Park, Buckingham Palace Gardens, Green Park and St James's Park, 1994
Ongoing proposal for the connectivity of the public realm and making the Royal Parks a true focus of the public realm in London.

Above: Farrell, The Nash Ramblas, a Farrell proposition to rediscover the route that formed John Nash's original set-piece masterplan from The Mall to the royal hunting grounds in the north of the city. This new public promenade, like the renowned Las Ramblas in Barcelona, would run from Regent's Park down to Waterloo Place, 2008

1. Nash Plan/monument. In celebration of John Nash, it is proposed to erect a 3-D model of the original Nash plan and buildings.

2. Waterloo Place. The Crown Estates and English Heritage have put forward detailed plans to restore the grandeur and pedestrian-friendly environment of this fine public thoroughfare.

The Central Royal Parks

The inner parks are quite different, of course, from the outer parks: they are much more truly part of the urban public realm. Each park has its own character. The 36 hectares (90 acres) of St James's Park – the oldest of the Royal Parks, acquired by Henry VIII in 1532 as a deer park and the site of the Palace of St James's – was originally marshland, where the Tyburn river flooded out and isolated the Palace of Westminster creating Thorney Island. The area was drained by Henry and laid out with formal gardens by James I to create the park, which is delightfully full of exotic birds

Park Crescent and Park Square, 1984
To celebrate the 200-year anniversary of John Nash's first plan for Regent's Park in 1812 there are proposals to create a pathway linking Park Crescent and Park Square as part of Farrell's Nash Ramblas.

such as pelicans. Surrounded by royal palaces – with St James's Palace and Clarence House to the north and Buckingham Palace dominating the west – it is very much the Royal Park, the state park. Green Park connects St James's Park to Hyde Park, which to most people's minds forms one enormous landscape with Kensington Gardens, although the latter's contrasting formality is still obvious in its tree-lined avenues and the regular outline of the Round Pond. Between the park and the gardens sits the Serpentine, which is the dammed line of the Westbourne river and takes a river-like shape (see 'The Tributaries' chapter for more on the Westbourne). At one end, the Italian gardens, in true London collage style, introduce an isolated and separate element of formalism.

This patchwork of formalism set within an informal landscape is very akin to an approach to urbanism that Nash and his one-time partner, the landscape architect Humphry Repton, always recognised. At Regent's Street and the route to Regent's Park, Nash was forced to work with the 'capabilities', as Capability Brown would call them, of the given terrain, rather than imposing the sort of man-made and unnatural geometric order epitomised by the classical gardens of Europe. Today, Regent's Park, to the north of Hyde Park, has moved from an aristocratic, gated enclosure to a public domain – with universities, colleges, the zoo, vast areas of football grounds and indeed a sports centre set within it, as well as continuing to house privately occupied villas and townhouses.

Cafés, restaurants, art galleries and theatres are permanent public presences in the parks and there is also an increasing recognition that, as parks are part of the public realm of the capital, they should provide a location for large-scale one-off

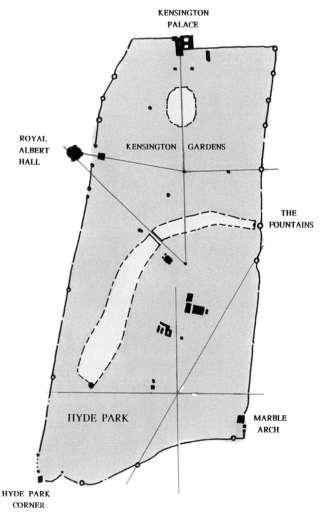

KENSINGTON
PALACE

ROYAL
ALBERT
HALL

KENSINGTON   GARDENS

THE
FOUNTAINS

HYDE PARK

MARBLE
ARCH

HYDE PARK
CORNER

the two best-known formal urban design set pieces in London: Exhibition Road with it universities and museums all the way up to Hyde Park, and Regent's Street which links St James's and Regent's parks. Increasingly, the great public realm of the central parks is being used for annual events such as the Frieze Art Fair with its tented campus in Regent's Park, major concerts in Hyde Park from the Rolling Stones to classical performances, and gatherings for large events, such as the broadcasting from Westminster Abbey of Princess Diana's funeral in 1997. The next great triumph of the parks as venues will be during the 2012 Olympics, with the triathlon in Hyde Park, cycling in Regent's Park, horse riding in Greenwich Park and beach volleyball at Horse Guards Parade alongside St James's Park.

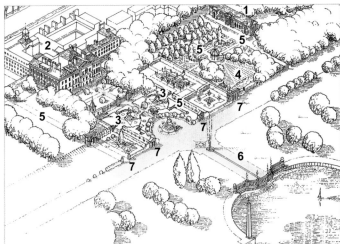

and seasonal events. The most famous of these was the Great Exhibition of 1851 in Joseph Paxton's Crystal Palace located on the south side of Hyde Park, where the tennis courts and bowling green are today. The event, led by Queen Victoria's consort, Prince Albert, influenced the layout of the whole of South Kensington's Exhibition Road and the formation of the great museums area. Consequently, it was royalty who directly influenced probably

Farrell, Links from Kensington Gardens and Hyde Park to the urban townscape beyond, 1994
A patchwork of formal links to the world beyond set within a largely formal landscape.

Farrell, Restoration of links between Kensington Palace and Kensington Gardens, 1994
The big idea underlying these detailed proposals, of reopening Palace to Park, is now being realised.

Key:
1. Hawksmoor's Orangery
2. Kensington Palace
3. New topiary gardens extending into the park
4. New sunken garden
5. New landscaped paths on to the Broad Walk
6. New direct link to the Round Pond
7. New gates

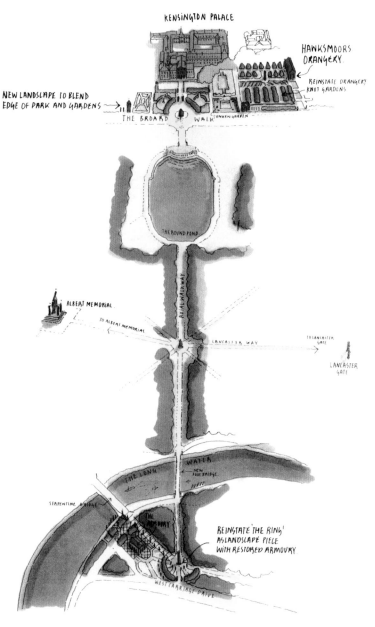

To say that the 20th century did not always well serve our urban relationship with the landscape would be true, but there are the beginnings of ideas to reawaken parts of it. These include the plan to link Hyde and Regent's Parks along the Regent's Canal through Paddington Basin. The crossing at Hyde Park Corner is now a joy compared with what existed for almost 50 years from the 1960s when a mini motorway intersection and its underpass were built, making Hyde Park seem inaccessible and marooning Marble Arch and Wellington Arch on islands at each end of Park Lane.

**Nannies and their charges
strolling in Hyde Park, 1900**
London squares were always meant to be
private enclaves, small oases, accessible
only to the residents that surrounded
them. Here, nannies walk in Hyde Park,
a typical scene of the squares at the time.

**Farrell, Reinstating links from
Kensington Palace to Hyde Park, 1994**
Rediscovering and reusing existing formal
axes in the park landscape, this 1994
proposition is now being partially realised
with the opening up of Kensington Palace
to the gardens.

St James's Square, 1754
The square with St James's Church,
and Piccadilly clearly seen in the distance.
The grant by Charles II of the freehold of
the site of St James's Square and other
adjacent property to trustees for the Earl
of St Albans was made in 1665. The
square itself took shape in the 1670s.

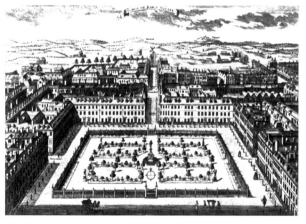

Municipal Parks, Squares, Cemeteries, Gardens and Fields

Outside central London the capital has many other great parks, not just the royal ones. There has been a long tradition of founding municipal parks, including Victoria Park (1845) in Hackney, Battersea Park (1853), and Brockwell Park in Herne Hill (1892), most of which were established in the Victorian era of philanthropy to offer some relief among the grime and pollution of working-class areas. The next scale down from the parks are the formal squares and the residential gardens with which London has been singularly innovative. London's first major square was at

Sutton Nichols, *Aerial View of Leicester Square*, 1754
The great house with the square surrounded by fine residences.

The changing layouts of London squares
Top: Monmouth House, south side of Soho Square, anonymous engraving
Built for the Duke of Monmouth, after the pattern of great houses that were related to squares and that were then sold to aspiring and wealthy people.

Above: Sutton Nichols, Soho Square, 1751
By and large these London squares allowed privileged access for the residents and remained for most Londoners merely a view. Although in this instance, Soho Square is now a green oasis in the West End for the enjoyment of the public.

Covent Garden, where in the early 17th century the Earl of Bedford established a piazza to complement his country estate. He used the square as a market to sell his estate's vegetables, reaping personal financial benefit.

The great squares that followed the Covent Garden piazza were those in Bloomsbury in the late 17th and 18th centuries. They were laid out as London's first suburbs; residential properties were sold with the benefits of the view onto the square and the use of gated private gardens in the centre. The idea of the enclosed fenced garden is not one that was thought up just to protect the privileged recreational pursuits of the residents who had a key – it was also a way of preventing large open spaces where rioting groups of peasants could assemble. Soon the residential garden squares were extending from Bloomsbury across to the centre at St James's, Grosvenor Square, Red Lion Square and Soho Square; then slightly further north to Cavendish, Montagu and Bryanston squares; and then east to Hoxton and Charles squares in Shoreditch. It is consistent with London's land ownership values that the city's most innovative and world-class urban design is made up of set pieces, patchworked across the city, mostly in aristocratic landed estates and for the sole benefit of residential neighbourhoods.

Looking at the squares today, particularly in Bloomsbury where I did a study to consider their continued evolution, they are now used for quite different purposes. The premises around Bedford Square, for example, are almost entirely non-residential; in Fitzroy Square on a summer's evening you will find marquees for corporate parties and events, as the buildings around are now occupied by commercial offices; and Gordon Square and Bloomsbury Square are now very much part of the university campus. Recently, there

was a debate about whether the paths of these squares should continue to be laid out as they were traditionally, when they were ideally suited for nannies with perambulators rather than for the accessibility of the general public.

Presently, many of London's garden squares continue to be somewhat inaccessible to the average Londoner, who regards and accepts them as contained pieces of very thickly treed landscape, as places to look at as rural artefacts, like wooded atolls that have floated in from Surrey or Hampshire – or perhaps as remnants of an imaginary great forest that covered all of London before the roads were built. Of course, this is not the case as the squares were newly planted, particularly with plane trees which now dominate London with their huge size and generous foliage. The first plane trees – though imported, we know it as the London plane – were planted in Berkeley Square in 1789 and were promoted as London's standard urban tree in the early

Ranelagh Gardens,
anonymous engraving, 1752
Pleasure gardens such as these were deliberately designed as places to visit for enjoyment. The organised landscapes, vistas and views were much more in the Parisian, Jardin du Luxembourg tradition, with limited paid access that allowed drinking, dancing and partying generally: places of leisure and entertainment for the

middle classes. Just as the Tivoli Gardens in Denmark were inspired by Vauxhall Gardens, they are believed to be the inspiration for Walt Disney's Disneyland.

1800s by the landscape gardener John Claudius Loudon. Some 200 years later these enormous giants may well be nearing the end of their life, but everyone is waiting to see the longevity of the Berkeley Square trees as a measure of how long we might expect these importations from southern Europe to survive in the London climate. They have survived so far because of their ability to withstand pollution and the close proximity of the buildings that surround them in the urban scene.

I think there are two features of London that are unique and special and add to the diversity of the city's green spaces. One is the great Victorian cemeteries that are themselves now nature reserves, including Highgate to the north and Brompton Cemetery in Earls Court, which are teeming with wildlife as well as being places for the dead. The other is the private gardens, not only those of private houses, of which there are so many right in the centre of London, but also the enclosed communal gardens which reversed the usual urban plan where they would be in the centre, to the front of the houses in the 18th-century style. Instead, particularly among the mansion blocks in areas like Ladbroke Grove and Maida Vale, built in the late Victorian and Edwardian eras, the communal gardens are positioned at the rear. Each house or mansion block has direct access through their back doors to tiny patios and then into communal gardens which cater for the modern pursuits of dog walking, barbecues or fireworks on Guy Fawkes' Night.

London today has gone a long way from its rural roots, when open rivers flowed through villages down to the Thames and when there were fairs on fields like Moorfields and Highbury Fields. Their names still exist today and the very idea that there were fields in the centre of London is an extraordinary continuity from the past, helping to give the city a hybrid feel of urban and rural, further endorsed by its polycentric nature, with its tube stations reaching out to a suburbia which is yet part of London. The names of the villages, such as Parsons Green, Wood Green and Highgate Village, also suggest a semi-rural nature. All the trees in the streets, the squares and the private gardens help to suggest that London is very green, but the green spaces are not at all evenly spread. There are large areas without a great deal of open space, in particular Islington, Wembley, Hounslow, Tottenham, Stoke Newington, Leighton, East Ham, Poplar, Dagenham, Camberwell and Mitchum, which have been described by Natural England, the conservation and landscape body, as suffering open space deprivation, having restricted access to green spaces and greenery.

It is probably not the amount of greenery or parks that makes London unique – it is the attitude, the idea that all Londoners think that they might still be in a collection of villages and in a somewhat adapted rural scene. The informal and irregular nature of the parks and their very centrality helps foster this idea. The position of the Royal Parks right in the middle of town may create a very difficult traffic plan and traffic management arrangement – as we all know, if one of the boundary streets that weave themselves between the parks gets blocked the effect upon all traffic in London is immediate and drastic – but they are there for the benefit of us all. The benefit is not just that the Royal Parks, great gardens and landscapes are there; it is that they are so well maintained. The standards of stewardship, husbandry and maintenance set a very high standard for any green spaces within the urban domain, and demonstrate Britain's continued love affair with the natural landscape.

Aerial view of Holland Park Avenue

Like Maida Vale, the whole of Notting Hill and Holland Park has large areas of private gardens like trapped landscapes. These communal private gardens, at the back of residential buildings, were revealed in the film *Notting Hill* (1999). They are accessible through small patios at the back of the houses or by locked gates.

Conclusion: London's Urbiculture

Urbiculture The development of cities and towns
(Oxford English Dictionary)

The land and how it is occupied, how people live on and
move across it is the direct result of man-made and landscape
infrastructural forces. These are what urbanist and architect

Christopher Alexander has called the 'fixed part of the system',
referred to in the Introduction, and developed further in the
other chapters of this book. There are so many different layers
of human activity, cultural, social and political, that have an
interaction with these 'fixed parts' of town planning that
it would not be possible to cover them all here, and indeed

this book does not attempt to do so. I will, however, develop here some outline thoughts that have personally intrigued me, albeit in a somewhat broadbrush manner – so apologies to all those experts, the sociologists, historians, constitutionalists, economists, planning lawyers, who will no doubt see my cavalier approach as, well, just that.

I like the term 'urbiculture' – I found it in the *Oxford English Dictionary* by accident. I did not know there was such a word, but it sat there with horticulture, agriculture and apiculture (bee keeping!) and readily evoked an approach, a way of doing things in the planning stewardship and governance of cities that needs to be nurtured and prized as a body of wisdom, or a skill base

necessary for all leaders and, indeed, ideally, for all citizens of any city. My vision of urbiculture would embrace aspects of governance and politics, and of ownership and stewardship of land. It would put 'place' high in the order of our cultural achievements. Place in our cities should be highly prized as it is the true constant client, as it outlives the people existing now. It would also develop a much better ranking in our priorities for town planning itself, long seen as a non-sexy, mundane endeavour – as a town planning that is proactive and excitingly creative and really genuinely engaging with communities, not as in the current, often cynical nod to 'consultation processes', that governance procedures and bureaucracy act out today.

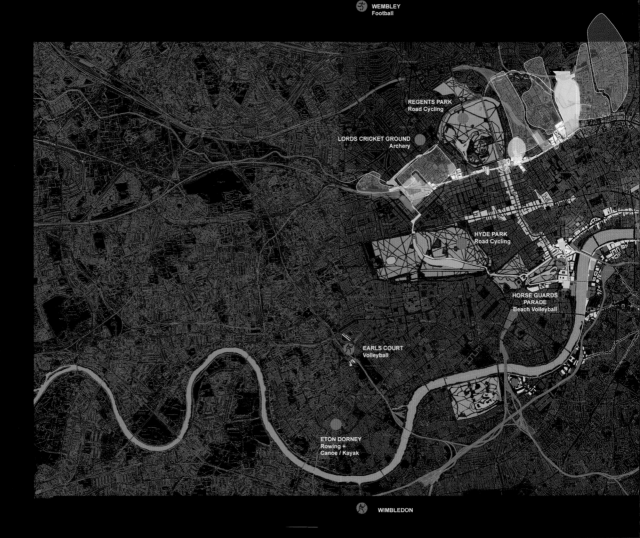

REGENTS PARK
Road Cycling

LORDS CRICKET GROUND
Archery

HYDE PARK
Road Cycling

HORSE GUARDS
PARADE
Beach Volleyball

EARLS COURT
Volleyball

ETON DORNEY
Rowing +
Canoe / Kayak

BARNES

WIMBLEDON

A Perennial Muddle? Governance and Place in the Capital

Let me look at governance and politics first. London's metropolitan character is a rather fudged or blurred one in terms of its governance, its public governance. While the Crown and landed estates, and some of the local authorities and institutions, managed themselves so well, and with such great continuity over history, local authority

**Farrell, London and
the 2012 Olympics, 2006**
The entire metropolis becomes
a World Festival.

government has had a fairly wobbly time. If there is a disjunction between governance and places, this was not always so. Parishes gathered around a church in a coherent neighbourhood and used to be the essence of urban (as well as rural) local government, but as that went in stages from small to larger boroughs, by the 1960s London had a legacy of boroughs that had been defined to suit political convenience, according to voting patterns and balances of communities and local taxes. When defining their boundaries in the

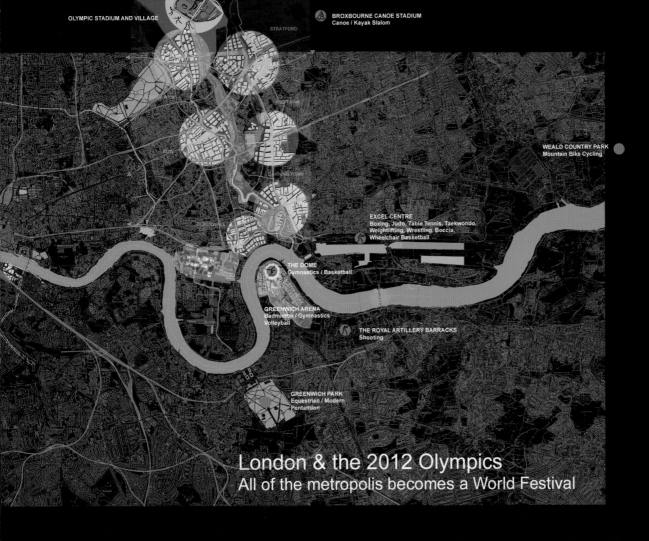

STRATFORD

BROXBOURNE CANOE STADIUM
Canoe / Kayak Slalom

CANNING TOWN

WEALD COUNTRY PARK
Mountain Bike Cycling

EXCEL CENTRE
Boxing, Judo, Table Tennis, Taekwondo,
Weightlifting, Wrestling, Boccia,
Wheelchair Basketball

THE DOME
Gymnastics / Basketball

GREENWICH ARENA
Badminton / Gymnastics
Volleyball

THE ROYAL ARTILLERY BARRACKS
Shooting

GREENWICH PARK
Equestrian / Modern
Pentathlon

London & the 2012 Olympics
All of the metropolis becomes a World Festival

1960s there resulted a deliberate mechanical concept that captured a range of tax and local rates so that there was a balance of offices, wealthy housing and poor housing in each borough.

The net result has been that on the ground there is a very arbitrary geographical arrangement particularly when one's own identity naturally wants to relate to a recognisable sense of place and mental geography. How can anyone tell where the boundaries, or the centres, are? Westminster, for instance, might be named after the old small city surrounding the medieval royal palace of Westminster, but it now extends miles north into the territories of suburban Brent and Kilburn. How does anyone really know when they have travelled through the boundaries of these boroughs, these new, politically invented 'places'. How does anyone tell whether they are in Camden, Islington or Hackney?

But if the smaller scale of parishes and boroughs has changed over time making them difficult to relate to, there has

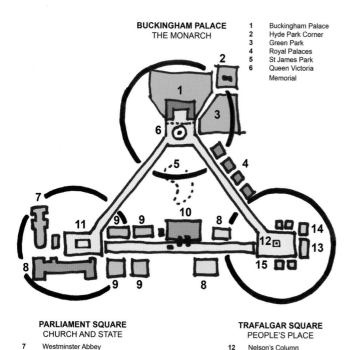

BUCKINGHAM PALACE
THE MONARCH

1	Buckingham Palace
2	Hyde Park Corner
3	Green Park
4	Royal Palaces
5	St James Park
6	Queen Victoria Memorial

PARLIAMENT SQUARE
CHURCH AND STATE

7	Westminster Abbey
8	Houses of Parliament
9	Ministries
10	Horseguards
11	Parliament Square

TRAFALGAR SQUARE
PEOPLE'S PLACE

12	Nelson's Column
13	National Gallery
14	National Gallery extension
15	Trafalgar Square

much of London's affairs. So with the whole tiering down from Crown to Parliament to mayor to boroughs, and to the public, the individual needs to have a committed course in local government politics before he can begin to comprehend just how his metropolis is run and who is responsible for what.

It has a certain kind of chaotic charm; a mixture of the feudal and the almost modern exist simultaneously. Just as a London street is such a mixture of styles and historical layers all cast in stone, so is our form of governance such that any constitutional structure is so complex and diverse it can probably never be written down. But the two mayors we have had, have set about their constrained task with an energy and enthusiasm that has caught popular imagination, and the effect they have had, such as London winning the Olympics, challenging big issues such as where airports should be, cycling within the centre and city-wide festivals, really have united London people. All of this has instigated the feeling that city life in the 21st century is capable of making London a more integrated and better-managed place.

Any discussion of London's pattern of governance and how it expresses itself on the land could not take place without the recognition that London is not just a metropolis, it is also a capital city. That sets it apart from any other great metropolis that is not, such as great cities like Glasgow, Manchester or Birmingham in the UK, or internationally Sydney, Melbourne, Shanghai, Bombay, New York, Chicago or Los Angeles. Having the centre of the seat of government at the centre of a great metropolitan city is very different, and different again to those specialist capital cities like Washington, Brasilia or Canberra. Physical expressions of the order of national governance in town planning are expressed in quite different ways; specialist cities like the above and most other

been an equally muddling tale of government at a metropolitan-wide level. It is not surprising that visitors from abroad or even London's citizens can be confused by the way the city runs itself; the terms mayor and lord mayor, for example, are used several times for different parts of the metropolis, and the additional newly invented title of the Mayor of London began in 2000 with Ken Livingstone, succeeded now by Boris Johnson. It is not only a very new invention of this century, his powers – compared with North American or Continental mayors or even major provincial city leaders – are really relatively limited. One is tempted to think of this as very typical British muddling-through: we have no constitution nationally, the Crown still rules aspects of church, army, state and Parliament; and the national Parliament at Westminster residing within the capital city of London still has a lot of powers over London with specific ministers still controlling

Farrell, Power triangle, 2009
There is a surprisingly clear physical expression in London's plan of the relationship of the primary components of power – as clear as any written constitution.

Crowds at the royal wedding, 1947
The link between the three great centres of power. Travelling to the wedding of Princess Elizabeth and Prince Philip, from Buckingham Palace (the centre of the monarchy), through Trafalgar Square (the people's square) and on to Westminster Abbey (the centre of religion and parliamentary power).

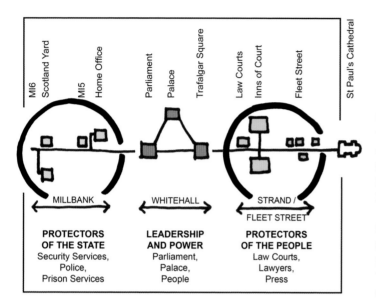

| MI6 Scotland Yard | MI5 Home Office | Parliament | Palace | Trafalgar Square | Law Courts | Inns of Court | Fleet Street | St Paul's Cathedral |

← MILLBANK →   ← WHITEHALL →   ← STRAND / →

FLEET STREET

| **PROTECTORS OF THE STATE** Security Services, Police, Prison Services | **LEADERSHIP AND POWER** Parliament, Palace, People | **PROTECTORS OF THE PEOPLE** Law Courts, Lawyers, Press |

Farrell, Patterns of power, 2009

There is a clear pattern in how the three central squares, expressions of the state, relate to their supporting institutions – all set out in a great linear route from Millbank to Whitehall to The Strand and Fleet Street.

major capital cities like Paris or Beijing have their order visually expressed in town planning in a very deliberate way with the presence of national government boldly expressed in an orderly way. This is seen in the White House, the Capitol, the Forbidden City or indeed New Delhi with Lutyens's extraordinary ensemble that moved from an empire capital to a capital of a self-governing united country fairly effortlessly as the physical objects of buildings and public spaces lent themselves to governance and grew from one kind of governance to almost its opposite with relative ease.

The Triumvirate: Hidden Order at the Heart of the Capital

What is most surprising and largely unrecognised is that there is a grand order at the heart of the capital. This remains hidden, underneath the surface. It is a kind of very British understatement.

British governance expresses itself here in London as a collaged triangulation, in set pieces that assemble all the elements of power, and it does so in a way that perfectly demonstrates how organic gradualism and evolutionary growth can achieve a structured pattern, a form of its own, just as any natural evolution, any bio-logical process can do over time.

There are three public spaces – Parliament Square, Trafalgar Square and the frontage space at Buckingham Palace – that for me set out all the key power relationships in a grand way and indeed in quite a clear way that is obvious once the pattern is recognised. The monarch and her/his palace gaze out across a great space, a grand enclosed theatrical stage set designed by Aston Webb in 1911 that is set around one of London's biggest statues, that of Queen Victoria. Although day to day much of it functions as a traffic roundabout, it is Britain's great place of state where royal weddings, funerals, coronations, great sporting achievements and war victories are publicly celebrated. Whenever the British gather for something that unites the people in a celebratory way, in a positive affirmation of the nation, they gather at the front of Buckingham Palace. There must hardly be a tourist that comes to London who does not at some point go through Green Park or St James's Park and enter this amphitheatre.

To the southwest is Parliament Square and around it the Palace of Westminster (the House of Lords and the House of Commons), sitting next to Westminster Abbey and St Stephen's Chapel. This is the national centre and focus for governance and religion, linked as they are in the British way of things – with the Crown being the head of the church since King Henry VIII.

Then to complete the triangulation, at the other end of Whitehall is Trafalgar Square, named, of course, after the battle

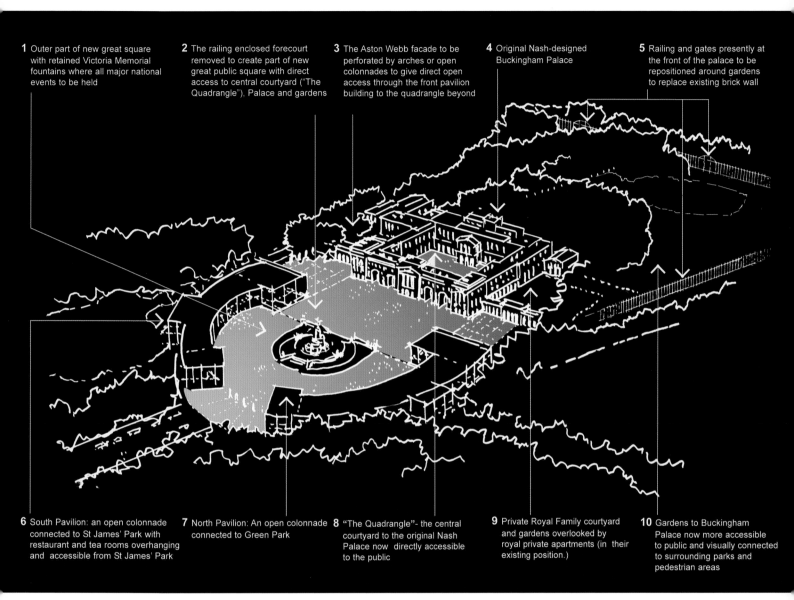

1 Outer part of new great square with retained Victoria Memorial fountains where all major national events to be held

2 The railing enclosed forecourt removed to create part of new great public square with direct access to central courtyard ("The Quadrangle"), Palace and gardens

3 The Aston Webb facade to be perforated by arches or open colonnades to give direct open access through the front pavilion building to the quadrangle beyond

4 Original Nash-designed Buckingham Palace

5 Railing and gates presently at the front of the palace to be repositioned around gardens to replace existing brick wall

6 South Pavilion: an open colonnade connected to St James' Park with restaurant and tea rooms overhanging and accessible from St James' Park

7 North Pavilion: An open colonnade connected to Green Park

8 "The Quadrangle"- the central courtyard to the original Nash Palace now directly accessible to the public

9 Private Royal Family courtyard and gardens overlooked by royal private apartments (in their existing position.)

10 Gardens to Buckingham Palace now more accessible to public and visually connected to surrounding parks and pedestrian areas

Farrell, Proposal for Buckingham Palace, 2001

Farrell's proposal for a rationalisation of the space in front of Buckingham Palace would change it from a giant traffic roundabout to a people place, reflecting its enormous importance to the nation (as well as to tourists).

that at the beginning of the 19th century established Britain as a great European and world power and literally enabled it to set sail on a century of dominance and expansion. It is very much the people's square, particularly with its improved pedestrianisation of late. This is a place where tourists gather, where anything independent of Crown and Parliament happens. This is a place where (usually well-mannered) demonstrations are 'permitted' with lesser and organised protests and also popular festivals and pop concerts. It is London's only properly public paved square and makes itself fully and freely available for events, organised and spontaneous. Symbolically this works because the crowds that gather are not outside the gates of the government and Parliament or those of monarch and Crown. Instead, gathered around this square are mainly art galleries and incidental embassies and other buildings that are rarely, if ever, the object of the protests themselves (see diagram on p 260).

Connecting these three great spaces, these three expressions of the poles of power are arranged like seats at a table, various family members or partners in crime or members of the board with all the right-hand men, as it were, physically ever present. The first government building next to Parliament is the Treasury – and of course the prime minister was first known as the First Lord of the Treasury, in Robert Walpole's time – and next to the Treasury, appropriately for a once empire, is the Foreign Office. The parade of ministries goes down Whitehall with the Ministry of Defence sitting next to Lutyens's Cenotaph, around which the military gather annually to honour the fallen, while opposite is Horse Guards, through an arch of which there is the great parade ground which sits facing the palace as a reminder to all that the monarch is head of the military in Great Britain. It is where the Queen takes the Trooping the Colour annually to reinforce and reaffirm this relationship with the military, and so her palace looks directly down to Horse Guards, the Cenotaph, the Ministry of Defence and the Admiralty.

Next to Buckingham Palace, the focus for the monarch and running down the Mall is another leg of the triangle, appropriately set out running down to Trafalgar Square, biased symbolically to the people's side. Here most of the members of the royal family reside – the Queen Mother lived at Clarence House, Prince Charles lives officially in St James's Palace – and they are set with other palaces running along the Mall like seats at a family dining table, like a family village estate, albeit of a regal kind!

The patterns reach outwards as Whitehall extends its influence some distance along the riverbank west and east in terms of national government and its expression within London's landscape. To the west, for example, are collected all the ministries to do with national security, intelligence and police. The Home Office sits just behind the Embankment which is the centre not only of home government, but also the police force and prisons. Nearby on the Embankment is MI5, the equivalent of the American FBI, I suppose; over the road further along is Scotland Yard, HQ of the police; and opposite that on the other side of the river, on the same axis west of Parliament, is MI6, Britain's equivalent of the CIA. Going in the opposite direction and travelling east from Whitehall, through Trafalgar Square, is that other great arm of national order, the legislature, defending people's rights (suitably distant from the police at the opposite end of the axis!). Here are not only the law courts, but the inns where the barristers, judges, solicitors and lawyers all reside, and beyond that is traditionally the fourth estate, the press on Fleet Street (though now mostly

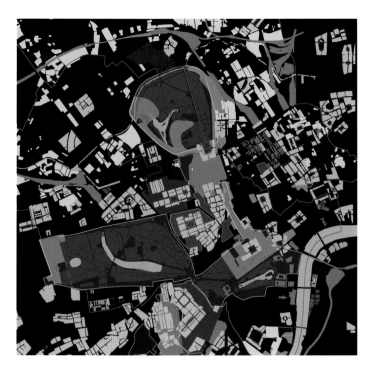

moved to outer London locations). It is almost as if the nation has arranged its family relationships, its orders of governance and constitution far more clearly written here in bricks and stone than it is on paper. If you want to understand power relationships here it is, woven into the patterns of plan forms of the capital city's streets, squares, palaces and buildings of state in the heart of the city of Westminster (see diagram on p 262).

London's Patterns of Stewardship and Land Ownership

How do the great land holdings affect stewardship, political influence and planning policy particularly within the central areas? The Crown Estate at the top of the social tree – with its palaces and legacy of Royal Parks and land holdings that make up large parts of Regent's Street and elsewhere – is a major force in continuing to shape London simply because in the manner

of true British compromise and the results of evolution rather than revolution, the management of its Royal Parks, commercial exploitation of land ownership and palaces has never symbolically or possibly even in reality, fully passed over to the private sector or municipal authorities. It is run by its own set of bodies, largely and quite frankly rather independently of most democratic processes so that the Royal Parks, the Crown Estates, the Crown Estate Paving Commission all take their powers and legislation back to archaic acts of Parliament and settlements between monarchs and Parliament at different points in time.

Then there are the greater landed aristocratic estates that cover substantial territories of central London and, by and large, have always been exceptionally well managed. They are not the runts of royal privilege; they were, and are, well laid-out landed estates, once agricultural and now streets and squares, always having an eye to the continuing creation of value and income. The stewardship of these is invariably excellent, with, for example, the Howard de Walden Estate and the way it manages Marylebone High Street leading it to receive many awards for being the best high street not just in London but in all of Britain. The choice of shops and kinds of goods, the street festivals, they are all part of this great estate continuing its enlightened stewardship of the land some 200 years or more after it was first built up. The Grosvenors, Cavendishes, Harleys and so many of the other estates have similar stories to tell of exemplary urban stewardship – albeit for those who are better off.

In contrast there are the large municipal estates, social housing and other local authority land ownerships – town halls, fire and ambulance stations, schools with their large areas of playground and so on. Again this is a large domain – and to

Farrell, Central London collage, 2007
The collage shows how much of central London is owned by a small minority. If this is added to the road areas, utilities and religious buildings, very little is left that is under 'normal' town planning control.

Large Single Landownerships in the 19th century and today

The City of London
The Portman Estate
The Crown Estate
The Cadogan Estate
The Grosvenor Estate

Palaces
Council estates
Universities
Public buildings
Hospitals
Great estates
Railways
Royal Parks
Borough boundaries

Farrell, Public Housing, 2007
The six major public housing estates
north of Euston Road: together they are
the same size as Milton Keynes, providing
housing for 250,000 people.

these should be added the estates of the various institutions and statutory undertakers, gas and electricity companies, bus stations, railways and their goods yards and sidings and stations, hospitals and, of course, universities and the great cultural institutions of the museums which dominate so much of areas like South Kensington and Bloomsbury.

Taken all together there is an astonishing pattern of concentrated land in central London, mostly in the form of these private

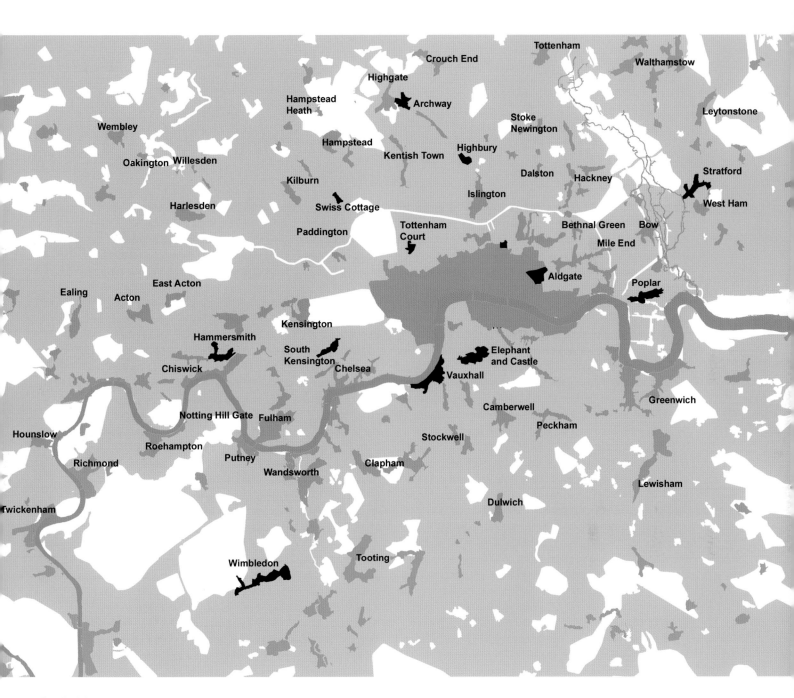

Farrell, 18th-century London, 2007

Showing its towns and villages within
the current plan of London.
Pink – 18th-century built form
Grey – current built form
Black – lost and endangered town centres.

and public estates that are managed formally and professionally by large and centralised establishment organisations. It distinguishes in many ways the core from the suburban periphery ring; the outer boroughs have always felt that there is a great difference in the attitude to their communities and land and stewardship, a huge difference between them and the inner part of London.

There are differing kinds of stewardship that derive from these land ownerships with their different management styles and residents' expectations and attitudes. The social housing, for example, arranges itself quite differently from the middle-class landed estates. It is quite surprising how spatial perceptions, assumptions and preconceptions dominate so much of how we read the shape and form of London. North of the Marylebone-Euston Roads, a quarter of a million people (the population of Milton Keynes) live in seven social housing estates. These are all half the density of the landed estates immediately to the south with substantially lower land values, much less mixed use, with fewer shops and services within them. They are much more likely to be single tenancy type and monocultural, and much more likely to be deprived of trees and a public realm.

It is surprising how dense some of the landed middle-class estates have become – Marylebone is twice the density of the social housing of the Lisson Green and Church Street estates directly opposite on the other (north) side of the Marylebone Road. The most densely populated local authorities in the whole of the British Isles are Kensington & Chelsea and Westminster, both of which go completely against all preconceived notions of density. In the popular imagination, density goes with high-rise buildings, poverty, crime, lack of open space, lack of cultural facilities and poor health. In fact it is completely the reverse. The highest life expectancy, anywhere in Britain, is in these two, densest boroughs; they are generally low rise, they contain all the central Royal Parks, have major university and museum campuses and art galleries and shopping centres, and have the highest property values and richest people in Britain. If it does prove anything it is that the patterns of physical domain are predictably inhabited by an alignment of wealth and privilege with perceived urban planning quality.

There is so much that is today so valuable in the city that harks back to the 18th- and 19th-century roots of the modern metropolis. The work of local conservation bodies, local government planning departments, English Heritage and campaigning organisations like SAVE, the Georgian and Victorian societies and the Twentieth Century Society has done a lot to conserve the values, to make places better, to convey that history plays a major part in place identity and therefore in London's future. There are many parts of the metropolitan and town-planning inventions that are struggling in today's world because of their inventive, experimental nature. London's infrastructure – the rail and underground systems in particular – requires considerable investment to bring it up to modern standards and to make continued sense of it. The process of creating order from disorder is ever continuing.

The major museums, for example, are busy reinventing themselves – through Lottery grants they are our contemporary *grands projets*. Unlike newer countries that are building their cities around new galleries and museums, London has an extraordinary treasure chest that it has inherited, such as the Victoria & Albert, Natural History and Science museums and, of course, the British Museum. But there are also spectacularly interesting small museums across London. To mention just two, at Lincoln's Inn Fields on opposite sides of the square, sitting to the north is the

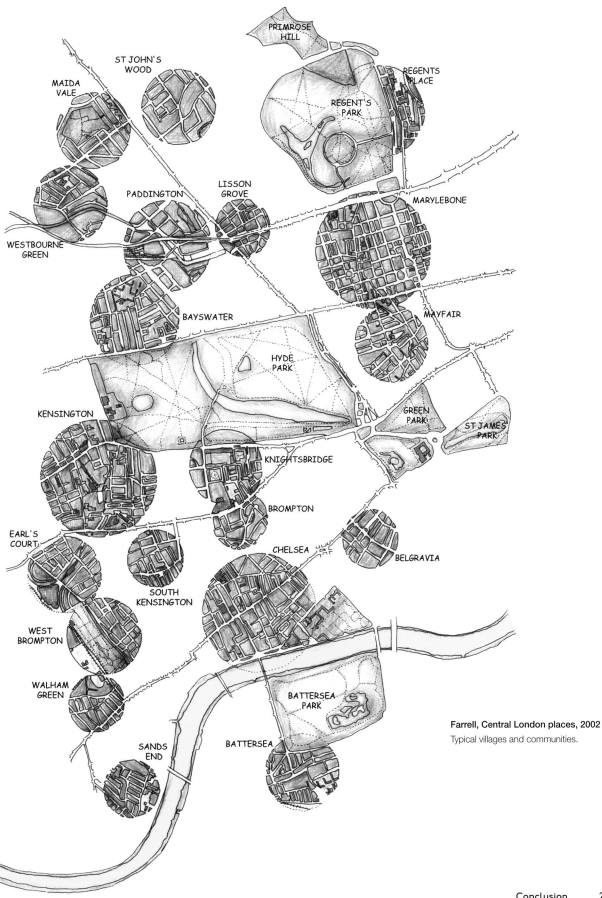

PRIMROSE
HILL

ST JOHN'S
WOOD

MAIDA
VALE

REGENTS
PLACE

REGENT'S
PARK

PADDINGTON

LISSON
GROVE

MARYLEBONE

WESTBOURNE
GREEN

BAYSWATER

HYDE
PARK

MAYFAIR

GREEN
PARK

ST JAMES
PARK

KENSINGTON

KNIGHTSBRIDGE

BROMPTON

EARL'S
COURT

CHELSEA

BELGRAVIA

WEST
BROMPTON

SOUTH
KENSINGTON

WALHAM
GREEN

BATTERSEA
PARK

SANDS
END

BATTERSEA

Farrell, Central London places, 2002
Typical villages and communities.

Highgate Archway in 1820.

Soane Museum, the collection of the great British architect's life and works; a veritable Tutankhamun's cave and opposite that, from a similar time in history, is the Hunterian Museum, inside the Royal College of Surgeons, where again is assembled a very personal collection, this time of anatomical specimens of one of the world's pioneers in medical surgery, John Hunter. Extraordinarily brilliantly displayed and explained, the Huntarian Museum is not just an exposition of the human body, it is also a thing of its time.

Both of these little museums, like all the great ones, are woven into the history and cultural fabric of London, they explain how the sciences and the arts and all the great institutions like London Zoo and Kew Gardens were contributing to the building and laying out of a metropolis where all that was found in the world was displayed and explained. The story of London's leadership in ideas and cultural development is expressed in physical form – you can still walk the galleries and exhibition halls of London's museums and see how the city's 18th-, 19th- and 20th-century knowledge of the world developed as the metropolis grew and grew. In these museums is the story of London. Much of this book is about the world outside, but inside the interiors not just of museums but of clubs, galleries, pubs, hotels, theatres and cinemas tell the city's story just as well. As Alberti wrote, (to paraphrase): 'The city is a large house and a house a small city'.

Discovering, Recovering and Regenerating Places in the City

Central to any study of the 'fixed' infrastructures and the human occupation and interaction with them is the concept of 'place'. And on any urbiculturist's priorities and skill set must be the nurturing, protection and enhancement of place, of its inherent reality, what it means to people, how it is perceived and defined. The various villages and towns that have grown to make the metropolis are in themselves made up of parishes, neighbourhoods and street blocks, varying considerably in density and social arrangements. How have some places survived and others been lost under the onslaught of so much infrastructural change over the last 200 years? How do you discover places in the larger field pattern of urban territory?

A particular study that fascinated me as it captured London's place-making within the wide urban pattern and grain, is one of the Edgware Road by the Centre for Advanced Spatial Analysis

Archway Tavern, 1820
Crossroads were always essential place-making hubs and vital focus points for the community.

Archway, a functioning town centre before the gyratory was built, 1950
Even ever denser urbanisation retained the 'place' as the community focus. All this ended in the 1960s with traffic 'improvements' giving priority to those passing through rather than those living there.

(CASA) at University College London (UCL). This is a street that is very familiar to me, as it is where I have lived and worked for over 30 years. The road itself is the Roman road of Watling Street but takes its name, Edge + wares, from being a long route into town, along the edge of which goods or wares were sold over the centuries to those travellers on their way in or out of London. So it still is a long string of settlements aggregated to form nodal points along the line. As the UCL studies have shown, finding the very physical, geometrical patterning of the streets guarantees the discovering of the places, the nodal points. From plan forms

The lost town centre of Archway

The increase in traffic since the 1960s has gradually eroded the town and villages around road junctions. Some disappeared altogether and others were severely compromised. For example at Archway, now a huge traffic gyratory, remnants of the centre remain with bus and tube stations in the middle of the roudabout; difficult to access, but physically still in the centre of the community. Plans are now developing to rediscover and remake this lost centre by reducing traffic, narrowing the roads, increasing the public realm and emphasising the pedestrian, and filling vacant sites with imaginative new buildings.

disappeared, too, and some are heavily compromised. The industrial revolution did not kill off these lost centres, but the car did. The beginning of this process can be seen in the 1940s when Abercrombie and others proposed a series of extraordinary eight-lane ring roads that smashed through the centre of what are now lost settlements: Hammersmith's centre moved to King Street; the heart of Aldgate and of Whitechapel are now roundabouts; Camden Town, Earls Court, South Kensington and Elephant & Castle all sit at the heart of place-busting busy gyratories. But some, such as Highgate and Hampstead, are untouched as they sit on hills with less public transport and their historic character and more articulate middle-class residents banded together to protect their 'place'. The remnants of some centres, such as Archway, remain on these gyratories with bus and tube stations in the middle of roundabouts.

The balance between movement, access and through-traffic which has to be set against places, the points of arrival, is one of the most difficult challenges of our time. How do you make the city efficient for movement yet preserve the value of its points of arrival, the very essence of why it is there in the first place? In many ways the Abercrombie Plan of 1943 captured the spirit of the middle of the last century that prevailed for several decades. The eight-lane motorway proposed to eliminate Camden Town, Primrose Hill, Maida Vale, Earls Court, Clapham, Kensington, Elephant & Castle and Highbury & Islington in a great ring road. The Marylebone-Euston Roads, junctions at Aldgate and at Swiss Cottage are all being looked at today to see what degree of restoration there can be to put back elements of the lost places, to rediscover a pedestrian domain and wrestle it back to the days when the place was eroded for the benefit of the car.

it can be predicted just where the shops are grouped, where the tube stations and neighbourhood centres are. Place can be deciphered from lines and patterns on computer mapping.

But, just as these junctions and movement concentrations create the nodal points that make settlements and places, in time they can by their very concentration, I have observed, also destroy them. As a fast-flowing river washes away its banks over time, ever increasing road traffic gradually erodes the gathered and focused activities of towns and villages around the junctions, such that some neighbourhoods and small towns have disappeared altogether. I have frequently asked 'where is Paddington?' In reality it has gone, evaporated. Road improvements in the 1960s eliminated one of London's historic town centres; some others

Historic Paddington
View of Harrow Road from Edgware Road
in the 1930s (top) and (below) showing
the half finished Marylebone Flyover to
the right of the picture in 1966.

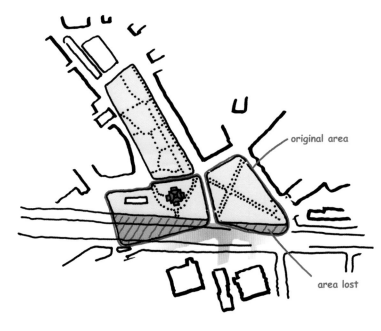

original area

area lost

The mid-20th-century notion that the city had failed, that places were easily dispensed with and that efficient movement must be met at any cost, was expressed well by Le Corbusier: 'The city is crumbling, cannot last much longer, its time is past. It is too old. The torrent of traffic can no longer keep to its bed'. A few decades later Le Corbusier was appropriately put in his place by the redoubtable and wise Jane Jacobs: 'Le Corbusier's dream city was like a wonderful mechanical toy, but as to how the city works, it tells … nothing but lies'. And she added: 'There is a quality even meaner than outright ugliness or disorder, and this is the dishonest mask of pretended order, achieved by ignoring or suppressing the real order that is struggling to exist and to be served' (Jane Jacobs, *The Death and Life of Great American Cities*, Penguin Books, 1994, p 33).

Jane Jacobs would be heartened to see London today as there has been such a revolution, a complete change, a complete turnaround in London's urban planning over the past 20 years. After decades that favoured devastating change with very little regard for what existed, there has been a momentous shift towards 'expressing' and 'serving' the 'real order' of London. The first signs of this shift were in the 1970s when the large motorways, the inner box widening of artery roads, were all beaten off by local communities. The first real significant and visible large-scale regeneration was at Covent Garden, where local community groups often led by local shopkeepers, restaurateurs and local community architects changed the whole fate of the area from total demolition to virtually none at all. The success of Covent Garden today is a great credit to that battle, to that major change in London's fortunes, and has been a model for all that came after.

This shift to a concerned urbanism which is not dominated by brand new 'grand projects' is one that looks at what is there, one that works with the grain. This shift has had an astonishing effect in the 1990s and early 2000s, when more money through the economic boom, particularly fuelled through Lottery-funded projects, was pumped into regeneration. The arrival of a new mayoral system in 2000 also gave impetus to London to improve itself, and in particular brought the 2012 Olympics to London with the promise that the legacy of the event would be urban regeneration of a key part of London's depressed East End – on an ambitious scale.

At Covent Garden, the Lottery funded not just the radical improvements to the Opera House, but also a whole urban set piece, completing the piazza with arcades, restoring and integrating the iron and glass Floral Hall and completing the urban block with mixed use – land that had been vacant for a generation since the market left. It is the small streets and alleyways, the medieval patterns of lanes, that make the character of Covent Garden along with the simple utilitarian workshops with large windows now readily occupied by creative industries, offices and

new shops as well as new residential flats right here in the heart of the town. The medieval organic pattern, with qualities we now cherish, was the very reason that the area was proposed to be knocked down because of the closeness of the buildings, their age and the 'inefficient' street layout.

Thus began in London the realisation of the value of what the city had; today whole areas, complete districts, have been rediscovered and regenerated. The list is much too long to recount here – but there need to be alternatives to the many building guidebooks that show the newest architecture. It is much more than the architecture that has been successful in London's environment of late. To name a few, Bloomsbury has benefited from the radical interior transformation of the British Museum, but also from the re-landscaping and upgrading of its squares – Bedford Square, Gordon Square and Russell Square – and University College London has plans to reinvent its own public realm. The museums of South Kensington have all benefited from imaginative Lottery projects and will now have a re-ordered public realm the length of Exhibition Road. Greenwich Palace and Park, Trafalgar Square with the National Gallery and National Portrait Gallery, the Southbank cultural centre and the area around Tate Modern, as well as the old Tate (Tate Britain) and its adjoining new art schools, all have been in essence primarily urban regeneration projects.

At a larger scale, whole districts have been transformed – Hoxton, Clerkenwell and Shoreditch to name a few further east, as well Forest Hill and Borough to the south of the river. Usually it is local communities and incoming 'creatives' that lead, and sometimes it is individuals. Out east, Lord Andrew Mawson, a great social entrepreneur, has been transforming the community

Aerial photo of Paddington Station and Basin severed from Paddington Green by Marylebone Flyover
The flyover passes right through the centre of Paddington dividing this former urban village – those civic elements that remain are separated by the motorway.

of Bromley-by-Bow; in Kensington & Chelsea local political leader Daniel Moylan has reinvented the street, its pavings, railings, kerbs and crossings, and made Kensington High Street a model, an exemplar for all London's pedestrian realm. Eric Reynolds, a pioneer urban regeneration entrepreneur, led the Camden Market regeneration to rival any Middle Eastern souk, revitalised Spitalfields and Greenwich markets and has created a complex – at the mouth of the River Lea around Trinity Buoy Wharf – of restored historical buildings and boats, a conference centre, living areas and a village of recycled container boxes for flats, offices and workspaces. John Scott, an antique collector and developer, almost single-handedly created a place – Turquoise Island in Kensington – set around new toilets and a flower shop, and went on to champion street art works in much of Notting Hill. None

of these was a professional town planner or architect, and all worked over time with local communities.

But the wide sweep of London's regeneration during these last 10 to 15 years has been by the community of all London. Like the whole history of London, it has been a pattern of organic change, collective change by many hands, that have brought it about by evolving the form, the shape of London. The metropolis is, in essence, a social creation, 'better as the giving birth of peoples in labour than as the gushing stream of genius', as Victor Hugo elegantly described past achievements, adding that these great works were the 'accumulation of centuries, the residue of successive evaporations of human society, briefly as a kind of geological formation'. London is itself, in itself, a great accumulated work, a masterpiece, more fine and noble

Farrell, Swiss Cottage
figure-ground (1893), 1999
The nodal point as a place with a natural
balance between traffic and pedestrians.

Farrell, Swiss Cottage
figure-ground (1995), 1999
The prioritisation of traffic over
pedestrians has eroded the nodal
balance, causing the 'place' to be lost.

an achievement than any individual great painting, concerto, opera or piece of sculpture – simply because it is an inspiring accumulation of, and for, all these things in the first place. In this book I have tried to identify the patterns and forms, to explain what the underlying harmonies and orders are, hopefully not just to help value and appreciate the city more, but to further encourage the process of nurturing and stewardship and to reinforce the case for change and progress to be built on what it is, what its true patterns and forms are, so that London's 'real order is served' in all future plans.

Swiss Cottage town centre, 2007
Swiss Cottage now has a new theatre, sports centre, library, housing and public green space, masterplanned by Farrell.

Masterplanning and place-making work by Terry Farrell

Re-planning 19th-century industrial and 20th-century infrastructural areas of London. Masterplanning and place-making work by Terry Farrell from the 1980s to the present day

A Outer London: Re-planning urban motorways and arterial approach roads – creating places and new communities
Brent Cross, Cricklewood, new urban communities, 2006–8 (1); Swiss Cottage town centre, 1998–2006 (2); Elephant & Castle, 2001–3 (3)

B 1960s inner urban road 'improvements', 19th-century mainline railways and canals
Masterplanning work to reintegrate these major infrastructure changes back into the urban realm. Reintroducing the urban pattern by making places and public realm: Paddington Station and canal basin, 1995–2009 (4); Euston Road and Euston Station, 1999–2009 (5); Kings Cross and St Pancras Stations, 1989–2005 (6); British Library masterplan, 2009 (6); Euston Circus, 2004 onwards (7)

C Rethinking urban set pieces; Palaces, parks and Crown lands
The Nash Ramblas, the John Nash set piece from St James's Park, through Regent St to Regent's Park, 1995–2009 (8); The Royal Parks,1973–2009 (9); South Kensington, Exhibition Road and museums, 1992–2005 (10)

D Central London's public realm, the landed aristocratic estates and London's high street
East end of Oxford Street, London's high street, 2004–7 (11); Bloomsbury Study: University lands, British Museum and historic squares, 2006–8 (12); St Giles's Circus, rethinking of 20th-century roundabout, 2007–9 (13)

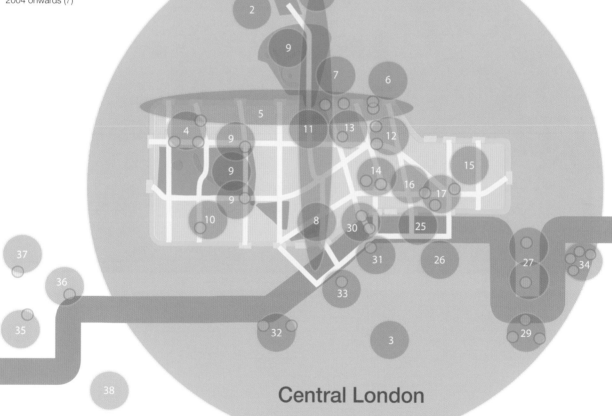

Central London

O Rethinking 19th-century canals and navigable tributaries around the River Brent and Chelsea Creek
Including associated industrial infrastructure to make mixed-use residential communities: Brentford Dock, 1989–90 (35); Lots Road, 1998–2009 (36)

P Outer London town centres
Working with local communities and conservation groups to protect and regenerate a sense of place: Hammersmith town centre in conjunction with the GLC, 1981–3 (37); Wimbledon town centre, for English Heritage and others, 1987–9 (38)

M Rethinking and re-planning a 19th-century railway station and railway bridge, and 20th-century South Bank
Reshaping, reinventing and urbanising: Charing Cross, 1985–90 (including concept work for the new Hungerford Bridge) (30); South Bank cultural masterplan, transforming and urbanising a mid-20th-century heavily infrastructural cultural centre, 1995–2001 (31)

N 19th- and early 20th-century riverside industrial areas
Effra masterplan (centred round the Thames tributary, River Effra, 1982–4 (32); Vauxhall Cross/MI6 building with new river walk, 1987–93 (32); Founder's Place/St Thomas' Hospital, housing and medical masterplan, 2001–9 (33); Greenwich Peninsula masterplan, 1989 onwards (34)

E New roles and new uses for London's great market buildings
Covent Garden piazza and Opera House masterplan, 1983–4; Comyn Ching urban regeneration, 1976–89 (14); Spitalfields masterplan for SAVE and local community, 1992 (15); Smithfield planning study and historic building retention schemes for English Heritage, 2006–8 (16)

F City of London urban streets and public realm
Masterplanning London Wall to rethink 1960s office buildings, 1986–92 (17); Paternoster, St Paul's, 1989–94 (17); Mansion House retention masterplan for SAVE and English Heritage, 1983–4 (17)

G Canal and navigable tributary waterways; regeneration and masterplan projects, Lea Valley
Waterway masterplans, Olympic legacy concepts and Prescott Lock, 2004 (18); Meridian Water for British Waterways and others, 2007–8 (19)

H Thames Gateway and Estuary Parklands: Europe's largest regeneration project
Independent concept work, 2002–7, Estuary Parklands champion for HM Department of Communities and Local Government, 2008–9, Overall vision masterplanner for the Homes & Communities Agency, 2009–10 (20)

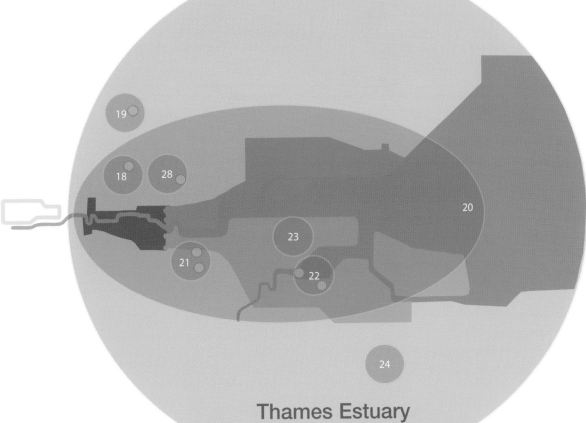

Thames Estuary

K 20th-century riverside industry and 19th-century railways comprehensively redeveloped in the last 40 years
Masterplanning work including new residential and office areas for local authorities and British railways: Thameslink rail masterplanning London Bridge to Blackfriars Bridge, 1994–7 (25); Potters Field Study for Southwark Council, 2007–8 (26)

L Reinventing London's docklands after their closure in the 1970s
Limehouse Studios, 1983 (27); Isle of Dogs waterpark for British Waterways, 2007–8 (27); Royal Docks masterplan, 1987 (28); Silvertown Quay and aquarium, 1996–2008 (28); Greenwich Pier, Palace and Park, 1996–2009 (29)

I Estuary post-industrial regeneration
Cement works and quarries: masterplanning new communities, masterplan concept work for new towns and residential areas for Gravesend, Ebbsfleet, Northfleet and Bluewater, 1997–2009 (21)

J Estuary naval towns
Following the shift of naval ports, regeneration within the overall Estuary Parklands project: Design Champion and masterplanner for Medway City, 2004–9 (22); Hoo Peninsula masterplan, 2008–9 (23); Wider County of Kent visioning work, 2008–9 (24)

Bibliography by Chapter

Introduction
Christopher Alexander, 'A City Is Not a Tree', essay online at www.rudi.net/pages/8755.
Philip Ball, *The Self-Made Tapestry: Pattern Formation in Nature*, Oxford University Press, new edition, 2001.
Heather Creaton, *Bibliography of Printed Works on London History to 1939*, Library Association Pub., 1994.
Charles Dickens, *Household Words*, Volume XVI, 1857.
Colin Rowe and Fred Koetter, *Collage City*, MIT Press, new edition, 1978.
D'Arcy Wentworth Thompson, *On Growth and Form*, Cambridge University Press, 1952.

Rural Upper Thames
Mavis Batey, Henrietta Buttery, David Lambert and Kim Wilkie, *Arcadian Thames: The River Landscape from Hampton to Kew*, Barn Elms Publishing, 1994.
Charles Dickens, *Little Dorrit*, Penguin Classics, new edition, 2003.
Charles Dickens, *Great Expectations*, Penguin Classics, Longman, revised edition, 2004.
Amanda Foreman, *Georgiana, Duchess of Devonshire*, Flamingo, new edition, 1999.
Mark Girouard, *Life in the English Country House: A Social and Architectural History*, Yale University Press, new edition, 1980.

The Urban Thames
Peter Ackroyd, *Thames Sacred River*, Chatto & Windus, 2007.
Felix Barker and Peter Jackson, *London: 2000 Years of a City and its People*, Cassell & Co, 1974.
JHO Bunge, *Tideless Thames in Future London*, The Thames Barrage Association, 1944.
WJ Loftie, *London City: Its History – Streets – Traffic – Buildings and People*, The Leadenhall Press, 1891.
George Mansell (ed) with JM Hirsh, *The Living Heritage of Westminster*, Westminster City Council, Westminster Chamber of Commerce, Cities of London and Westminster Society of Architects, 1975.
Gavin Weightman, *London River: the Thames Story*, Collins & Brown, 1990.

The Docklands
Dockland, North East London Polytechnic and Greater London Council, 1986.

Estuary Thames: London's Engine Room
Thames Gateway Parklands Vision 2008 brochure available at http://www.communities.gov.uk/publications/thamesgateway/parklandsvision.

The Tributaries
Nicholas Barton, *The Lost Rivers of London*, Quality Paperbacks Direct, 1993.
Colin Rowe and Fred Koetter, *Collage City*, MIT Press, new edition, 1978.
Richard Trench and Ellis Hillman, *London Under London: A Subterranean Guide*, John Murray Ltd, 1984.

Canals
Anthony Burton and Neil Curtis, *The Grand Union Canal Walk*, Aurum Press, 1993.

Bridget Cherry and Nikolaus Pevsner, *London 3: North West*, The Buildings of England, Penguin Books, 1991.
Terry Farrell, 'Buildings As A Resource', *RIBA Journal*, May 1976.
Charles Hadfield, *British Canals: An Illustrated History*, David & Charles, 7th edition, 1984.
Edward Jones and Christopher Woodward, *A Guide to the Architecture of London*, Weidenfeld & Nicolson, new edition, 1992.
Herbert Spencer, *London's Canal: An Illustrated History of the Regent's Canal*, Putnam & Co Ltd, 1961.

Railways
Christopher Hibbert, *London: The Biography of a City*, Penguin Books Ltd, 1969.

The Tube
Antony Clayton, *Subterranean City, Beneath the Streets of London*, Historical Publications Ltd, 2000.

Inner Roads
Peter Ackroyd, *London: The Biography*, Chatto & Windus, illustrated edition, 2000.
W Crawford Snowden, *London 200 Years Ago*, a Daily Mail Publication.
Alastair Service, *London 1900*, Granada Publishing Ltd, 1979.

Outer Roads
Colin Buchanan, *Traffic In Towns*, Report of the Steering Group, HMSO, 1963.

Pedestrians, Cyclists and Buses
Harold P Clunn, *The Face of London*, Spring Books, 1932.
Ken Glazier, *London Transport Garages*, Capital Transport Publishing, 2006.
John Reed, *London Buses, a Brief History*, Capital Transport Publishing, 2007.
Philip Wallis, *London Transport Connections 1945–1985*, Capital Transport Publishing, 2003.

Landscapes, Parks and Gardens
Dana Arnold, *Rural Urbanism: London Landscapes in the Early Nineteenth Century*, Manchester University Press, 2006.
Paul Mellon, *The London Town Garden 1700–1840*, Yale University Press, 2001.
Galinou Mireille, *London's Pride: the Glorious History of London's Parks and Gardens*, Anaya Publishers, 1990.

Conclusion
Victor Hugo, *The Hunchback of Notre-Dame*, Wordsworth Editions Ltd, 1993.
Jane Jacobs, *The Death and Life of Great American Cities*, Penguin in association with Cape, 1964.

Website Sources by Chapter

Rural Upper Thames
www.kew.org Site for Royal Botanic Gardens, Kew. See in particular the history and heritage pages.
www.royalparks.org.uk Outlines the history and architecture of Richmond Park.
www.thames-landscape-strategy.org.uk Organisation set up to conserve, promote and enhance for the future one of the world's great river landscapes between Hampton and Kew.

The Urban Thames
www.bbc.co.uk/history/historic_figures/bazalgette_joseph.shtml A profile of Joseph Bazalgette.
www.somersethouse.org.uk See entries on 'Tudor Palace' and 'Since the Eighteenth Century' for a history of the palace and development of the area.
www.vauxhallgardens.com Site dedicated to the history of Vauxhall Gardens by curator David Coke.
www.pepysdiary.com For Samuel Pepys visit to Cherry Garden in Bermondsey, see entries for 13 June 1664 and 15 June 1664.

The Docklands
www.portcities.org.uk For an account of Charles Dickens's visit to Canning Town in 1857.

Canals
www.canalmuseum.org.uk Site for the London Canal Museum, which is located at Battlebridge Basin on the Regent's Canal in King's Cross. Provides a history of Regent's Canal and Grand Junction Canal.
www.camdenlock.net For background information on the development of Camden Lock.

Railways
www.nrm.org.uk National Railway Museum, home to the UK's national rail collection. Includes online exhibitions of collections, special events and information for visitors.

The Tube – London Underground
www.20thcenturylondon.org.uk See entry on the Metropolitan railway.
www.ltmuseum.co.uk London Transport Museum, with a comprehensive online picture/photo library.

Pedestrians, Cyclists and Buses
www.english-heritage.org.uk English Heritage exists to protect and promote England's spectacular historic environment and ensure that its past is researched and understood.

Landscapes, Parks and Gardens
www.royalparks.org.uk Responsible for administering and maintaining London's Royal Parks. Provides information about the parks, their amenities and forthcoming events.

General Bibliography

Christopher Alexander, *The Phenomenon of Life: The Nature of Order*, Book 1, Routledge, 1st edition, 2004.
Christopher Alexander, *Process of Creating Life: The Nature of Order*, Book 2, Routledge, 1st edition, 2004.
Philip Ball, *Critical Mass: How One Thing Leads to Another*, Arrow Books Ltd, 2005.
Simon Foxell, *Mapping London*, Black Dog Publishing, 2007.
Stephen Inwood, *A History of London*, Macmillan, 1998.
Richard Mabey, *The Unofficial Countryside*, Collins, 1st edition, 1973.
Roy Porter, *London: A Social History*, Penguin Books Ltd, new edition, 2000.
Chris Stringer, *Homo Britannicus: The Incredible Story of Human Life in Britain*, Penguin, 2007.
Gavin Weightman and Steve Humphries, *The Making of Modern London*, Ebury Press, 2007.

London-Related Bibliography by and on Terry Farrell

Colin Amery and Charles Jencks, *Terry Farrell*, Architectural Monographs, introduction by Terry Farrell, Academy Editions/St Martin's Press, 1984.
Lightweight Classic: Terry Farrell's Covent Garden Nursery Building, World Architecture Building Profile No 1, 1993.
'Manifesto For London', *Architectural Review,* Sept 2007.

Marcus Binney, *Palace on the River: Terry Farrell's Design for the Redevelopment of Charing Cross*, Wordsearch Publishing, 1991.
Terry Farrell, *Thames Gateway Parklands Vision*, Department for Communities & Local Government, 2008.
Terry Farrell, *Place: A Story of Modelmaking, Menageries and Paper Rounds*, Laurence King, 2004.
Terry Farrell, *Buckingham Palace Redesigned: A Radical New Approach to London's Royal Parks*, Papdakis, 2003.
Ten Years: Ten Cities, The Work of Terry Farrell & Partners 1991–2001, foreword by Sir Terry Farrell, introduction by Hugh Pearman, Laurence King, 2002.
Terry Farrell & Partners with essays by Robert Maxwell and Terry Farrell, *Sketchbook 12.05.98*, Rightangle Publishing, 1998.
Terry Farrell Selected and Current Works, introduction by Clare Melhuish, Images Publishing, 1994.
Terry Farrell Urban Design, introduction by Kenneth Powell, Academy Editions and Ernst & Sohn, 1993.
'Terry Farrell & Company', *A+U* special feature, December 1989, pp 37–132.
Piers Gough, *Blueprint Extra 09, Three Urban Projects*, 1993.
Charles Jencks and Terry Farrell, 'Designing a House', *Architectural Design*, 1986.
Rowan Moore, *Terry Farrell in the Context of London*, introduction by Deyan Sudjic, published to coincide with the exhibition at the RIBA Heinz Gallery, 14 May to 13 June 1987, 1987.
Kenneth Powell, *Vauxhall Cross: The Story of the Design and Construction of a New London Landmark*, Wordsearch Publishing, 1992.

Index

Picture Credits

All archive material has been sourced and provided by Terry Farrell's office. The author and the publisher gratefully acknowledge the people who gave their permission to reproduce material in this book. While every effort has been made to contact copyright holders for their permission to reprint material, the publishers would be grateful to hear from any copyright holder who is not acknowledged here and will undertake to rectify any errors or omissions in future editions.

l = left, r = right, t = top, b = bottom

Front cover artwork © Robbie Polley

pp 1, 23, 39, 46, 50(t), 66, 67, 172, 173, 177(t), 251 © Historical Picture Archive/Corbis; pp 2, 79, 84(b), 119(b), 150, 195, 237, 239, 240, 241, 248 © Skyscan/Corbis; pp 3, 4, 41, 61, 62, 85(b), 103, 115, 116, 117, 119(t), 127, 133, 140, 141, 149(r), 183, 194, 205, 214, 217, 223, 224, 229, 231 © Hulton-Deutsch Collection/Corbis; pp 6, 73, 185 © Construction Photography/Corbis; pp 8-9 © Monsoon/Photolibrary/Corbis; pp 10, 12, 17(t), 19, 22, 24, 26, 28, 36, 38(tr), 49, 50(b), 51, 53, 55(t), 60, 63(t), 68, 69, 75, 77, 78, 82, 83, 84-5, 88(r), 92, 93, 95, 96, 97, 98-9, 100, 101(b), 104, 105, 106, 111, 118, 120, 129, 130, 131, 136, 137, 139, 145, 146, 162(b), 163, 165, 170, 171(t), 174, 179, 180, 181(r), 182(b), 186, 187, 190, 193, 199, 201, 204, 208-9, 210, 211, 213, 215, 216, 218, 219, 242, 243, 244, 245, 246, 247, 249, 250(l), 258-9, 260, 262, 263, 265, 266, 267, 269, 271, 273, 276, 278, 279 © Farrell; pp 11, 48, © Corbis; pp 14-5 © Centre for Advanced Spatial Analysis, University College London; p 16 © The MIT Press; p 17(b) © Centre for Advanced Spatial Analysis, University College London and Environmental Research Group at Kings College London; p 18 © Martin Wooster and Weidong Xu, King's College London. Original Data: NASA/GSFC/MITI/ERSDAC/JAROS, and U.S./Japan ASTER Science Team; pp 20-1, 72, 88(l), 166-7, 234-5, 255 © Jason Hawkes/Corbis; p 25 © Pool Photograph/Corbis; p 27 © Hoberman Collection/Corbis; pp 29, 153 © Swim Ink 2, LLC/Corbis; pp 29(tr), 30, 31 © Kim Wilkie; p 33 © Angelo Hornak/Corbis; p 34 © SGAERIAL; p 37 © Museum of London; p 42 © London Aerial Photo Library, Gly/London Aerial Photo Library/Corbis; pp 43, 64-5,

70, 134(b), 169, 225, 250(r), 261 © Bettmann/Corbis; p 47 © Christie's Images/Corbis; p 52 © Nicholas Hare Architects LLP; p 54 Reproduced by permission of English Heritage. NMR; pp 55(b), 58, 151 © Farrell/photo Nigel Young; p 57 © Bo Zaunders/Corbis; p 59 © Lifschutz Davidson Sandilands Photo: Ian Lambot; p 71 © Julia Waterlow; Eye Ubiquitous/Corbis; p 74 © Annebicque Bernard/Corbis Sygma; p 80 © Peter Young/Fotolibra; p 86 © Renaissance Southend Ltd; p 87(b) Thames Gateway South Essex by Pixelwork Ltd; p 89 Reproduced by kind permission of Southend Museums Service; p 90 © The Gallery Collection/Corbis; p 91 © Dae Sasitorn/www.lastrefuge.co.uk ; p 101(t) © Pipers; p 107(t) © Professor Graham Shane (1970-71) from the book *Collage City* by Colin Rowe and Fred Koetter, published by The MIT Press; p 112-13 © Ludovic Maisant/Hemis/Corbis; p 121 © British Waterways, courtesy of waterscape.com; pp 122-123 © Roberto Herrett/LOOP IMAGES/Loop Images/Corbis; pp 124-25 © Steven Vidler/Eurasia Press/Corbis; p 134(t) © Merthyr Tydfil Libraries; pp 135, 238 © Stapleton Collection/Corbis; p 147 © Arup/Zhou Ruogu Architecture Photography; p 148 © Yann Arthus-Bertrand/Corbis; p 149(l) © Andy Rain/epa/Corbis; pp 157(b), 158, 159, 160, 162(t), 177(br), 192 © TfL, from the London Transport Museum Collection; p 161(l) © 2006 Tom Carden all rights reserved http://www.tom-carden.co.uk/p5/tube_map_travel_times/applet/; p161(r) courtesy of mysociety.org; p 171(b) © Robert Holmes/Corbis; p 175 © PoodlesRock/Corbis; p 176 © Jeremy Horner/Corbis; p 177(bl) © Underwood & Underwood/Corbis; p 178 © Michael Nicholson/Corbis; p 181(l) © Richard Cowan of M3 Consulting; p 182(t) courtesy of Traffic In Towns HMSO 1963; p 189 courtesy of *The County of London Plan 1943*, Macmillan Publishing, 1944; p 191 © National Motor Museum; p 196 © Mike Finn-Kelcey/Reuters/Corbis; p 197 © Colin Garratt; Milepost 92 ½/Corbis; p 198 © Matthew Polak/Sygma/Corbis; p 200 © AA Media Limited 2009. © Crown Copyright 2009. All rights reserved. Licence number 100021153; p 203 © John Harper/Corbis; p 207 © Felipe Trueba/epa/Corbis; p 212 © Atkins; p 220 © Patrice Latron/Corbis; p 221 © E.O. Hoppé/Corbis; p 226 © Arthur W.V. Mace; Milepost 92 ½/Corbis; p 227 © Lindsey Parnaby/epa/Corbis; p 233 © Richard Baker/Corbis; pp 256-57 © Robert Morden/Getty Images; pp 274-75, 277 © Blom Pictometry.